HUNTING
THE
TIGER

The Fast Life and Violent Death of
the Balkans' Most Dangerous Man

CHRISTOPHER S. STEWART

Thomas Dunne Books
St. Martin's Press ⚏ New York

THOMAS DUNNE BOOKS.
An imprint of St. Martin's Press.

www.thomasdunnebooks.com
www.stmartins.com

Library of Congress Cataloging-in-Publication Data

Stewart, Christopher S.
   Hunting the tiger: the fast life and violent death of the Balkans' most dangerous man / Christopher S. Stewart.—1st ed.
      p. cm.
   The Early Years—1. John Wayne dreams—2. Taking Europe—3. How we change—4. The case of the elusive man: A reporter's search—5. The smiling bank robber—6. We got you! No you don't!—7. Breakout—8. Hitman—9. The man Arkan didn't kill, Part II: Warlord—10. My fixer Milan and our search for truth among Serbia's crime lords—11. Cruising in the pink Cadillac—12. Lord of the soccer warriors—13. The Tigers—14. What I learned at Red Star Stadium—15. War!—16. The danger out there—17. Camp Erdut—18. Vukovar: I killed twenty-four Ustache!—19. Because war pays—20. Meeting the Tigers—21. My name is Trax; Arkan made me do it—22. Don't give a damn—23. Man of the people—24. Pop star—25. War's over, Part III: The assassination—26. This is Serbia, you wouldn't understand—27. Going legit—28. The end—29. If I had a magic wand—30. The kill.
   ISBN-13: 978-0-312-35606-4
   ISBN-10: 0-312-35606-4
   1. Arkan, 1952–2000. 2. Guerrillas—Serbia—Biography. 3. Yugoslav War, 1991–1995 —Atrocities. 4. War criminals—Serbia—Biography. 5. Paramilitary forces—Serbia. I. Title.
DR1321.A75S74   2008
949.703—dc22
[B]   2007038918

First Edition: January 2008

10 9 8 7 6 5 4 3 2 1

To Amy, of course, and Skylar

CONTENTS

PART III: THE ASSASSINATION

ACKNOWLEDGMENTS

This book began with a conversation with PJ Mark. I didn't think I could do it. But PJ talked me into it, and I'm grateful for his encouragement and loyalty and most of all for his smart ideas along the way.

At St. Martin's Press/Thomas Dunne Books, John Parsley was an exceptional editor. His wit, insight, and devotion to my book challenge everything I've ever heard about the business-first world of publishing. Thank you.

Eric Gordy was my go-to guy for everything Balkan, especially pop culture and politics. I'm grateful for the hours he spent talking me through the region's tangled history. He also read an early draft of the manuscript. Without him, the book would have been a lesser creature.

When I traveled to Belgrade for the first time, Milan, my fixer, met me at the airport, and for three years he didn't leave my side. He made important connections and watched my back and became my friend. He risked a lot for me, and he deserves serious props, more than I can articulate here. In Serbia, I also owe thanks to a diverse crowd who offered their wisdom: Marko Nicovic, Marko Lopusina, Jovan Dulovic, Milan St. Protic, and Dobrivoje Radovanovic.

Of course, you can't write a book without friends and collaborators.

These folks helped not in one explicit way but in many ways, all of them unique and invaluable. A million thanks to Scott Anderson, Michael Burger, John Falk, Brett Forrest, Jason Gay, Andrew Goldman, Ron Haviv, Walter Rep, Andrew Rice, Jen Saba, Lockhart Steele, Stacy Sullivan, and Elna Svenle.

In addition to John Parsley and PJ Mark, I'm indebted to Betsy Cummings and Abrahm Lustgarten for close readings of the manuscript.

My greatest thanks is reserved for my family. First to my parents, Don and Sis, and brother, DJ: Though they didn't always understand what I was doing, they never stopped cheering me on. Thank you. Naturally, my wife, Amy, deserves the biggest credit here. The book took me away for long stretches. When I wasn't in the Balkans, I was off in my head. I missed a lot and Amy carried the weight at home. It is to her and to my daughter, Skylar, that I dedicate this book, especially to Amy who even at the end of her very long days stayed up reading draft after draft, saving me from my own personal abyss, and offering keen editorial ideas that made this book what it is. As much as it is my book, I'd like to say that it is also hers.

HUNTING
THE
TIGER

PROLOGUE

1

His name was Zeljko Raznatovic, but when I first came to know him, most of the world called him Arkan.

I met Arkan—or at least his shadow—on a sweltering summer train ride through war-battered Serbia. It was July 1998 and my girlfriend and I had been backpacking through Europe for about a month. Most of the trip was like any other postcollege adventure—sunburned days spent wandering ancient streets, boozy nights in tiny outdoor cafés lit by strings of naked bulbs, dancing that went too late, the occasional Gypsy run-in, hangovers that didn't quit—until Arkan's men entered our world and changed everything.

Arkan was a Serbian warlord. Images of his baby face had been appearing regularly on CNN and BBC that summer, and much of the world, including the United States, believed that he and his private militia, the Tigers, were responsible for torturing, raping, and killing thousands in the Balkan wars of the early 1990s. There was also talk of other criminal exploits, how, in an earlier life, he had been one of Europe's most prolific thieves, a communist hit man, an escape artist, and an international mob boss on the scale of Al Capone. The general feeling was that Arkan had to pay for his crimes, all of them—or be killed. Arkan didn't give a damn about what anyone said.

He broke up the world into strong men and weak men and lived his life accordingly.

I didn't know any of this back then, of course. When we landed at the empty train station in Thessaloniki, in northern Greece, I didn't even know we were going to Serbia. The trip wasn't planned, but trips like this never are.

We had told the man at the ticket counter we wanted to travel north to Budapest. Temperatures hovered around 110 degrees, with humidity like a rain forest. I remember sweat dripping down the man's chunky forehead. He smiled, but it was a sinister smile. "You think you have pretty faces?" he asked.

"Excuse me?" I wasn't sure if I'd heard him right. Was he speaking English? He was large and bloblike, with thick eyeglasses. His ratty white button-down was almost soaked through, and patches of chest hair curled out from his lower neck, like field grass.

"You don't want to go through Serbia," he said finally. "People die there." Then, for no apparent reason, he made a pistol with his right hand and fired it off.

It was weird, but I nodded and didn't ask.

He mapped out a northern route for us to Hungary. Instead of going straight up through Serbia, we would first travel east through Macedonia and then go north through Bulgaria and Romania. "I save you," he said, laughing. "Thank you," we said, and paid him the U.S. equivalent of about $20 in Greek drachma.

He had some trouble getting the machine to spit out the tickets, and the hassle made him visibly angry. He shook his balding head, banged the machine, wiped his face, swore in Greek. In the absence of official tickets, he decided to write them out in pen on what looked to be two take-out fast-food stubs.

In retrospect, I should have seen it as a sign that something was completely wrong. Of course, there were other things that weren't quite right after that, like the fact that he directed us to a train car holding goats and chickens, and that our assigned seat numbers didn't even exist. We were young, however, and perhaps most important, traveling on a tight budget like every other *Lonely Planet*–armed backpacker, and all we cared about was escaping the punishing heat and humidity and making it to Budapest by the next day.

So we boarded the train. Of the hundred or so other passengers, we appeared to be the only backpackers, let alone Americans. Most of the passengers appeared to be peasants with sun-beaten faces and ratty clothes. The train was littered with cigarette butts, wrappers, and crumpled papers. Windows were either permanently closed or permanently open. Soon we found an empty cabin of six seats. The walls, like the outside of the train, were scarred with colorful graffiti in languages I didn't know, and the plastic-tiled ceiling was stained with moisture and caving in. "What do you think?" I wondered. My girlfriend looked at me. "Your call." The departure bell twittered. We didn't get out. We stayed. That was our mistake. My big mistake.

2

The first hour or so of the trip was undramatic, just another picturesque tour through provincial Europe: grassy fields, an occasional shepherd, and tiny villages whisking past. Pretty. In fact, so pretty and brimming with green life that it was strange and almost obscene to imagine the evil that lurked out there.

We passed into Macedonia and left its capital, Skopje, just as day drained into night, but instead of heading for Bulgaria we soon found out from a Polish man who spoke broken English that we were crossing into Serbia. Whatever motivated the ticket man to send us into what was an emerging war zone not yet on the public's radar, I'll never know—but we'd been duped.

Deep in the countryside, at an unmarked station in Serbia, the train came to a snorting halt. Men with guns emerged from shadows and boarded the train. We heard screams. Metal hitting metal. Eventually two men barged into our cabin.

They resembled the Billy Goats Gruff—short and scrunched with bad teeth, dirty fingernails, and ragged beards. Both wore high-water gray pants with blue button-downs stained black and brown and missing buttons. One had a mashed-up fighter's nose and a revolver tucked in his leather belt.

These were the conductors. They did not welcome us. "Ticket or jail," said the fighter when we explained that we only had the handwritten tickets. The fighter pointed out the window at the decrepit concrete building that acted as the station. We had no dollars for bribes. Only Greek drachmas, which were worthless.

That's when his revolver popped out and everything started to turn ugly.

The fighter looked into my eyes and looked at my girlfriend. Behind him soldiers slung with automatic weapons carted off two passengers tied up with a rope. Fights erupted between the soldiers and the passengers. I saw a soldier put his boot on the back of a fallen man's head. We heard more screaming. A crying woman passed our cabin, her dirty hands desperately reaching out for something left behind.

They didn't throw us off. Not yet. Stuffing his revolver back in his pants, the fighter leaned in close to me, pressed a fat index finger to my temple, hard, and then murmured, "Painful trouble. You understand?"

3

This would be my first taste of Serbia's horror, my first look at a country crippled and broken by fear. Until this time, I had only heard stories about this part of the world, distant and improbable stories of war, which had been waged on and off for centuries—from the wars with the Turks, Austrians, and German Nazis to the blood-soaked civil wars in the 1990s, where Yugoslav brothers fought brothers over religion, where genocide was probably committed, and where even now there were freshly shoveled mass graves hiding thousands of bodies.

The train moved on. What had we gotten ourselves into? I chain-smoked a pack of cigarettes in less than an hour, I scuffed the dirty floor, at one point I turned to my girlfriend and asked, "Should we get off the train before full night comes?" She shrugged. Her lips were chaffed from grinding her teeth on them. "We could probably catch a train going back the other way. Or walk."

We stayed, decided to take our chances, and full-on night came. Crawling north, the train seemed to stop every twenty minutes or so, with Serb soldiers climbing on and off. Some sported green uniforms that looked military; others wore commando-black jumpers that seemed less official, maybe paramilitary or just local thugs. Most were young, college aged, with pimply faces and spotty beards that hadn't quite filled in yet. I noticed that some had patches on their arms. One that stuck out featured the face of a tiger. Again, we tried to explain that we didn't mean to get on this train. "We're Americans," I said a million times. They laughed and went through our bags, stealing a watch, a pen, and some stupid shot glasses and key chains from a gift shop near the Acropolis.

The other passengers were even worse off. Every stop had its unique horrors. I witnessed men's faces bloodied from pistol whippings, women in head scarves separated from children, slapped, and dragged off to "train station jail," which is how the Polish passenger described the guarded makeshift rooms at nearly every stop. When I asked him why they kept taking people off, he simply replied, "This is Serbia," as if that would explain it.

At one stop a soldier took his rifle butt and cracked open the skull of an old man. From the window of our cabin the two conductors watched the man writhe on the ground and looked back at us, shaking their heads, as if to say, see what you've gotten yourselves into.

The conductors came and went. "Painful trouble," they said, laughing, the fighter tapping his revolver. At several stops they took our passports and handed them to the soldiers, as if to suggest that something should be done about us. Our passports would disappear for ten, twenty minutes, then reappear with a cocky kid soldier. "Who the fuck are you?" one of them sneered. "CIA," guessed his sidekick, toying with a pistol. "We hate CIA." Then they broke up laughing.

I smoked more cigarettes. My head hurt. "We're fucked," I kept saying to no one in particular. "Please stop," begged my girlfriend. I was out of cigarettes.

My overwhelming fear was that the conductors or soldiers could do anything they wanted with us at any moment. We could be thrown off the train, or beaten; they could rape my girlfriend, and throw me in jail; they could simply kill us. And for what? No one back home would even know. We were somewhere we shouldn't have been.

Through the first few hours I tried to remain outwardly calm. I started to think that if it came to it, I'd fight the bastards off. I thought more seriously about an escape. We could jump off the train when it slowed to a creep before a station, disappear into the woods, and make our way back south. Inside, I felt sick. I thought we were going to die.

4

And then it was my turn. Around 1:00 A.M., at some nowhere station, two soldiers led me off the train. Except for armed men, there was nothing but forest as far as I could see: just an impenetrable sea of rolling blackness with crickets squawking a loud kind of desolation song. My girlfriend tried to follow, but other thugs snatched her arms. A rough man in black who reeked of alcohol took me from the soldier and walked me down the tracks.

I remember the stones crunching under my Nike trail shoes. We passed a lopsided and crumbling one-room stone building, where a knot of uniformed men played cards at a table and drank, a swirl of smoke overhead. Drunken laughter punctuated the night like gunfire. Farther down I was shown into a dank, lightless room where shadows of men and women commingled in a corner. The stench of urine burned my nostrils. On a closer look I could see that some wore handcuffs and others were tied with rope. The man in black took my passport. "You stay here," he said before leaving.

I waited in that room for at least half an hour, wondering what to do, what my girlfriend was doing, what her father would think if he knew where I'd taken her. I tried not to breathe in the awful stink, but then the thoughts took over, and I must have forgotten about it. Would we make it? Where would we be a week from now? I tried to think about the future, made silly promises to go to church if we got out of this. Around me, the shadows groaned.

Finally a soldier appeared and, without explanation, returned my passport and pointed me back to the train. Crouching in the corner of our cabin with no lights, I found my girlfriend dressed in a baseball cap, a scarf, a sweatshirt, and a pair of my jeans, which she'd pulled on over her shorts. Tears streaked her tan face. She looked like she'd aged. "What happened?" I asked. While I was gone another gunman had forced her into an empty car, but she'd kicked him, screamed, and managed to scramble away. "They're going to come back," she said. "Don't worry," I said, though I knew she was probably right.

At daybreak fifteen heavily armed men—some with official uniforms, others not—jammed into our cabin, including the two conductors. Though we didn't have a clue as to what was happening, the fighter-nosed conductor made hand gestures suggesting he wanted the armed men to cuff us and take us away.

Then something very strange occurred. A tall young man showed up. He was around our age, nicely dressed—white button-down tucked into pressed jeans. "No pain, no gain," he said to us cryptically, smiling before turning and speaking to the men.

Later my girlfriend would say that her mother, who had died of cancer several years earlier, had had something to do with the intervention. I don't think she meant that her mother actually had entered the young man as a spirit, but that somehow she was there. I like the sound of it, but I'm not so sure.

Still, there was something about the young man. How does he just step into the middle of a crowd like this and not get shoved away?

But he had. As he began interacting with the soldiers in their language, the tension in that very cramped space started to lessen, as if a plug miraculously had been pulled. He gestured at us and then at the men's guns. He laughed, and a couple of them cracked a smile. Why screw with them? he seemed to ask.

The only thing I could think of was that this young kid was connected. Maybe he was the son of an organized-crime figure in the region. Or maybe he headed up his own gang. It was far-fetched, but not implausible.

The conversation lasted about five minutes. My girlfriend and I just sat there. Until, finally, the fighter-conductor said, "OK." Then he took our passports, stamped something on them, and handed us two official tickets. He was letting us go. As if making up for all the trouble, the fighter put a hand on my shoulder and muttered, "Good trip." Then they were all gone.

That was it. We never got a chance to thank the passenger. I don't even remember the name of the station. I still can't come up with any good reason for his decision to save us. Sometimes things just don't make sense. The last we saw of him he was outside the train walking away in the bright morning sun. Then, slowly, seeming to heave, the train pulled out of the station and we continued north toward Belgrade and then on to Budapest.

5

I remember the tiger patches most. Several of the pimply teens and twentysomethings with guns had the image of the growling yellow beast stitched to their upper sleeves. This was the patch of Arkan. The man himself was not on the train, but whether directly under his control or just imitators, these thugs symbolized his reach.

It was a hellish ride, lasting twenty-plus hours in all, with the worst of it in southern Serbia, mainly around Kosovo. What I saw firsthand on that stretch of the ride—the beatings, the seemingly arbitrary imprisonments, the guns, the fear on the faces of the other passengers—was just the tip of the iceberg of what was actually happening in the region, what Arkan and his men were doing and had been doing to local Albanians, Bosnians, Croats, and anyone else who wasn't an ethnic Serb.

Who was Arkan? Arkan was an outlaw, though that's a little too Western storybook for the real man. He spent his teens and twenties darting through Europe with fake passports—robbing banks, escaping prisons, assassinating for Tito, the then Yugoslav leader. At twenty-three, he was on Interpol's most-wanted list, and everyone seemed to know about his adventures. Goran Vukovic, a contemporary Serbian gangster, was convinced that there had never been a better bank robber. "Of all of us, Arkan robbed the most banks," he said. "He walked into them almost like they were self-service stores—banks were his specialty, as well as escapes from prison."

By 1988, Arkan was Serbia's thirty-six-year-old mobster king, piloting a pink Cadillac, sporting flashy suits and gold Rolexes, and flashing large-bore revolvers. At home he kept a pet tiger and dozens of fighting dogs. No one got in his way, not even the police. Three years later Yugoslavia, once a country made up of six republics, slipped into civil war, and Arkan organized a Serbian paramilitary crew. He called them the Tigers, inspired by a pet tiger. Unofficially, the Tigers' mandate was to help Serbia's president, Slobodan Milosevic, fight for a "Greater Serbia," though Arkan had his own demonic visions. Composed of as many as ten thousand well-armed, well-trained gangsters, ex-cons, and soccer fans, the Tigers rampaged through Croatia and Bosnia in satellite-equipped SUVs and old Russian tanks, executing thousands of Croat and Muslim men, women, and children.

He was, of course, no ideologue. He joined the war for power and money, and the Serbian state silently backed him. Looted businesses, stolen cars, and smuggled oil and cigarettes (among other black market products) eventually made Arkan one of the region's richest men. Later, when he married Yugoslavia's biggest pop star, Ceca—Serbs called her the "Madonna of the Balkans"—local papers began referring to the couple as the country's "Charles and Diana." Later they were referred to, more appropriately, as the Sopranos of Serbia. Some day, Arkan promised friends, "I'm going to make a movie about my life."

What intrigues me about Arkan is that his story is not only the story of a monstrous gangster and warlord, but also of Yugoslavia's epochal fall into bedlam, deviance, and destruction as the country transitioned away from forty-five years of communism. It is the story of an incredibly ghastly man who became the fear-inspiring symbol of a treacherous world swallowed up by a culture of mafia and war-styled crime and violence and an insidious streak of nationalism that sparked all the fighting and finally broke up the country.

Arkan thrived on war. He was an apocalyptic guy. When Yugoslavia officially divided and fighting petered out in Croatia and Bosnia, he sent his Tigers to southern Serbia, mainly in Kosovo, where Milosevic was butchering and purging the native population of Albanians. My train ride took me through the heart of that war.

By 1999, Arkan was an international phenomenon. He was one of Serbia's most popular men, a superstar warlord showing up daily on the covers of tabloids, but he was also a wanted man, a man on the run. People followed his lurid trail of blood and money as a perverse kind of entertainment. CNN shadowed him wherever he went, and politicians from the United States to Europe called for his end. "The Hague" had indicted him on 24 counts of war crimes; 177 countries had his criminal records; and the United States had put a $5 million bounty on his head. Richard Holbrooke, the U.S. special envoy to the Balkans, was one of Arkan's most visible opponents, describing him as a "freelance murderer" and a "racist fanatic run amok," and urged the world to stop him—or else.

Shortly after my train ride I wrote about that wild trip for a U.S. publication. Out of curiosity, I tried unsuccessfully to organize an interview with Arkan. After his indictment that spring he'd been defending himself vigorously on all the major international networks, including CNN and BBC. Not surprisingly, he was a masterful media spinner. He spoke five languages fluently, was good-looking in a suburban dad kind of way, with his soft face and retreating hairline. One of the more memorable exchanges was with Charles Gibson on ABC's *Good Morning America,* where he called The Hague's lead prosecutor "a bitch" and threatened to unleash his Tigers on the United States. "You want your machinery, your world propaganda, the media, to think that I'm a bad boy, to show that I'm a killer, that I'm this and that. Well, I'm telling you, I'm not," he said, as the world watched. "To tell you in the clear English language, I don't give a damn for indictment of The Hague. . . . I am a Serbian patriot, and the people in Yugoslavia, they simply love me, and I love them." Not long after that interview he abruptly and improbably, for the most part, went silent. It seemed that the history of what he'd done had suddenly enveloped him. Dark forces began to coalesce. Besides international law wanting his head, there were also rumors that President Milosevic had decided that Arkan had grown too powerful.

Then it was over. On January 15, 2000, Arkan was assassinated in a spectacular gangland murder. Three years later I read that his pop-star wife, Ceca, had been linked to the suspects in the assassination of the country's first democratically elected prime minister. What sort of family was this? They were alleged killers, thieves, mobsters—and major stars.

When she emerged from several months in jail Ceca talked to few people about her life and times with Arkan. After some failed connections, a fixer set up a meeting with her, and I returned to Serbia for the first time since the detour I'd taken in 1998.

6

Ceca lives in a garish seven-floor mansion that Arkan had built mostly during the war years—a miniskyscraper with blue-and-white trim, bulletproof windows, a Willy Wonka–styled glass elevator, and a gang of armed men patrolling a ten-foot stone wall. She is tall and slim with surgically enhanced breasts and razor-straight brown hair that trails halfway down her back. The walls inside of her mansion are plastered with portraits of Arkan in military garb and giant paintings of World War I death scenes. When I asked her about life with Arkan, she fidgeted with an oversized diamond on her right hand for a moment, and then answered, "If I were to tell someone outside of this place about all of that, they wouldn't believe me."

During his life Arkan had become subsumed in a supermyth, an understandable phenomenon for someone with such an outsized existence. Before his assassination few would have talked candidly about him. Talking meant death. It was a common mafia code in Belgrade, a city that for a time seemed to be dealing with a new assassination every day. Even today, years after his murder, there exists a deep reluctance to speak about him and what he did. Several of his ex-associates told me simply, "It is healthier to let the dead rest." Others prefaced conversations with requests for anonymity. There are also still terrifying people out there, from mobsters to war criminals, who are willing to die for him, or at least for his name. As a former Tiger once warned me, "Be careful what you say. We've got our eyes on you."

I kept going back, however, more than a half dozen times. I located old friends, ex-gangsters, soccer fanatics, politicians, and family, among many others connected to him who wanted to talk. What Ceca and these others told me over a few years of conversations only increased my interest in Arkan, his crimes, his murder, and the painful death of Yugoslavia. As Ceca explained once, a lot of what happened "sounds too crazy to be true."

PART I

———

THE EARLY DAYS

1

JOHN WAYNE DREAMS

1

Belgrade is an unfortunate city. For hundreds of years, Ottoman conquerors repeatedly entered and destroyed Serbia's capital, wearing it down to bone and gristle. In the twentieth century, the city was bombed more times than any other major European metropolis, excluding Warsaw. The Austrians shot it up, the Nazis shelled it, and so did the Allies. In the 1990s, there were civil wars, assassinations, mafia kings, and more bombing, this time by NATO planes, payback for the country's genocidal operations in Kosovo. It was a frightening place to be then, awash in black market goods, guns, and crazed warlords, and some got to calling the city Mordor, the name J. R. R. Tolkien gave to his depraved shadowland.

Today, having spent much time in a state of conflict, Belgrade is still a battered and corrupted place. Similar in size to Philadelphia, it is home to about 1.5 million people and sits at the confluence of the Danube and Sava Rivers. Ugly and gray, the city is dotted with blown-up buildings, grim apartment blocks constructed in the sixties and seventies, half-built condominiums, and shantytowns, with little left architecturally from earlier centuries. Rusted Lada sedans and noisy city buses bump along the potholed streets that rise and fall. Gypsies dwell in the damp shade of the Branko Bridge,

which divides the old and new parts of Belgrade, their ashen faces and ema-
ciated bodies huddled around garbage burning in oil drums, with only the
brown river water to wash in. Amid the visible poverty there is also garish
wealth, late-model Mercedeses and Audis with bulletproof windows, heavily fortressed mansions, and glitzy restaurants and nightclubs inhabited by
sharply dressed gangsters, reform-talking politicians, and surgically modi-
fied pop stars.

Arkan is one of the city's saintly warriors. When he died thousands attended his funeral on a freezing midwinter day in 2000. As the black vehicle
transporting his casket glided into the central Belgrade cemetery, people
reached out to grasp him one last time. Television cameras rolled, reproduc-
ing images of the dreary scene all over the world. Tears were shed, and baskets of flowers and sticks of incense were piled atop his grave at the peak of
a hill. Even today, there are always fresh flowers on his headstone, with candles flickering in the open air. The gravesite, still guarded by his men, is
mentioned in travel guides, and it's not uncommon to find tourists there,
snapping pictures or saying prayers. The organizers of his assasination remain unknown.

After everything that has happened to this country and to this city, after
the civil wars, after all the pain and killing, after the imprisonment and then
the death of former Serbian president and dictator Slobodan Milosevic, and
after the promise by new politicians to heal, reconcile, and move on, Arkan,
even in death, remains a visible force in Belgrade. His beret-wearing mug is
painted in bright colors on the concrete side of a high-rise apartment building. A similar portrait is wallpapered on the Obilic Football Club stadium.
Tabloids regularly feature him and Ceca on their front pages, and teenagers
worship his tough guy ways like American kids talk excitedly about 50 Cent,
as some gangster to be glorified. A considerable number of people also believe that he is still alive, out there somewhere in the world, waiting to make
a comeback, to wreak his revenge. As a Red Star soccer fan in his twenties
told me one night at a local nightclub, "Arkan is fucking God."

2

No one seems to know exactly how Arkan acquired his famous nickname. I
asked dozens of people, and heard several different stories. According to one
version, Arkan was the name that appeared on a forged Turkish passport he

A Belgrade wall in front of Arkan's Obilic soccer stadium, where the warlord is memorialized.

employed during his bank robbing and hit-man days in Europe, and it just stuck. Marko Lopusina, in his book *Commander Arkan,* proposes another idea, that he took the name in his twenties after a tiger in a favorite comic strip, though I could never identify that comic. In general, Arkan did like tigers because, as an old friend of his told me, tigers were "beautiful and gentle and could also kill." Still others conjectured that the name was a shortening of the Latin word *arcanus,* meaning secret, a theory that I subscribed to, not because I found it more convincing than the others but simply because that's what his life was.

Although Arkan occasionally dropped hints about his early adventures, much of those days are as vague as the origins of his nickname, shot through with conflicting accounts and tinted by myth. When I asked Ceca if she knew anything about his life before she met him, she said cryptically, "I only know what I read in the papers." So, I wondered, you weren't at all curious about what he did when he was a kid? "Not really," she said and shrugged. I didn't believe her, but that was beside the point. I did hear many stories, some more than others. It was in these told and retold stories that the fog of mystery slowly began to melt and give way to a clearer, if not truer, portrait of the man's youth.

Arkan was born on April 17, 1952, in the Yugoslav National Army barracks in Brezice, Slovenia, a town famous for red wine and thermal baths. His father, Veljko, was a decorated colonel in the national military, based in Brezice at the time. There were three older sisters, which meant that the family was always fighting for space in tight apartments. Early on, comic books seemed to provide passing pleasure, as did science-fiction novels, but movies, especially American and European spaghetti Westerns featuring headline actors such as Gary Cooper, John Wayne, and Clint Eastwood, were said to have been his refuge. Yugoslavia was in fact one of the only communist countries that imported Hollywood films, making Arkan a lucky communist kid. In these cowboy flicks, people said, he found role models. He transformed those grainy black-and-white Western narratives into his own Technicolor dreams. Like those great outlaws, he knew from an early age that he wanted to be big, perhaps like John Wayne.

Soon the family moved to Zagreb, and then to New Belgrade, north of the Sava River, and finally to old Belgrade, where they occupied a cramped walk-up in the city's crowded center. It was a busy time for the country, as it moved into an age of industrialism. Tito (Josip Broz), an ex-machinist and champion fencer, was the country's anointed communist leader, after he and his partisan army muscled out the Nazis and Fascists in 1945. Dreaming of a unified country, he had put a lid on the dangerous ethnic rivalries between Serbs, Croats, and Bosnians and forced his people into full-throttled work mode. Whatever atrocities had happened during the war or before, he didn't give a damn. Leftover nationalists were killed, imprisoned, or driven out of the country.

Tito made Belgrade the capital of the new Yugoslavia, which consisted of six republics and two semiautonomous provinces. After having been obliterated by the Germans in 1941, Belgrade needed a face-lift—and it happened fast. From 1950 to late 1960, the city experienced a quadrupling in population, with peasants from the countryside flooding in, moving from houses into small state-subsidized apartments with state-subsidized health care and state-subsidized vacations. In what became known as the age of "Belgradization," blocks and blocks of concrete high-rises mushroomed up everywhere, especially in New Belgrade. Streets were laid out and paved, hospitals rebuilt, schools erected, and factories opened.

People labored long hours for the state at low wages, digging away in

mines, manufacturing automobiles, and working in the government bu-
reaucracy. After Tito abandoned Stalin's domination, from 1954 to 1975 industrial jobs grew at an average annual rate of 4.3 percent, and Serbia's
industrial working class grew from 1.1 million in 1947 to 6.3 million in
1985. Wagewise, the industrial jobs beat farming peppers and cabbage any
day, though the money wasn't going to make anyone rich—or completely
happy. Still, the new age was a change, or at least it felt like a change. So
what if there was only one shoe store in Belgrade, or that you could buy
only Super Rifle jeans and not Levi's, or that no one sold Coca-Cola? There
was no time to think about that.

Outside the Raznatovics' window you could hear the quotidian cycles of
Belgrade life, the chatter of the sidewalk, the whistles of policemen, the
droning sound of buses and cars and vendors bumping along March 27
Street, one of the city's busiest thoroughfares. At night, especially in the
summer and fall months, when the kosava winds tunneled in from the east,
the dusty streets were packed with dark faces, people coming and going
from state jobs, trying to get places, to get home, to get out, to get settled.

I remember what Marx said about communism, it "is not to make a man
better but to change his nature." Arkan would not have liked Marx. He certainly wasn't about to have his nature changed—not ever. Seeking an edge,
he decided to rebel. He rebelled against the state roles, the careers, the so-
cially programmed assumptions about how life was meant to be lived in
communist Serbia. Rules were for suckers. The people who followed them,
hell, they were just like deer stuck dumbly in high beams.

While other kids woke, slipped into bland uniforms, and went to school,
where they genuflected to the communist leader and learned about "Brotherhood and Unity," Arkan wandered. When he showed up at school he was
supposedly a good student with a quick mind who appreciated a good argument, but school wasn't for him. He skipped classes, hung out on the street
with delinquent friends, and went with pretty girls to Kalemegdan Park, a
sprawling green oasis in the middle of the city. There were other things, too.
He hustled, played cards, got in fights, and threw coins.

The city tightened in on him like a noose. He had to get out. As city lore
goes, he ran away for the first time when he was nine years old, long before
most boys got to first base with their girlfriends. With his dark hair cut
short, he traveled eleven bumpy hours to Dubrovnik, at the southern tip of
the Croatian coast. Most likely he traveled by a series of overnight buses
and trains, although there is one story that he stole a car. Once there, he
stopped at a camp perched at the crown of a craggy hill, with a view of the

Adriatic. Europe was a boat ride away, but from there it seemed like you could reach out and touch it.

Officially, it was tough, if not impossible, to leave Yugoslavia back then. Tito only issued priority passports, as he needed his good comrades to stick around and help build his personal empire, which was fast becoming more decentralized as it broke away from the Soviets' postwar influence. Still, that didn't keep Arkan from dreaming. The kid had lots of dreams.

Standing there on the coastline, he could almost see it: his future outside of the deadening miasma of Yugoslavia. Across the gleaming water there were wheelbarrows of money to be made. There were roads paved with Levi's and lakes of Coca-Cola. That first night you could almost see him sitting there, staring out at that big black rolling mass of sea, thinking about what was in store for his life, perhaps imagining his future existence: Young gun John Wayne takes Europe.

Unfortunately, it was over before it began. His father, who had apparently intercepted a letter from Arkan to his mother, arrived soon after to transport the young delinquent home. Still, even if it was a long ride back to Belgrade with a dour father, Arkan had gotten what he needed, and that was the taste of freedom. After that, the dream of chasing life outside of Yugoslavia would never diminish. It would only mature—like a cancer.

3

Teenage Arkan stood out. He was taller and always talking, running his mouth about whatever was on his mind. His charisma was expansive. He always had a plan and people were drawn to that, like a gravitational force. A slim kid, he had narrow shoulders and a disproportionately large, square head with soft unlined features, like a prized pupil or a choirboy. Some friends called him Hybrid—because of his large head and slim stature. Most remember that he favored white T-shirts and jeans, just like James Dean, and pomaded his hair. His baby face was one feature that he'd never shake. Even in his thirties and forties, it stuck with him, becoming a kind of personal trademark. When he started turning up in newspaper headlines, journalists would refer to him as the "baby-faced bank robber" or the "baby-faced butcher."

Gradually, he drifted toward the world of gangsters, not an easy world anywhere, but especially not in Yugoslavia. Crime was infrequent in the federation. Tito paid his state policemen well to prevent corruption, and he employed a rigid federal security apparatus that was as good or better than any omniscient Big Brother. Harsh punishments were customary, forcing hooligans to retire young or stand in front of a firing squad. Stealing could cost you many years, even life, in jail. Rapists were executed, just like murderers. "You'd lose your head if you were bad back then," Jovan Dulovic told me one day at a backyard café in Belgrade. Dulovic was a respected crime reporter at the weekly magazine *Vreme,* in Belgrade. "One judge gave a robber the death penalty," he said.

If you made it big as a criminal, you most likely did it outside the Yugoslavian border. Dulovic recalled the local legend of Sis Mis and Bora Madora. To some of the younger wannabe criminals at the time in Belgrade, they were tantamount to the Beatles, the band that got the party started. In their early days, Sis and Bora robbed hotel suites and restaurants and underground casinos. It was never enough. Yugoslavia was poor and the profits were meager compared to the money elsewhere in the world. So Sis and Bora hopped a train and went west—without passports. According to Dulovic, they rode under boxcar trains, clinging to the carriage, choking on dirt and rocks, their hands, no doubt, numb. When they arrived in Paris they didn't waste a second, snatching purses and robbing people in city parks and public toilets. What they found out: Parisians were loaded! Word of this revelation got back to the streets of Belgrade, how they made truckloads of cash, how it was as easy as plucking dollar bills from trees! They were Bonnie and Clyde and thieved for years without getting caught. Then, like two smart criminals, they retired rich.

Colonel Veljko Raznatovic must have seen his son "Arkan" moving toward the thug life, and he tried to rein him in. The colonel was a sparkplug-shaped man with a Spartan sensibility. His whole life had been devoted to the Yugoslav military. During World War II, the colonel led an army battalion in the retaking of the southern Serbian town of Pristina that Italian Fascists had occupied since the war's early moments. His victory was total. Days later, inspired by victory, he fell in love. As he led his men on a patrol around the town square, he spotted a woman giving a procommunist speech. She had dark hair and a pretty face and he had to have her. So he sent his police force to arrest her. When she arrived at the barracks he didn't mince words, asking her for her hand. "The army was everything to him," Arkan once told a reporter. "He waged war, and married like a soldier."

Arkan's mother, Slavka, was a tiny, elegant woman, and she always supported her son—always would. Same with his older sister, Jasna. But the two women couldn't stop the hard-nosed colonel. He wanted his son to join the military, just like him, and he was determined to make that happen. Whenever Arkan resisted, the colonel didn't just swat him on the backside or send him to his room without dinner. He was a harsh disciplinarian. He believed in tough love and duty. "He would simply pick me up and hurl me on the floor with all of his might," Arkan recalled later in an interview. For the most serious infractions, as when Arkan joked one morning about Tito dying, which wouldn't happen until 1980, the colonel yanked his son up by his skinny ankles and, like a snagged fish, dangled him out of the apartment window until he begged for mercy.

The discipline probably strengthened Arkan, but I suspect it also screwed him up. The question was how much. What interested me about Arkan through these early days was how he went from being just another kid who dreamed of bad guys to being a real bad guy. What event or what influence steered this kid down one hell-making road over another? My guess is that Arkan's father was a big factor in shaping his life. You have someone coming down on you, like the colonel, pressing you from all sides, slapping you around, hanging you out of apartment windows—it's going to change you.

Still, if Arkan was goaded into a frenzy of acting out, it was not solely because of a monster father on his back but also because, as a growing man with an inflated sense of where he was going to go, he saw no profit in the dispirited and hard-faced in communist Yugoslavia. Arkan took the hits, shrugged them off, maybe even laughed. Then rebelled some more, knowing that his time would come.

Arkan was twelve or thirteen when he started lifting purses and wallets in Belgrade's parks, and then he branched out to holding up nearby shops. During that time he met other young wannabe gangsters, guys who he'd work with when he finally made his way to Europe. There was Candyman, Karate Bob, Zika the Nerve, and Vule the Taylor. Crazy Horse was another, an ex-wrestler with red eyes, and the police were after him in the late 1960s for a string of robberies and for beating a foreigner who had slept with his girlfriend. Like Arkan, all these guys were hungry wolves. It would be this nonstop hunger that got almost every one of them killed.

Being a gangster was a lot like being a rock star. That was their mantra. They lived hard, but loved the living better than anything else. There were girls, there was money, and there was—freedom. Death, however, was a shadow forever threatening to swallow them up. In the end, life for these guys was measured in seconds, not in years or decades or centuries. They probably knew they weren't going to get old, but at least they had their own lives. Arkan would always tell his men later on, "I'd rather live a day like a lion than twenty years like a fucking sheep." A personal mantra, it was similar to how Edith Hamilton described the ancient Greek's attitude in her book *Mythology:* "Life for him was an adventure, perilous indeed, but men are not made for safe havens. The fullness of life is in the hazards of life."

Though Arkan probably could be a little bit of a prick, talking his big game, it didn't mean that he didn't have any reason to brag. When he started turning up on the radar of law enforcement, he didn't make it easy on the police. He was calm, cool, and an exceptionally smooth operator. He was also fox fast. As one officer later explained to *Duga,* a Serbian magazine, "He was unusually strong for his age and agile, never dirty or slovenly, always clean and properly dressed. . . . If he had gone out for any sport, he certainly would have had extraordinary results. That was just the way he was, capable of anything."

He did get into kickboxing, but oddly, unlike many other Serbian males, he didn't appear to be interested in entering competitions to see who could beat up more people. He seemed uninterested in winning a flimsy blue first-place ribbon or a silly bronze plaque congratulating him on a victory. His decision to become a kickboxer appeared more motivated by his grand career ambitions than a feeling for sport. He was preparing himself, creating a lethal tool.

He sweated it out in the local gyms against real men, men bigger and older than him, who instructed him in toughness, machismo, and tenacity, and taught him how to stay alive. He got knocked down and bloodied. He was a kid with attitude, a kid who wouldn't stop running his mouth, and probably got beaten down a lot, but he jumped back up. He worked his legs into fine weapons that snapped open and shut like switchblades. He lifted weights, did push-ups and pull-ups, and toned and enhanced his young body. His hammer of a head was anchored to his iron shoulders, and his hands were little balls of steel. His arms and forearms became lightning quick, suggesting to enemies that they were fast and strong enough to squeeze off a grown man's neck.

He stayed out late. When he came home, other men were returning from their late shifts at oil fields and tire factories. The men were a few years older than him, their bodies bent over in exhaustion. Maybe for a second, with that stolen loot wadded in his pocket, Arkan would pause and watch as they passed: specters of a life that would have been his if he'd stayed on course.

But maybe not; maybe he never had second thoughts about where he was going. Maybe he just went straight on, like a bullet. Because—those men bent in half—they were just plain fools.

The reality was: Who really knew how long those fools would have their jobs? Rumors would eventually spread about the "political factories" that Tito had built to employ the masses, and how those factories were sucking the economy bone dry. Secretly, people worried. The economy had its stable moments, then it jerked and sputtered, like an old car in the freezing winter months, especially after 1966, when the economy lurched from one crisis to the next with bouts of inflation and high unemployment. In subtle ways, young criminals like Arkan probably noticed this darkening and prepared for the worst. They of course saw the state workers' cheap and worn-out clothes. They saw the melancholic faces, and those dismal images only fueled their drive to control their own destinies.

It wasn't that Arkan was poor or deprived. By Yugoslavian standards, his family was considered privileged middle class. The military provided his family with superior state-owned apartments, enhanced health care, and a dependable paycheck. That was a lot back then. Arkan had a decent life available to him, with assurances of a future life in the military. Which made me curious: Why didn't he just toe the line and stick with what he had coming? I asked Milan St. Protic, a Serbian scholar and former Yugoslav ambassador to the United States. "He was a military brat," said Protic. "Kids in the military were known to be some of the worst criminals, mainly because they could get away with a lot. More than most people." Being in a military family was a lot like being the son of the boss: You could screw up and test the boundaries more than others, until the boss decided that you'd gone too far and snapped back.

The record shows that Arkan was arrested for the first time in 1966 and sent away to a juvenile detention facility not far from Belgrade. He stayed there for about a year, and when he got out, the colonel had had enough. The colonel bused Arkan to the seaside town of Kotor, in Montenegro, where the young misfit was supposed to join the Yugoslav navy. Somewhere along the way, however, Arkan changed trains, or buses, with other plans in mind. He was heading to Paris!

As most accounts go, it was Arkan's first real taste of what life could be like outside of Yugoslavia. What it was like to break free. He was fifteen years old and thousands of miles away from home. There was wealth—and French women! The miniskirts, the see-through dresses, faddish at the time, with big gold-chain belts. Exhibitionism! On the streets students were rioting about

Vietnam. Sartre, having just rejected the Nobel Prize for literature, was behind a heady café scene. The possibilities were endless. What does a man do?

Here he refined his "light touch." I asked the former *Vreme* reporter Dulovic about this period. He laughed. "Arkan was like Tom Sawyer, constantly looking for the next big adventure," he said, taking a long drag on one of many cigarettes. "I remember this one picture of him holding wads of cash in his hands. He's standing with his arms outstretched and looking victorious. He was young and good-looking, with flowing black hair." Dulovic shook his head. "He was really something."

4

Two years later, in 1969, Arkan was back in jail. He was seventeen years old and his life was on hold. After the Parisians shipped him home, Serbian police arrested him for several burglaries, and a judge sentenced him to three years, one of his longest stretches behind bars. He was sent to a detention center for boys in Valjevo, Serbia, about an hour from Belgrade. Valjevo was a temporary home to around one hundred other male prisoners, ranging in age from sixteen to twenty-five and serving sentences for everything from car theft to rape. Like similar detention centers, Valjevo imposed a strict communist culture. Inmates were taught practical blue-collar trades, including plumbing and car mechanics. Food was predictably tasteless but more edible than in the adult facilities. There was soccer in the courtyard and chess inside and shelves full of books and plenty of portraits of the great leader, Tito.

Dobrivoje Radovanovic was a psychologist at Valjevo when Arkan did his time. Radovanovic would be the first—and last—adult in an official role to get close enough to witness the criminal mind of the teenaged Arkan. Radovanovic, who would later become the head of Belgrade's Institute for Criminological and Sociological Studies, would see signs of the master bank robber and brutal murderer Arkan would eventually become. "It was an interesting moment, looking back on it," the psychologist told me years later. "Seeing Arkan then."

According to Radovanovic, Arkan spent time working on his body, playing soccer in the courtyard, reading sci-fi novels, and watching American Westerns. "The cowboys in those Westerns were his idols," he said. "They were idols for many fourteen- and fifteen-year-olds, but I think the difference is that Arkan eventually realized that he could be even better than them."

At Valejvo, Arkan gained downtime to think and grow. He also made connections with other violent criminals. To his prison overlords, he was stern, tough, and unrelenting on anything that he considered to be an infraction of what he believed. He was also fastidious about his appearance in prison—his face always freshly shaved, his shirts and pants always laundered. "Everything around him had to be clean and ordered," Radovanovic remembered. He recalled that in his cell all of Arkan's clothes were folded, T-shirts made into perfect squares and pants turned into nice rectangles. His books were stacked neatly in a corner.

It came as no surprise that it was impossible to teach Arkan. In the classroom, he spoke out of turn endlessly. "You'd try to teach him and he cracked jokes," Radovanovic told me. "Like he'd interrupt a lesson and say, 'That's stupid, Professor. Everyone knows that.' Or he'd tell me to be careful what I say, like a threat."

"It wasn't that he was unintelligent," he went on. "He was bright. Almost too bright. Not book smart, but born smart. It was a pure kind of intellect."

However, he wasn't instantly respected among the inmate population. There were kids who wanted to beat his face in. "At first, some of the prisoners treated him like a woman," said Radovanovic. "He had a very high voice, and some laughed at him for that."

If anyone harbored doubts about Arkan's prowess, he quickly fixed them. The turning point was one day when a much bigger kid told him to shut up in class. They were tired of his outbursts. "You're talking like a woman," the prisoner sneered. "Are you a woman?" Arkan thought for a second. Then he picked up a chair and smashed the boy in the head, according to Radovanovic, sending him bleeding to the floor.

The act earned him immediate respect, and soon he organized his own crew—one of two or three gangs in the prison. "He became a leader," said Radovanovic. "Even though there were guys much stronger than him, many were drawn to him. He had a way with words. He was articulate and seemed to have bigger dreams and could talk about it. In this way, he was different."

Throughout his stay there, Radovanovic performed a battery of psychological tests on the young man. He conducted these tests on all inmates, which was an attempt by the state to understand the prisoners at a deeper level, what drove them to do what they did. His conclusion was that Arkan's behavior stemmed from his father's strict military discipline. "His father's harsh treatment created a man who was obsessed with the rule of his own laws," Radovanovic told me. "Arkan was a man who didn't have control when he was young, and because of that he strove to have total control when he was older and out of his father's house."

Radovanovic paused. "He despised his father and loved his mother," he continued. "All along I think he wanted to be a momma's boy. He yearned for his mother's world, a family, the hearth."

That life would never happen, of course. Radovanovic, in the end, perceived what he called "the classic portrait of the criminal mind." There was little the prison facility could do to reform him. Arkan, the psychologist told me, "was almost destined to do the things he did."

5

When Arkan was released from jail in 1972, he received a call that changed his life. It was Crazy Horse, calling from somewhere in Italy. He had a business going and thought Arkan might want in.

"Talk fast," said Arkan, who was twenty.

"I'm talking big money!" Crazy exclaimed.

"Seriously?"

"Yeah, real fucking money!"

"Now you got my attention," Arkan said. "What's the story?"

Italy is a thief's paradise, Crazy told him, talking a thousand miles a minute. People are rich! You know what rich is? The women are curvy and olive-skinned and beautiful! And easy! "The legs and curves!" he declared. The food, of course, was just icing on the cake. He had come up with a mantra: "Why steal cars from your neighbors when you can steal them from Italians!" It sounded like a fucking commercial. Crazy laughed his crazy guttural laugh, chuck-chucking like a Mack truck's engine turning over. "Fucking milk and honey," he shouted into the phone. "These streets are running with milk and honey."

All this sounded great, but it almost didn't happen. Soon after, Arkan was arrested for armed robbery, probably a last-minute effort to collect some travel money. The judge, having already seen him not long before, slapped him with a ten-year sentence in Padinska Skela prison, a dreary adult facility minutes from Belgrade. If he hadn't been the son of a military officer, the situation might have been much worse.

Still, no matter how you cut it, it was bad. He didn't have ten years to spare. Arkan sat in jail for a couple of weeks, and then he was gone, the first of many grander escapes to come. He climbed the security wall and ran. He didn't go home. He hardly slept. There was no time. Some people say that he stole a car, drove it to the Slovenian border, and crossed into Italy on foot. Others say he did like Sis Mis and Bora Madora, clung to the undercarriage of a slow-chugging passenger train and rode it, Spider-Man–like, out of the country.

Whatever happened, he fled Belgrade in 1972. His future would be bold: There would be epic crime sprees, bank robberies, girls, gambling, and multiple Houdini-like prison escapes. In the process he'd become one of Europe's most wanted men. History would be made, and remade, and a decade would pass before his return.

2

TAKING EUROPE

1

The story of his departure began, as these things do, with a simple, undeniable desire: a man's desire to be more self-reliant, to be distinctive, to provide fully for himself, maybe even for a family.

As the economy in Yugoslavia began to sag in the late 1960s, Tito swung open the long-closed borders and told his people that, if they needed to, they could go out into the world and try to make a living somewhere else. So hundreds of thousands packed their bags and left, carrying with them great hopes of improving their lives. They traveled west looking to fill labor gaps—to Holland, Italy, West Germany, Sweden, and Canada. Known as *Gastarbeiter*, the German term for guest workers, the new immigrants worked in shipyards, oil refineries, and gun factories; wherever they were needed. They worked hard, formed their own communities, and stashed their weekly cash payments away in mattresses, cupboards, and shoe boxes. By 1970 Yugoslavia had one of Europe's highest emigration rates, with 20 percent of the country's labor force employed abroad, and by 1980 there were over a million Yugoslavians working in foreign lands.

Not all of the workers were honest, or had noble intentions, of course.

Some used the new distance to plot against Tito. Others organized gangs and began to extract money with force—muscle, bats, knives, and guns. Sweaty factory floors? Forget about it. Fourteen-hour days sloshing around in oil and grease? Idiotic, because, as these new criminal immigrants saw it, that hard labor stuff, that was petty cash, and there was no time to watch years go by, because every day you got closer to your grave, and they'd already wasted a good chunk of their lives languishing under Tito. The criminals were in a rush to make money, in a rush to live large, to buy a nice suit, a gold watch, a fast car, a big house, and they did whatever it took to get these things—they cheated, robbed, and even killed.

When Arkan began to wander in the 1970s, he didn't stay anywhere for long. It seemed to be an operating rule for many of the aspiring Yugoslav gangsters, which makes it hard to track him as he darted this way and that across the continent. Over the months and years, he would make countless detours while he picked pockets; robbed houses, jewelry shops, and banks; and stole cars. He would bounce from gang to gang, woman to woman, city to city, country to country. Years would blur, as would people and places. Once he left Belgrade, he was a man on the run.

Most agree that after leaving Padinska, he made his way to London sometime in the summer of 1972. These were the sleepy days, before his John Wayne dream became real. If anything, it seems that London func-tioned for him as a sort of stop-off point, a pause before the bigger storm, when he left one life behind and took up another.

Old acquaintances told me that he moved in with a friend in the Chelsea part of the city. The roommate was unemployed and known to live off a dozen or so girlfriends. "A real ladies' man," a Serb named Dragan Stovic told me one afternoon years later in Belgrade. Dragan, a pseudonym, was a student at the London School of Economics at the time. "No one was as good with the ladies as this guy," he said.

During the day Arkan roamed the busy streets, met with friends, shored up criminal contacts, maybe dreamed of his life to come with a résumé full of crime. Some claim that he secured a part-time bellboy job at a local ho-tel, while others say he robbed apartments for enough money to tide him over until he got to Italy.

At night people saw Arkan at the Yugoslav social club in South Kensington. A small restaurant and bar that served national food and drink, the place occupied the ground floor of a nondescript building and was perceived by many in the large Yugoslav émigré population as a kind of home away from home. There were dissidents, diplomats, actors, dropouts, secret agents, dishwashers, and gangsters. Of all of them, the gangsters stuck out, Dragan recalled. It wasn't that there was a huge population of them. It was just that they were garish about everything. They arrived driving BMWs and Mercedeses, most of them stolen, with plates from Sweden, Germany, and Italy. They were always looking for something, always hungrier than the others. You could see it in their super-snazzy clothes; in their sleepless, bloodshot eyes; in the way they downed shots, drank bottle after bottle of plum schnapps, and tore through steaks like wolves; in the way they'd be there one week and then gone the next.

There was Vule the Taylor, who, in addition to leading a crew of itinerant thieves, made jeans. There was Johnny the Jumper, who ran stolen cars across the continent. There were numbers guys, cigarette and drug traffickers, and human smugglers. There were "suit guys," who stood around the upscale shops along Bond Street, offering to steal anything for half price. There were the guys who ran protection rackets at the city's factories, and there were dozens of petty thieves aspiring to grander things.

When Arkan began showing up at the club with these men, he had grown and was now just under six feet tall. He was muscular from exercising and kickboxing and as narrow as a beanpole, with long, wavy black hair. He dressed like a dandy, flaunting a penchant for expensive shirts and custom suits with big lapels and bell-bottoms. Some nights he wore a leather trench coat. Dragan recalled a two-bullet pistol, with a mother-of-pearl handle. "He'd pull it out of his Italian leather boot and show you he had backup," Dragan said. "He liked his gun. It was a statement."

Arkan was a different sort of gangster. He spoke gently, was articulate, wasn't markedly boastful, and came off as a thinker. He didn't drink or smoke, something the others did in excess nightly.

What's that you're drinking? Some sort of colada? someone might ask him at the club, eyeing up the viscous orange-colored drink in his hand.

Peach nectar, he would answer.

Seriously?

Peach nectar, he would repeat, probably giving a death stare. Problem?

If anything, expatriates in London like Dragan remember this early stage in Arkan's career for its exceptional oddness. One night stood out in particular. There was a house party in Chelsea. When Arkan arrived, some sort of 1970s rock music was blasting, and there was a group of partygoers freebasing heroin in a circle on the floor. "He walked right up to the people," Dragan recalled, "and said, 'That stuff is bad for you. Do you know your body is going to go to shit? Come on,' he said, 'let's ventilate this room.' It was very strange. No one really knew what to make of him." Strange was an understatement. The only people talking that way in the 1970s were straight-arrow assholes and religious freaks. Which one was Arkan? He was probably more a straight-arrow asshole, but the difference between him and the other straight-arrow assholes is that later he would kill you if you disagreed.

Dragan said that he spoke very little, if at all, about what he was doing in town and what his future plans were. Few people knew much about him. He went by different names—Arkan, Zeljko, and sometimes Marko. When he met girls, he introduced himself as a commodities trader, or a general manager of an international company, or a diplomat. "I'm Andy from Chicago," he might say. He employed different accents and spoke at least four other languages: Italian, French, German, and English. He was a Frenchman or an Italian or a Brit, depending on the night, the occasion, or the woman. The general consensus is that Arkan stayed in London for no more than a couple of months and then was gone, poof, like that. "Arkan was always hard to figure out," Dragan told me. "At one party, at this girl's house, he was standing in the corner, looking very aloof, like he had other things on his mind. That's how I remember him. Aloof. And that was the last time I saw him . . . then he started turning up in the news."

2

"Crazy" was born Dacovic Milutin in 1951 but picked up the name Crazy Horse when he was just a kid—because, as he told me later, "I was strong and liked to wrestle and couldn't sit still." Tall, tattooed, with a square face, a strong nose, a square jaw, and broken teeth, he looked like he had just stepped out of a Genet novel. He had quick hands, was always ready for a brawl, and had a bad temper amplified by the gallons of whiskey he sucked down.

It was 1967 when he landed in Italy. Getting there hadn't been easy, or fun. Like Arkan, he'd spent several months in a Belgrade prison, doing time, he said, for beating a man who had stolen his lover. He escaped, took a bus to the Yugoslav border, and crossed to Italy on foot. A day later he was in Trieste, and in ten days he was in Rome. Early on, he made money off the streets, hustling and picking pockets, and as he learned the language he began mingling with the Sicilian mob. If you didn't make good with the Sicilians you could kiss your career good-bye, he said. Crazy was charismatic. He could talk his way into anything, and he had the muscle and guile to back it up. The Sicilians allowed Crazy to handle his own protection rackets, which turned out to be lucrative. As he put it to me almost forty years later, "I did favors for people. Everyone had a problem, so I solved the problems."

By 1968, Crazy, in his estimation, was a small but precise force in Rome. Occasionally he sighted the filmmaker Federico Fellini on the busy streets and secretly imagined that his burgeoning life was the stuff of great crime movies. His idols were French film bad guys, Jean-Paul Belmondo and Alain Delon. Crazy was bold like them and good-looking like them, but the difference was—and sometimes this annoyed him—he was living the real life. He was arrested more than fifty times, and he couldn't even remember how many times Italy had kicked him out on immigration violations, but he kept coming back, wanting more. He was insatiable. It showed in everything he did. Later, the Sicilian family boss offered him an apartment downtown, a sign of respect. That's about when Crazy reached out to Arkan and a slew of other Serbian men and started to organize his own squad. "I called all my criminal friends and told them about Italy," he recalled later on. "There was so much money to be made."

The men arrived with and without visas, jumping the borders, stowing away in the guts of cargo ships or riding on the tops of trains. Crazy directed them to family-run lodges, ones with only a handful of rooms where backpackers on a shoestring budget might stay. Living on the fringes was a necessary precaution for his budding crime syndicate. As Crazy told me, you needed a place where the managers didn't snoop around or ask for travel documents. The fewer people who knew about their presence in the city the better. He said the idea was to be as close to nonexistence as possible. Otherwise you'd have the police breaking down your doors or, worse, rival gangs waiting for you to step out, and then shooting you dead in your tracks.

The rivals were numerous. They included, of course, the Italians; then, the Albanians, who moved drugs and engaged in a lot of human trafficking from Asia; and the Russians, who dealt arms. There were other Yugoslavian crews as well, with their hands in a little of everything, from smuggling cigarettes and jeans to selling heroin and pimping. Of the Yugo crews, there was Ljubomir Magas, a steely bastard who beat up anyone who looked at him wrong, and there was a Montenegrin who carried around a single grenade in his pocket in case he was captured. There was also Karate Bob, a flamboyant pimp with the most beautiful ladies in Italy. The list goes on.

Crazy dubbed himself "teacher," now a ringleader with a handful of guys under his command. "I taught them the ropes," he told me. "Showed them the towns, how to do what we needed to do to get paid." The crew operated across Italy, jumping on trains or using stolen cars, and made monthly jaunts to other parts of Europe, including Switzerland, Germany, and Belgium. The money was always good, he said. Damned good at times. It was hard work, but worth it. "We woke at 7:00 A.M. and worked all day. At night, we dressed up in the best fashion—Armani, Versace—and went to nightclubs," he boasted. "We drank and smoked and fooled with girls and talked about our exploits of the day, guy talk, what we scored, the take. Every night, two, three in the morning we were doing this. And then up at seven again to do it all over. Every day was like that. We didn't sleep. We could have slept back in Yugoslavia."

Then Arkan came, and life was different for everyone.

3

Crazy remembered Arkan materializing in Rome in late 1972, though he can't say for sure. Like the others, Arkan settled in at a boardinghouse near the city center. The room probably wasn't much different than his associates' places, a stained single or double mattress on a bent-up frame, a sink jammed into the corner, a tiny closet with an extra set of linens, and a foot rug dropped on the old creaky wood floor, perfect for muffling late-night sounds, so when he came and went at odd hours, no one would hear.

When Arkan finally sat down with Crazy, he announced that he was ready. "What's the deal?" he wanted to know. As he stared across the table, Crazy saw a kid with a lot of guts but not much else. "He was just a beginner," said Crazy. "He was naive and young and needed someone to teach him."

"There's a lot of money to be made," Crazy told Arkan, his voice sharp and fast as gunfire. "And I know how to make it."

"That's why I'm here."

"Good. Let's do something."

As Crazy explained, he was Arkan's first and only real mentor. Whether that's entirely true is hard to tell, but Crazy was in Italy and did have a reputation in Belgrade for bringing in new talent and teaching that new talent the rules of the criminal game. In fact, newspapers in Belgrade wrote about his criminal activities and, when I asked other former gangsters about Crazy's credibility, most said that he knew what he was talking about, though he did have a tendency to exaggerate his place in the world, especially when he had some whiskey in his blood. As one younger Serb told me, "He's a drunk, but he did his time, paid his dues."

Crazy told me that he taught Arkan almost everything he knew: where money could be made, and where there was trouble with the police. He told him who smuggled jeans and cigarettes and how, and who was bringing in heroin and cocaine. One week he might have taken him to Milan, where he showed him crowded tourist areas like the Duomo and the glassed-in arcade Galleria Vittorio Emmanuele II, where a blind man could get rich in the enterprise of picking pockets. Another week he showed him the upscale neighborhoods in Rome and Vatican City.

As others his age pursued advanced degrees in economics and literature or got dead-end jobs, Arkan earned a Ph.D. in street skills. Soon he was developing his own repertoire. When he scoped targets, he dressed as if he were going to a law office, wearing a fancy Italian suit and carrying a briefcase or some other leather bag. He carried a pocket-sized notepad, Crazy said, and, when he needed to, paused to scribble down descriptions about how a particular house might be entered, noting details like the distance from the ground to a first-floor window and whether there was a steel gate or a wood door, and how many people appeared to be living in the residence. When there were too many people on the streets, he most likely stood in front of the villa and stocked away the salient details in his brain while pretending to be quietly taking in the sun and the blue sea sky, a man simply contemplating a beautiful Italian day. "Arkan stored things in his head, like a computer," said Bratislav Grubacic, general manager of Belgrade's VIP News Services. After sundown, he'd organize a crew of men and steal everything he could carry. "He was a madman."

Robbery appeared to suit him very well. It played up to all of his talents: the muscle; the quickness; the independence; the fearlessness; and also the superhuman knack for sizing up enemies, predicting their movements, and exploiting any perceived weaknesses. What separated him even more, most people pointed out, was his devotion to success. He was more devoted than anyone else, and would work harder, no matter the consequences.

Shops became his specialty. He robbed dozens—gold shops, pawnbrokers, and groceries. The banks would come later. He wore masks, stocking caps, wigs, or fake mustaches. Disguises gave him confidence, and also pleasure. His real innovation was bike riding. The crew would try to persuade him to take a car, laughing at the idea of a robber on a bike. They'd offer backup, but he carried a gun—the lady's pistol with a mother-of-pearl handle—and that was all he needed. Besides, sometimes things were better done alone, and he seemed to enjoy doing things on his own, riding through the streets of Rome, Milan, and Trieste, feeling the sun on his face and the freedom of the open air.

He grew bolder, testing out his new skills, like a superhero just finding out that he had a super power. He came across as unorthodox, even a little nutty. When he entered a place this knowing grin would sometimes curl over his baby face, the crime reporter Dulovic told me. "As a robber he was a gentleman," Dulovic explained. "He'd go into a store or a bank and say to the beautiful woman at the counter, 'You're so beautiful, please be gentle and so kind and give me some charity.'" Then he'd draw his gun.

It was all part of a grander strategy: to separate himself, to get rich, and be powerful. Arkan "went to Italy focused on the job at hand, which was to make money and rise in the world," said Grubacic, the newspaper editor. "It was all a part of the big plan."

It wasn't long before the police were onto his trail. According to Crazy, Arkan eventually was arrested in Rome for armed robbery, but somehow managed to slip away, though I could never verify this. Still, by most accounts, Arkan had begun to rack up arrest warrants in 1972 and 1973, and investigators referred to him as "The Italian" because he was one of the only Serbian criminals who spoke the language like an Italian, and also sort of looked native.

When Crazy's crew partied at night, Arkan typically stayed around the semidark rooms at the pension, doing push-ups on the floor, planning for future heists. He did have women, like most of the transient men around him, though none stuck around long. When the money started rolling in, he grew fond of gambling. The small-time games didn't hold much appeal, of course. Instead, he played games in private apartments and in hotel rooms, with tens of thousands of dollars on the table. If there were high-stakes games in Switzerland or Germany, he'd evidently hop in a car or take a train and go. Sometimes games lasted for days, and he'd return to his Italian crew, red-eyed and bent over in exhaustion, his pockets either stuffed with cash or frayed and empty, with tens of thousands of dollars of debt making him anxious to do another big job.

4

He knew one thing for sure: If he wanted to advance this lifestyle he was going to need some stronger backup, certainly stronger than Crazy and his crew. That's where the Yugoslav State Security, or UDBA, came in. The UDBA was Yugoslavia's super spy agency, similar to the Soviet Union's KGB. It's believed that Arkan made contact with the agency in 1972 or 1973, allegedly through his father's friendship with the agency's head, Stane Dolanc. As this story goes, Arkan's father, Colonel Raznatovic, decided to put him in touch with the UDBA in hopes of salvaging some honor in his son's life.

No one seems to know exactly where the first meeting between Arkan and UDBA operatives took place; a number of theories are out there. He could have met them in England, Germany, or Switzerland. The agency, organized by Tito's Interior Ministry to take down Yugoslav émigrés with a terrorist bent, had underground cells in almost every Western European country, in secret apartments, in the smoky back rooms of bars, and in national restaurants, like the one in London.

The agency already had a file on Arkan, according to Bozidar Spasic, who was high up at the UDBA at the time, and in charge of many of the international operatives. Being a domestic and international spy outfit, the UDBA had eyes in many places. And, as most official accounts indicate, they were impressed with his résumé. Spasic, who is now a private detective in Belgrade, told me that the decision to forge a deal with Arkan was uncomplicated. Certainly it helped that Arkan's father had been a top colonel, but there were other factors, too. "He was a good source for us," Spasic explained to me one fall day in 2004, "because even at sixteen he acted like an adult criminal. He had the necessary skills to do the jobs."

When Spasic spoke about "jobs," he meant "dirty jobs." "Like assassinations," he said, looking into my eyes to see if I'd flinch. I didn't. Spasic was a compact man with square shoulders and graying hair. Arkan, he said, would become a hired killer for the UDBA. It was a deal struck with the devil—but a profitable one. In return, the spy organization, Spasic claimed, would offer Arkan a new life whenever he got too deep into crime and needed a trapdoor.

Among its services, the UDBA provided fake passports, forged documents, and phony driver's licenses. They also provided money, guns, and ammunition. If he ever got into trouble with the law in Europe or anywhere else, the agency would be there to help him wiggle out, even when it meant organizing a prison escape—and there would be many prison escapes. Back then, of course, no one at the UDBA—not Dolanc, not Spasic—had a clue that hiring Arkan would be one of the agency's biggest mistakes.

Arkan knew the connection was an invaluable one, but could he deal with killing a man when the time came? That was a seminal question. A responsive killing was one thing, but premeditated killing was entirely different. You put thought into the act. You made a plan, sought out your target, and then put a bullet in that unsuspecting target's head. It required a special kind of moral calculation, one that required a man to separate his life into light and dark, and to be okay living with the dark, even justifying it.

Still, there's no doubt that the new relationship was a source of fresh energy. Once operating alone or with small, disparate gangs, he was now a man with a clandestine government agency behind him. The relationship, cultivated by men like Spasic, supplied him with the confidence and resources to do whatever the hell he dreamed of—and his dreams would become outsized.

The agency didn't need him right away. They told him they'd be in touch. We'll have something for you soon, they promised. Who, when, and where, they didn't say, but they'd find him.

Soon, they said.

Take your time, he could have easily responded. I have plans in the meantime.

And they could have just as easily have said, We'll be watching.

5

His first reported murder didn't have anything to do with the UDBA. According to a Serbian magazine called *Profil,* the murder took place on February 1, 1974, in Milan, when Arkan and two armed partners strutted into a family restaurant. It was around lunchtime. One man guarded the door as the other man and Arkan, sporting a sawed-off shotgun and a pistol, with a stocking covering his face, approached the headwaiter.

"Signori, Signori," Arkan announced to the man, with a tinge of black humor. "There are no problems. This is just an ordinary robbery."

Then he turned to the room and proclaimed, "For those who listen to us, there is no reason to be afraid. I beg you to be so good and generous and buy your own lives."

Arkan waved his guns, according to the article, and demanded that the guests begin to put their valuables into an open bag that one of his men was taking around the room—bracelets, necklaces, watches, cash, whatever they had.

Meanwhile, the owner of the restaurant suddenly materialized from the kitchen, wondering what was going on. According to *Profil,* he asked out loud if the men were shooting a movie. Had no one informed him? Was his restaurant going to be famous?

Arkan didn't give the man a chance. The shotgun leveled and his finger went down on the trigger and that was it. What else could he do? The guy came in, surprised him, and, with the adrenaline coursing through his veins, boom, the gun went off. The force of the blast struck the owner, cutting his upper body almost completely in half, like you might chop off the midsection of a small tree, which sent him to the floor in a bloody pile.

Silence engulfed the place—the guests and even Arkan's crew. What the hell had just happened? It took time to translate. After the seconds began to accumulate, everyone in that room, even Arkan, started to understand that they had, whether they liked it or not, entered into frighteningly new territory. Whatever anyone else in the restaurant was feeling didn't matter much. What mattered was that for Arkan life would be different after this.

Moments later Arkan dropped the shotgun to his side, slipped the pistol into his waistband, and ran out of the place, vanishing from those people's lives forever.

Although the police wouldn't get him, his thoughts surely would. At twenty-one, he was now suddenly more than just a thief. What he'd allegedly done was just a prelude to a much colder character that would evolve in the years to come. If he could kill once, he could kill again, and again and again. This was certainly a turning point, like that transformative moment where you look at old pictures of yourself and you don't look the same anymore.

There was no turning back. His real life was just getting started.

3

HOW WE CHANGE

After Arkan headed for Sweden, Crazy started thinking about leaving Italy himself. He was sick of the gangster life and ready to put it behind him. Not just for a week or a month or a yearlong vacation, but for good. It had been fun and profitable, but it had also been draining; he was burned out. "I was exhausted," said Crazy through a translator, when I met him in Belgrade in 2005.

Crazy still had an angular, tough-guy face and was boxer stocky, with arctic white hair. He wore a tailored blue suit, and though probably once expensive, the sleeves were slightly frayed and his white shirttail hung out the back. His eyes were shot with red from drinking J & B. He had a tattoo of a red rose on the top of his left hand and, when he took off his coat and rolled up his sleeves, an American flag materialized on his right forearm.

"I decided to leave Italy and everything else," he said. "Life was getting too complicated." What he meant by complicated was that the game was getting dangerous: Territorial disputes between ethnic gangs were popping up all over the place, and people settled conflicts most often with guns. The old days when two gentlemen settled a score over espresso in the back of a sidewalk café—that was so yesterday. There were other things, too. He didn't feel like going to jail anymore and, most important, dying young didn't exactly appeal to him as much as it once had. He wanted to live, and living meant getting out.

He told me that in 1972 he sold the apartment in Rome and packed up the $100,000 or so he had left from his life as an outlaw and said a final good-bye to friends. He bid farewell to his crew and to the country, which he loved and had called home, the women, the wine, and the food. With his fugitive status in Serbia long expired, he boarded a train and made the long slog home to Belgrade. He was thirty-two.

He told me he rented an apartment with leftover money in one of the gray super high-rises in New Belgrade—fifteen-, twenty-, and thirty-story buildings, some with footprints as wide as Manhattan blocks, which loomed like an invading army over the city's exhaust-choked horizon. As luck would have it, there was also a ground-floor space available for rent. Built in the 1960s and 1970s, the building was cheap and in good condition, Crazy said. So he snapped it up, put some money into renovation, and opened the city's first Italian restaurant, which he still owns today.

The main building, however, hasn't aged very well. It possesses the sad feeling of a ghetto. The concrete exterior is covered in graffiti; most prominently someone has scrawled in bold, FUCK YOUR MOTHER. The cement planters outside, once filled with flowers when the building went up, are now overgrown with weeds or loaded with squashed beer cans, cigarettes, or stray condoms. In front of Crazy's restaurant, the sidewalk is broken up and weeds creep through cracks. Many of the other stores on the ground floor—there was once a flower shop, a copy store, and some offices—appear shuttered.

When you walk into the restaurant, however, you walk out of one world and into another. It's clear much time and imagination has been invested in the smallish space. The walls are covered with pictures from *The Godfther* movies. There are mirrors, a wall of wine, a small wood bar, glass-topped tables, and a pond the size of a kiddie pool, with some plant life and a miniature waterfall.

Crazy manages the restaurant and doubles as a waiter. An old woman, who looks like his mother, serves up all sorts of pastas and pizzas. Wine and coffee is imported from Italy. When the temperature warms, there is a forlorn patch of concrete outside for tables and umbrellas. Although only a quarter of the place filled up for lunch that day, it didn't seem to bother Crazy. More than a business venture, the restaurant is a place to meet old friends, drink, eat, and reminisce about the good old days.

"Boy, I made a lot of money back then," he boasted, his mind traveling back to the Italian days. He whistled. "There was lots of money over there in Italy. I became Italian. Sometimes I went to Switzerland. There were lots of banks there. Lots and lots of money."

"It was so long ago," he told me, before adding, "I miss it." When he said this there was an evident sadness in his voice, as with anyone else who finally comes to terms with the fact that the bright years are long past.

He got up and walked around the restaurant. I wasn't sure if he'd come back, but he did. "It's been a long day," he said, shaking his head. He explained that his mistress had broken up with him, and his wife and he were fighting. "Do you know what that is like?" he asked.

"To lose a mistress? Or to fight with your wife?"

"Both," he said. I shook my head. He called for another J & B and water. After about two hours of talking with me, Crazy had downed about seven J & Bs. In the twenty or so seats, there was now only one couple eating. He served them pizza and wine and they told Crazy they enjoyed it. "The people that come here love my restaurant," he said, as if trying to convince me. I ordered a pizza—and it was pretty good.

Then he abruptly shifted gears. "Once a man came in here and asked why my shop is so empty," he said. " 'You know why?' I asked him. 'All of my friends have been assassinated. I'm alone here, with my memories. Fuck off.' "

When Arkan left Italy, Crazy wasn't sure if he'd ever see his so-called student again, though he did do his best to keep track of him, mainly through newspapers and common friends. "I was his teacher, but he outgrew that," he said. "We were on the same level in the sixties and seventies. Then he became a millionaire, with all of his villas, and I became a waiter, with no bodyguards. I drank, I saw girls, I didn't have much money, but I slept peacefully at night."

He did see Arkan again. About twenty years later. On that day Crazy did one last thing for his student: He saved his life, but that story would have to wait. Crazy didn't want to talk anymore. He was tired, the J & Bs were getting to him, and he had to deal with his women problems. "Another time," he said before getting up and disappearing into the back. Which was fine, because there were other things that happened to Arkan in the years in between.

4

THE CASE OF THE ELUSIVE MAN

A man wanted to tell me a story about Arkan. He called it "the famous story, the one I wouldn't forget."

There were conditions. Before he said anything he made me swear not to use his name. "Names are not good here," he said. "That is the first thing you need to understand."

The man was in his fifties and wore a brown trenchcoat, his face heavily lined and his nose flat and wide as a lion's. We sat at a dreary bar in downtown Belgrade, not far from Arkan's compound. It was late. The bar was just a hole-in-the-wall with no signage outside. About a dozen others sat in the midnight shadows, in booths and at the long wood bar. The Smiths burbled out of the stereo.

I heard this so many times as I traveled through Serbia. You must protect my identity. Once we leave each other, I don't exist in your life. I'm gone, my face forgotten. Got it? My sources pleaded with me. Some made the hand sign for a gun, aimed at the mouth. "Arkan has men who protect him, even in death," they said. "That is no joke."

They told me I should be careful, too. It is easy to get lost in Serbia, they said. One man actually used that term: "lost." What he meant was that if you ask too many questions about Arkan, you'll end up at the bottom of the Danube River. This is what Serbia became to me: a place where I could get "lost."

"So," the man asked me, "do you agree?" I told him I had already forgotten his name. I made the sign of zipping my mouth shut.

"Did you hear the one about Arkan in Frankfurt?" he asked, raising his bushy eyebrows. "It's the story of Arkan and the flowers."

I didn't know that one, and he seemed pleased, smiling as he sipped at a straight whiskey. He leaned toward me, as if in secret.

"So," he said. "Arkan walked up to this woman at the bank counter. She was beautiful and he handed her a bouquet of roses and he told her, 'You are so gorgeous.' Fucking guy. When she put the roses to her nose, he pulled the gun on her and told her to give him all the money."

"Excuse me," I said. "Roses?" I scribbled it down on my notepad. It sounded too much like Hollywood.

"Yes," said the man. "Roses! You don't believe me?" He made a sour face.

No, I didn't believe him. "How do you know this?" I asked. I always threw the question out there, even though I knew the answer before it came.

"I know," said the man. "Everyone knows this one."

Of course they do. He was right. I heard the story four more times, though the amount of money he stole in the Frankfurt robbery ranged from $60,000 to $125,000 U.S. dollars. Still, what was I supposed to think about it? I couldn't verify it: There were no newspaper accounts and no criminal records, but did that necessarily make it untrue?

"Did you hear the one about how he robbed three banks in one day?" asked another anonymous Serb. He said he was living in Italy in the 1980s and was in a position to know these things.

"What?" I asked.

"In Stuttgart."

"Do you know the year?"

"I don't, but it's true. He did. Boom. Boom. Boom. Like that," the man said, clapping his hands. "He was very, very good. There's no question about that."

The fact is, many saw Arkan's life in Europe from 1972 to 1983 as a Hollywood drama, and because of this few really knew what exactly had gone on. The reports were scattered and he was difficult to track. He seemed to move every other month and sometimes every week, coming and going on trains, buses, and stolen cars. The incessant wandering made Jack Kerouac and Neal Cassady's crisscrossing of America look amateurish. Favoring countries with flourishing Yugoslav diasporas—Germany, Austria, Holland, and Sweden—he tended to blend in and disappear. It certainly would have been easy to mix him up with the dozens of other criminals and their operations. When he stuck around a city or town, he occupied no-name pensiones or shoddy hotels, or shacked up with local girls. Rarely, if ever, did he have a room or apartment of his own. In fact, there's no indication that in all of his travels in Europe he ever owned or rented a place for himself.

There was other stuff, too, such as his constantly changing identities. By the time he left Crazy behind Arkan had dozens of fake identities in rotation. One week, for instance, he might be a German tourist, the next an Italian businessman, later a British diplomat. He knew the languages, had official backup documents and stories. He sported fake mustaches, wigs, hoods, and balaclavas. Sometimes he allowed his hair to grow long and curly—like John Travolta in *Saturday Night Fever,* as a witness to one of his crimes would say. For Arkan, going from one phony identity to the next would become as easy as putting on a new suit. In this way, he could become invisible.

So how was I going to find out what he did and didn't do in Europe? It's especially problematic if you don't even know whom you're following. All of this made the facts about Arkan hugely complicated, a quandary that would only grow worse with the passage of time. As he plunged deeper into crime, as more people chased him and even more people talked about him, the details of his life would become more stretched, twisted, bent, and even eroded, like something left outside in the winter. If his life were a photograph, it would be out of focus. Sure, there were things that we know he did. That's why half a dozen countries would soon have alerts out for him in the 1970s and 1980s, and why Interpol, the international police agency, would describe him to *The New York Times* as "the most qualified bank robber in Europe." For all the things we know, there must be a hundred other acts that we don't know, things committed by an alter ego built into a fake passport. Then, of course, there were all the things that he didn't do that were attributed to him, just because they began to fit the spectacular mythos of Arkan.

"There was the bank robbery in Antwerp," another old friend of Arkan's told me one morning on the phone. Of course, I couldn't reveal his name.

"Antwerp? I didn't know he robbed a bank in Belgium."

"He did." The man was delighted that I hadn't heard. "One day he was sitting around a café with a few friends talking about how they were going to take the money from this bank around the corner. You know they spent a lot of time at cafés," he said. "But that day, you know, they were making calculations, discussing how to go in and do it. They'd actually been talking about it for a few days, and Arkan got sick of all the talk, got up, and left. Twenty minutes later he returned with a couple bags of cash and said, 'This is how you do it.'"

"He'd robbed the bank?"

"Just like that."

"How much did he get?"

"Twenty or thirty thousand, I don't know."

"That's a lot."

"But that wasn't the point. The point was that the other guys were pussies. They just spoke about doing a big heist but never did it. He wasn't afraid of anything."

I heard a lot about pussies. Usually the pussies were people who challenged Arkan but ended up backing down. Like the story another anonymous source told me about the police in Frankfurt. In early 1983, Arkan and a partner were running from the German police after a post office heist. Suddenly, in midstride, Arkan had second thoughts. As my source explained, "Arkan asks, 'Why the hell are we running? We shouldn't be running from these German pussies.' So they turn back and pull their guns on the police. The police, of course, are taken off guard and don't know what to do. Arkan tells them to take off their clothes. They steal their money and run off, laughing about the police standing naked in the road."

Of them all, Branimir Gugl probably had the best story. He even said I could use his real name. Gugl was a Belgrade attorney and had at one time represented Arkan, as well as former Serbian president Slobodan Milosevic. "The casino robbery in San Remo was one of the robberies I remember most," Gugl told me one night in a red-lit café in central Belgrade. "The place was on the water and he arrived in a speedboat."

I wrote it down, though I sort of laughed.

"There were five hundred people there, including workers and players," he went on, firing up a cigarette. "Arkan drove up in the boat, parked it, and walked right in with his gun and took all the money from the bank."

How could a man single-handedly rob a casino? I wondered. It was not like *Ocean's Eleven,* where he was operating with a team of highly talented individuals with state-of-the-art technology. He was one man with a gun. Gugl chuckled. He wore a dark bespoke suit with a crisp white shirt. "He even took the money from the players," Gugl said, nodding. "Probably five hundred people were there."

"Five hundred?" I asked.

He produced a Cheshire smile.

"I don't believe it."

"He did. I know this story. He told me it. He went in, got the money, and then he was gone. He was that good."

There were times, after sitting with these men in the dimly lit bowels of cafés and bars, when I had to rush out and get some air. It was too much. Where was the truth? I wondered. What did Arkan really do? What do I believe? Who was this man?

His time in Sweden began to provide some answers.

5

THE SMILING
BANK ROBBER

1

Gothenburg, Sweden, slouches along the hilly coastline of the rough-and-tumble North Sea. Built by the Dutch, the stately port city was home to a Volvo plant and some of the country's principal shipyards. It had always been an epicenter for industry, drawing workers from all over the world and priding itself on its blue-collar soul. There are canals; a famous wooden roller coaster; a downtown park where people like to sit, drink beer, and lull away time after work; rolling streets of quaint three- and four-story wooden houses; and a sprawling university. Being smack in line with the jet stream, the city experiences protracted periods of rain and gloom, not unlike Seattle. In the summer months, Gothenburg being so far north, it's daylight almost around the clock, and it's hard to sleep.

Arkan glided into the city for the first time in March 1974, a month after the alleged murder in Italy, when the trees were just starting to turn green again after a long, gloaming winter. Records show that he registered at a modest hotel called Lundgren, not far from the train station. Suspicious that police would be tracking him, he signed in at the front desk with a fake Belgian passport, according to police reports. His false name: Mirko Saric.

It was a busy moment in the city's history, with foreign workers pouring in to fill a yawning labor shortage. Although other countries on the continent had struggled to rebuild and replace infrastructure after World War II, Sweden, as a neutral country with a population of about eight million, had emerged from the war with one of the few unwrecked industrial bases on the continent, and was now seeing an astonishing growth of about 4 percent a year. Factory floors needed filling and there weren't enough Swedes to do the unappealing jobs. So the country reached out across the borders and drew up labor agreements similar to Germany's *Gastarbeiter* program. Italians arrived first, followed by Hungarians, Turks, and, finally, the Yugoslavs in the late 1960s. Since then hundreds of thousands had come and the Swedish streets reflected the new emigrant life, especially in Gothenburg.

With the new workers came the concrete jungles, rising from the earth like icebergs on the city's outskirts. This was just a fraction of the million units of housing planned for construction over the next decade. The complexes were ugly three- to eight-story concrete buildings, devoid of character, mainly located on the city's borders and reachable by an extensive transportation system that included trams and buses. To the immigrants, the concrete jungles were home. To Arkan, the jungles were a good place to recruit. Not only that, when things heated up, the jungles would be a good place to hide, even disappear.

Although there was a pronounced frenzy among the bulging immigrant community to make a living and to get ahead, Gothenburg was a pretty easygoing, quiet place. People would even refer to the city as Edenic. Folks got along. Even with all the immigrants coming in, racial tension scarcely existed. Transcendental meditation was in vogue. So was the rock group ABBA. Hard crime was virtually nonexistent, and because of that people didn't have to think about looking over their shoulders and most front doors weren't locked. Murder, at the time, was almost unheard-of. It wasn't until the late 1960s that the police in Sweden began counting stolen cars. Compared to the rest of Europe, Sweden had one of the lower rates of incarceration. It was an open society, unusual for a world that was deep into the Cold War. With a social democratic government, the country was known for its *folkhem* model, where every citizen was cared for and considered important.

More than enforcers, the police were perceived as caretakers. There was no SWAT team, and the police hadn't even started carrying pistols until 1965. Many officers still traveled on foot or by bike. To Arkan, Sweden was an unlocked bank vault, protected by a bunch of panda bears.

Johannes Knutsson, a professor at the National Swedish Police Academy, remembered those early years. "Before Arkan, there were few instances of firearms," said Knutsson. "We were a society of hunters, with mad hunters in the countryside, but armed criminals weren't that common." The arrival of Arkan changed all of that. "He was one of a number of criminals that brought Sweden into high-crime society," Knutsson told me. "He was very notable in that way."

The era of the smiling bank robber was about to begin.

2

It didn't take him long before he met a cute Swedish girl. Her name was Agneta. According to most, Arkan picked her up at a nightclub, though one person told me that the two met at a local jail where Arkan was being held overnight and Agneta was employed as a social worker. Whatever the case, the girl must have taken an instant liking to him and he to her, because before long Arkan had collected his things and moved into her city apartment.

Days ticked past. At the new apartment, Arkan poured over area maps, acquainting himself with the city and the city's suburbs, noting middle- and upper-class neighborhoods. He consulted locals and took long drives through the areas he planned to hit. Agneta's apartment appeared to become a kind of informal headquarters. Arkan would do what Crazy did in Italy, but bigger. He made phone calls to friends in other countries and urged them to come. He would begin with small stuff, like robbing apartments, and as he learned the terrain and the way the police operated, how long it took them to respond and what sort of response they made, he would then move on to riskier undertakings.

What of his crooked history he shared with Agneta is impossible to confirm, and how much she would participate in his criminal future is even murkier. When I asked people from Sweden about her, no one seemed to know much at all except that she was Arkan's girl. The one thing that I could verify is that she never went to jail, even though she appeared to be an accessory by, if anything, proximity. In the years to come she wouldn't talk about Arkan or what he or she did, even when he was long gone.

When his players began appearing from abroad, and from the city's concrete jungles, the cramped apartment probably felt a lot like a bus station. There were between two and five men there, depending on the day and night. That's not including "the girls" who would come by. Sometimes, the visitors crashed on the floor. The men stayed for days, or weeks. When you read police reports about the time, the scene felt sort of like an improvised but functional hippie commune, with people coming and going all the time, doing whatever they pleased. When the men weren't talking stakeouts and money they stormed the town and chased girls, though Arkan was still known to abstain. Swedish girls, it was said, liked Yugoslavian men. Compared to the native boys with their ubiquitous blue eyes and bushy blond hair, the Yugoslavs, with their black hair and dark eyes, were no doubt novel and mysterious.

3

Arkan and his men worked as if they were always hungry and would never be satisfied. At least two or three places were hit a night. They stole cash, rifles, televisions, jewelry, gold, furs, and whatever they could get their hands on. When one house turned up nothing, they went to another, even if it was unplanned. The hunger for robbing didn't quit. Occasionally, local people came to them about a prospective job. When a man who was recently divorced told the crew about his ex-wife's stash of SKr 60,000, about $9,000, Arkan accepted the job and was happy to pay him 20 percent for the information.

The crew came down on the city like a freight train out of the sky. At times it seemed like the police were dozing or on a permanent vacation, just like the owners of the apartments and houses the men visited at night. In three weeks the crew committed more than fifty robberies in and around Gothenburg. It wasn't exactly *The Italian Job*, but it was enough to earn envy. Stolen goods were pawned and the money that came in was spent on suits, fast cars, and gambling, all of which must have conjured a fascinating image among his fellow Yugoslavs living in the dreary concrete jungles and toiling away at the shipyards.

"Arkan would gain the image of a kind of godfather," said Walter Repo, an investigative journalist who specializes in crime. "His story here is the classic one of a guy who goes from pickpocketing to millionaire. And for the young Yugoslavians fighting to get into the Swedish system, Arkan was someone who gave them hope."

The more crimes he committed, the tougher it became for him to end this life, to go back and be honest, or to be just some guy looking for legitimate work. This feeling must have held up for him even when his experiences had unpleasant endings, when he was imprisoned, when he was beaten up, knocked unconscious, told to go home and quit. He became hardened. He couldn't be stopped, and it must have gotten him to thinking that as long as he kept doing what he was doing, he'd always be fine.

And why not? On April 19, 1974, after having been in Sweden for just over a month, he moved on to more perilous adventures, testing just how far he could go. With two men he hijacked a bank courier. A friend had told him about the opportunity, saying it would be easy. It was supposed to work like this: After the bank courier picked up money from a Saab dealership, the men would intercept him, grab the cash, and bolt. Simple.

As it turned out, there was nothing straightforward about the job, mainly because he was still just a kid learning the ropes.

It started out as planned. The courier arrived on time, went into the dealership, and returned with the money. When the courier emerged with the bag, however, he wouldn't give the damn thing up. Arkan and his men attacked and the courier put up a fight, screamed, threw rights and lefts, and attracted the attention of a few people eating at the restaurant across the street, who decided to come over and help. Meanwhile someone else called the police, and seconds later a siren screamed in the distance.

What the hell? Arkan, or one of the other men, fanned a gun at the crowd. Stay back, they shouted.

By the time the criminals extracted the courier's bag and were speeding away, the police were there, chomping at their tailpipe. A car chase ensued. Reports didn't indicate how long the chase lasted, but it didn't end in a crash or death. As soon as shots started coming from Arkan's car, the police let him go. Although it wasn't exactly a smooth escape, Arkan would indeed learn from this: The police were easy to scare. The Saab was abandoned for a boxy Ford Taunus and back at the apartment the robbers counted the money: $2,000. Not a bad snag at the time.

Nevertheless, there were bigger takes out there. Arkan knew this, and he tossed out the idea of banks. That's where the money was, he told his countrymen—and he knew from experience. Can you see the money?

Are you crazy? The men probably checked his face to see. Maybe he was. Maybe he wasn't.

But he was serious.

Who's in?

Sweden's banks were next, and this was where the real test would come.

4

Arkan was not the first distinguished bank robber in Sweden. That distinction goes to Clark Olofsson. Olofsson was most famous for the Norrmalmstorg bank robbery in Stockholm in 1973, and before that he had been in jail for murdering a police officer and for other armed bank robberies. In the Norrmalmstorg case, his friend Jan-Erik "Janne" Olsson, who was armed with a machine gun, first walked into the Norrmalmstorg bank and took four hostages, all bank employees. After the police showed up, Olsson demanded that they bring Clark Olofsson to him, along with two guns, two bulletproof vests, a fast car, and the kronor equivalent of $750,000.

When Olofsson arrived, the two men locked themselves and the hostages into a bank vault and waited for the money and everything else. Hostages would later recall Olofsson, who had dark shaggy hair and looked a little like Jim Morrison, singing Roberta Flack's "Killing Me Softly." The money was stalled and the crisis stretched on for five days, until the police broke into the vault with gas, freed the hostages, who were uninjured, and arrested the two men. Later, Olofsson would get involved in a relationship with one of the female hostages, giving the name to the famous Stockholm syndrome, where a hostage identifies with the hostage takers. Other hostages would express sympathy with Olofsson, claiming they were more endangered by the police forcing themselves into the bank. The two men would become celebrities, or "pet criminals" to liberals and radicals of the time, setting the stage for Arkan's armed heists and the wonder that his actions would elicit.

Much like Olofsson, Arkan emerged as a pioneer of crime in Sweden. It wasn't the way he looked, of course. At twenty-two, he was much younger than the criminals before him, and he looked like an electronics salesman or some schmuck in the high school band. Although he still had that squishy baby face, something about him demanded respect and deference. No one denied his gravitas. He was the general, and the men he assembled over time would morph into bigger, more sophisticated gangs, planting roots and expanding throughout the country and Europe, a lot like the great organized crime syndicates of Chicago and New York. Alums of Arkan's initial dealings would rise from petty crimes to bank robberies to tightly networked clans that smuggled narcotics, cigarettes, and arms into the nation of Volvos. Although Arkan wouldn't be directly involved in the later smuggling operations, Swedish authorities and newspapers would cite him through the nineties, and even later, as, if nothing else, a spiritual leader to the Yugo-slavian gangs that had taken over their country. Arkan would change Swe-den. There was something unstoppable about him, like Caesar Augustus, who said, "I found Rome brick and left it marble."

The banks, however, made his name. His first was on May 17, 1974, the Gotabanken in downtown Gothenburg. A Yugoslav named Zivorad No-vakovic, a.k.a. "Sassa," joined him. The plans he worked out were signifi-cant, as they would serve as a template for future heists. With minor adjustments, a heist unfolded like this: He scoped out the bank, drew up a floor plan, counted customers coming and going. Later he stole a getaway car and drove it from the bank to the police station and back in order to know how long he had before the cops arrived. He figured out an escape route and went over it a hundred times. Precision was important; it was the only thing that separated you from prison—or death. At night he lay awake considering alternative plans: If a, then b, c, d; if not a, then x, y, z.

On that spring day, as the days grew longer, they arrived not long after the Gotabanken opened its doors for business. The car was left idling at the curb, its warm exhaust curling up into the brisk morning air. Inside there were only three tellers, just as they expected. As Sassa staked out the door, packing two automatic pistols, Arkan approached the tellers. He wore a ny-lon stocking over his head. Sassa had a mask, but it fell off during the rob-bery. "Good morning," Arkan said in perfect English. He had a high voice, a kid's voice, which must have made the teller think this was some kind of joke perpetrated by high school students. Then he flashed his Colt .45, one of his favorite guns, and it glimmered in the overhead bank lights. "Now let's have the money," he said calmly, as he jumped over the counter and produced a bag. "Hurry up."

The teller passed over stacks of bills and Arkan inspected them for ex-ploding dye packets, making note of the passing time. After the drawer was emptied, he gestured at the vault, which was also emptied. Before he left, he said, "Thank you very much," a parting comment that, from what people said about him, he probably meant, and that actually sounded sincere.

The getaway was a cinch: no alarms, no screams, no police. They drove the car a few blocks and then abandoned it for a tram, which they rode for a couple of stops before picking up another car. Easy. At the Lundgren hotel, they counted the loot. It was just about $4,000 U.S. It was nothing by Thomas Crown standards, but the amount wasn't really the point: The point was that he'd pulled it off. He was a bank robber now.

According to the police, he went out the next day and hit another bank in Gothenburg, and the post office—he would later deny these crimes. Cops swarmed, feeling the heat of their enemy's presence. Even though he was a young thief, Arkan knew when to stay in town and when to get out. That was another one of his specialties. Plus, he had money now and could afford to take his new girl away. Flush with kronor bills, he went on a holiday with Agneta, first to Oslo, then to Copenhagen, and finally to Greece. He gambled, visited a nudist colony, and gambled some more. The gambling brought in a supplementary income, but in his brain he no doubt carried images of those heists and the effortlessness with which he'd managed them. Soon those thoughts of easy money were pulling him back, like the earth pulled by the moon. He wanted more. That would become one of his vices: not knowing when enough was enough.

5

When Arkan returned to Gothenburg that summer, reports indicate that he was driving a light blue Mercedes 180 sedan, a beautiful luxury car. Piloted down the road, it was the kind of car that practically glided. The deep, curved, leather seats seemed to be customized for his broad, muscular back, and there was plenty of room in the foot well for his long, thin legs. Arkan had purchased it from a fellow Yugoslav for about $2,000 dollars, a deal at the time. It was registered in Belgium, but that didn't mean anything, because he'd probably secured the paperwork through one of his spy connections. Steering was effortless because of the way the car turned fluidly, almost intuitively, on its own. The leather wheel was easy on the hands. It was, for sure, a car to be appreciated: Its powerful engine humming along the highway, faster than the others; its gleaming dash with the stereo tuned to a rock station, the tunes floating through the superlux cabin; and its incredible comfort on longer trips.

He'd expended a great deal of effort to get to where he was in the world, too much to deny himself the luxury, even though the moment probably called for being low-key, especially because his robbing partner Novakovic was now in police custody. Nevertheless, stuff like that didn't seem to faze him. It was like dandruff, nothing to be worried about. Just flick it off the shoulder and it was gone.

When Agneta left for a trip to Italy later that summer, he began scheming again. He called two Serbs he'd met somewhere in his travels and encouraged them to come for a visit. One was Petar Skoric and the other was Ivica Obradovic, who called himself "Cipi." Arkan told them there was money to be made. Allegedly, the two men didn't agree right away to commit any crimes. What they did say was that maybe Sweden would be a good change for them. They talked about the possibility of getting work, maybe at one of the big shipyards, but what inspired them in particular seemed to be the notion of easy Swedish girls.

Soon after, Cipi and Skoric came. They visited night clubs and gambling joints and looked for dates. Oddly, the men would later refer to Arkan in police documents as Marko. Perhaps Arkan never told them his real name. It wouldn't be that unusual, as he was known to employ fake names even with his close associates. The thing was, in this business, anything could go wrong, so you had to be careful.

On September 6, Arkan woke the men early. They'd been asleep on Agneta's couch. "Let's go now," he told them. He wore a .22 caliber revolver and the men didn't argue. They didn't say that they were tired or hung over after having been out late the night before drinking, chasing girls, and gambling. They rose and muttered, "OK."

Whether Skoric and Cipi knew about the bank robbery he had planned for that morning is uncertain. The men said they didn't, though that's hard to believe considering Arkan's penchant for meticulous preparation. Still as Skoric would tell Swedish investigators later, it was unwise to question Arkan. He "was not the kind of person that you contradict or ask things unnecessarily. He gets really mad easily and asks that his friends do what he says. If something doesn't go his way, or if someone asks something unnecessarily, he flares up and shouts and screams."

The men trudged out to the street and climbed into Agneta's red Mazda. She had given him the keys while she was away. There was a slight bite in the air, as autumn was quickly descending upon the city, with the slasher winds from the North Sea getting stronger and colder. Arkan handed everyone blue women's stockings, and Skoric was given a thick rope. "Do this, you need it," he told the young man. It was almost 11:00 A.M. as Arkan steered the car onto the road. While driving, he didn't say much of anything, and the men didn't press for details.

After twenty minutes or so they glided into a parking lot and came to a halt. They were in downtown Kungalv, the tiny leafy suburb of Gothenburg. The lot was on a slight promontory, with a view of the town. Switching off the car and looking down the hill, Arkan pointed at a squat building that housed the national bank. "We will go in there," he explained straightforwardly to the men, "and take some money."

The men looked at one another, made funny faces, unsure. Who was this man? they seemed to ask.

Sensing their reserve, Arkan pressed them. "You need money, right?" he said.

"We do," said Skoric. He paused, and then added, as if realizing that there was no backing out now, "Every human wants money."

It was around noon when the men's faces disappeared under blue stockings, and they stormed the bank, plunging into a situation that would have consequences far greater than any of them could have imagined. Although three customers had arrived before them, an unforeseen happening, it didn't matter now. As Arkan went straight to the tellers and flashed his pistol, Skoric tied up the customers.

Time blurred, as it did in any high-stakes game, and soon it was over, the men were outside and then speeding away.

Back at Agneta's, the money was counted at a kitchen table. It was a bigger take this time around: the Swedish kronor equivalent of $10,000. Which must have made the crew happy, especially Skoric and Cipi, who were still a little baffled about what had just happened.

If there was a party, it was broken up minutes later as a squad of police officers broke through the front door and charged the tiny room. "Get down! This is the police! Get down!"

Skoric and Cipi didn't have a chance. In a matter of seconds they were snapped up and handcuffed. Not Arkan. Arkan leapt up from the table, shoving bills into his pockets, the pistol into his waistband, and whatever else he could grab, and vanished. Still, he left a lot behind for the police.

What he left behind told the story of a man who was more James Bond than your ordinary criminal. First there were all the fake papers: a Norwegian passport and driver's license in the name of Eagle Rostart; a Swedish passport with the name Petar Fransom; a Yugoslavian passport and driver's license for Marko Markovic; a Belgian passport for Marceil Decoque; and a British passport for Simon James Evert. Then there were lots of odds and ends: a box of Browning shells; a pistol; ladies' stockings that had been cut down for disguises; a stiletto; four tie pins in pearl and gold; gold cufflinks; and more than a dozen gold rings. Who was this man?

Meanwhile, Arkan was headed north. Sticking to shadows, he made his way quickly to the train station, where we know from police reports that he hopped on a train to Stockholm. He did not know if Cipi and Skoric would tell the police anything. They would suffer or betray him. In Stockholm, he went to a friend's apartment, a woman named Margaret. What his relationship was with the woman is unclear, though some reporters I spoke to suggested it was likely romantic.

He didn't lay low for long. It wasn't his way. Just like a kid with ADD. As he waited around the apartment, making love to Margaret, or not, wondering what Cipi and Skoric were saying and if the police would find him, the walls began to close in and he had to get out. Several days later he was scheming again, scoping out banks and asking around for people to help.

He met a man who called himself Whiskey. Whiskey knew the city like the crumbs on his bedroom floor he was too lazy to pick up, and he signed on as a getaway driver. First, they hit the Scandinavian Bank in Stockholm. Whiskey waited at the curb while Arkan did his work. Instead of a duffel bag, he took the packed bills the teller handed over the counter and stuffed them into the lining of his sports coat, which he had sliced open the night before. In a few minutes, it was over.

The take was about $17,000, which Arkan blew on "new clothes," according to police documents. The job went off so swimmingly that he and Whiskey went back to the same bank a month later, and walked away with $12,000. Of that take he gave Whiskey his cut and then went on a kind of spring break, traveling to Oslo, Paris, and London, where, as he told Swedish investigators three years later, "I went on a shopping spree" and "threw away the money."

There is a strong possibility that he later spent some time in Amsterdam, where he met with friends and began organizing the foundation for a smuggling network, which he would execute in full years later. He spent weeks on the road, and at some point he married Agneta, and later she was pregnant with a son. Little is known about this time with Agneta, though occasionally, she popped up in crime reports as "my Swedish wife."

6

In 1975 Arkan was twenty-three years old with a new son named Michael. He had some ten warrants out for his arrest in Sweden, a couple in Italy, and law enforcement was hunting him in Belgium and the Netherlands. His flare for the gun didn't go unnoticed. In fact, it seemed to herald a changing climate in Sweden, with imitators beginning to appear on the scene.

According to country statistics, robberies would double between 1975 and 1977. The same with crimes against persons, which included assaults and murders. Gradually, the country began to lose its once isolated and supreme-seeming innocence. Most notably, there was a passenger plane hijacking, an embassy bombing, and later the country's prime minister was assassinated. Arkan would steer clear of the country for four years—having little, if any, communication with his new wife and son. In the time spent away, he was plotting his return. If Act One had shocked the Swedish authorities, Act Two was going to knock them out.

6

WE GOT YOU! NO YOU DON'T!

A rkan was arrested in Belgium in the spring of 1975. Belgian police caught him robbing a jewelry store, though the details of where and how are vague. He was sentenced to ten years and sent to a high-security prison in Brussels, where he sat and wondered what had happened and how he would get out.

Two years passed before three unexpected visitors showed up. It was early, just after 9:00 A.M. on April 26, 1977, when the men lumbered into his cell. They explained that they were part of a Swedish investigative team— Karl Gustav Pfeiff, a prosecutor; Ingemar Stromvall, chief of Gothenburg police; and an interpreter. The men told Arkan that they had followed his criminal career in Sweden, and now it was time for him to give them some answers.

The men sat down at a table, and the session began with Arkan's first big crime, the car hijacking, and traveled through his days as the smiling bank robber, and then doubled back to those first weeks when he had robbed apartments and homes. Most of the men's questions were up front, no curveballs. They asked about each of his crimes, as if going down a numbered list, and Arkan was shockingly candid.

In the transcript, which was translated from Swedish, Arkan's tone is at once polite and arrogant, with a weird overlay of crackpot eagerness. Reading it I often got the feeling that I was hearing a young man who was not overly bright but had plenty of self-esteem. He seemed almost pleased that the men were there, and that he had a chance to elaborate on his crimes. It was as if a plug had been uncorked from his head and all this great pressure was suddenly hissing out. Many of his admissions began with the words: "I openly confess that I was the man" who committed that crime.

That he openly confessed, however, was not the most noteworthy point of their exchanges. Nor were the point-by-point retellings of his crimes. What most intrigued me about the conversations was Arkan's commentary, and the random anecdotes that he sprinkled throughout his storytelling.

Some heists were better than others, he explained. A few disappointed him because the scores were smaller than he'd imagined. He cited the bank courier hijacking as an example. In that case, a friend had given him all the details to pull off the job and promised that the score would be at least $10,000. In reality, the bag he and his partners wrestled away from the courier that day contained only around $1,000. "The man was supposed to get one-fifth of the loot," Arkan told the men. "But he got nothing, because the loot was much thinner than he'd said."

During the proceedings Arkan never attempted to play down what he'd done. If anything it seemed to me that he tried to emphasize his importance, especially his potential for violence. With every robbery, they asked him if his gun was loaded, as crimes committed in Sweden with loaded guns had much steeper penalties attached. Arkan had a chance to duck the question when it arose. But he didn't. Instead, during the Gotabank heist, he told them, "My revolver was of course loaded. You cannot do it differently."

Arkan's point was obvious here: He was not afraid of these men.

He demonstrated a flare for the sensational. In two months, he bragged that he and his crew "committed over fifty robberies" in Gothenburg. When he spoke of a jewelry shop where he'd robbed twenty diamonds and a Rolex watch, he rubbed their face in the fact that the shop was "50 meters [162.5 feet] from a police station!"

Recalling specific details was exceptionally amusing for Arkan. He seemed to take a perverse sort of pride in going beyond the basic reconstruction of a crime. For instance, about a robbery in a suburb of Gothenburg in the spring of 1974, he told the inquisitors: "We arrived at the place in a Ford Taunus. It was about 8:00 P.M. We broke down the door in the basement and went to the cupboard and I found a Colt .45 and .22 caliber. I used the Colt later for my robbery on April 19. We took 100 kilos of ammo and those two guns. We took everything that we thought of value, particularly watches, rings, and furs. We put everything in a wood box that was there, and after a few trips we returned to my room at the hotel Lundgren."

When points escaped him, he toyed with the Swedes. For example, he remembered pilfering a color television at some point in the spring of 1974, but "with all of this time that has passed and my good will, I cannot say the exact city and place. I do remember that [the television] was big and on wheels." He remembered another robbery, but again the details were blurry. "I can only tell you that it was a beautiful two-story villa and that we took quite a lot of jewelry from that place."

Although he confirmed the participation of his countrymen in all the crimes—basically ratting out every single one of them—he vigorously protected the women in his life, including the girlfriend in Stockholm and his wife, Agneta. He told them that Agneta was either working when he was committing crimes—and unaware—or out of town.

There were moments where he seemed ingratiating, as when he mentioned, for no apparent reason, a couple of other people who were peripherally involved in his criminal empire. Perhaps they had betrayed him and he was just settling scores three years later. Perhaps he was just getting kicks. Arkan explained that he'd given a Stockholm man named Jada "4,000 kronors from a robbery," and that "Jada knew the money was from a holdup." He even mentioned where they could find this Jada character. "He lives close to Stockholm with his Finnish girlfriend, right off highway A3." Then the final blow, if they needed a description: "Jada didn't work regularly," said Arkan, almost laughing to himself. "And it's easy to see because he has a big stomach."

He spoke with the three men in the mornings, took a lunch break around noontime, and again spoke through the afternoons. Three days passed, and then they were done. Before the men collected their files and prepared to return to Sweden, there was a conversation about extraditing Arkan on multiple counts of heinous bank robbery, among other crimes. The feeling was that he had done significant damage in Sweden and should pay for it there. Arkan would later say that he hoped for this option, as he wanted to see Agneta and his son, Michael.

In the end that didn't happen. The men went home with Arkan's confessions, but they didn't act fast enough to process his extradition. Arkan defied them, as he would defy many others in the decades to come. A year and a half after the interrogation, and just over three years into the decade-long sentence, he broke out of jail. It was 1979. This would be his second known break, the first outside of Serbia. According to press accounts at the time, the opportunity arose when the prison attendants started a strike about work conditions. In the ensuing confusion Arkan managed to slip through loose security, scale the complex wall, and drop down to the other side into the free world. A man named Carlo Fabiani joined him. Later Fabiani would partner up with Arkan then turn on him. Whether the Yugoslavian State Security helped Arkan escape is unknown.

7

BREAKOUT

1

Fabiani was nine years older than Arkan. In police reports, he personally described himself as an artist, or a draftsman, but also admitted to being a professional criminal. After escaping, the two men split up briefly before rendezvousing later in Italy, some say on a beach in the north. There Arkan brought up Sweden and his plan to go back.

Through the years it became considerably clear that one of Arkan's greatest assets was his charisma. If he wanted to convince you of something, he did it with aplomb, describing the brilliance of an idea, infecting you with the idea, as a preacher infects his people with godly visions.

He explained to the Italian that he was planning a trip north in a few weeks. As he saw it, there were loads of cash left in the country's bank vaults, and it was meant for the taking, their taking. Can you see that money? he most likely asked Fabiani. How about joining me?

They shook hands.

The two met again a month later in Copenhagen at the Royal Hotel, a five-star Radisson property built in one of the flashier skyscrapers in Denmark's capital. From there they loaded up their cars (Fabiani was in his Fiat and Arkan drove a notably unsexy Oldsmobile) and boarded a ferry to Oslo, where customs inspections were known to be loose, and then drove into Sweden. In Gothenburg, they regrouped at the train station and hooked up with a third player, a man named Slobodan Kostovski. Kostovski was, according to crime reports, a Serb and an old friend of Arkan's.

At first the conceit was to hit Gothenburg again, but as Arkan talked more about what he wanted to do, and as they drew closer to the city, he seemed to have second thoughts. It wasn't only the police looking out for him, but there was another variable: Agneta. Over the last couple of years, he had drifted from her, and their relationship was crumbling. Between prison time, running, robbing, and gambling, it seemed Arkan didn't have time for a wife and kids. When he did see her, things didn't always go so well. They argued, probably like all young couples argue—about money, about stable jobs, and about the future. At one point Arkan had had enough. After one feud, he grabbed a hot iron and slugged her in the face with it, an assault that would go down in classified Interpol reports, according to a woman familiar with his file.

Now in Gothenburg again, the last thing he wanted to do was run into her. (According to police reports the two officially separated sometime later that year, in 1979.) Who knew what she would do? It was a gamble that he decided not to take. So they drove to Stockholm.

As they headed north on September 4, 1979, the heist that would change the men forever began to feel like it wasn't meant to happen. First, Fabiani came down with the flu, not to mention a creeping pain in his back, and then in Stockholm the men couldn't find a hotel. Everything was booked. Bellhops shrugged their shoulders. What can we do? Ever heard of planning in advance? Eventually, an agency at the central train station sent them to a boardinghouse in the suburbs, where the three men were forced to squeeze into a single room.

That night they began to plot. The target: SE-Banken at 38 Birger Jarlsgatan. As he had before, Arkan surveyed the site, envisioned escape routes, and drove them out, checking times and drop-off points. Later that night the men stole two cars, one a red Alfa Romeo. Hours passed before they returned to the hotel. They didn't sleep long. When they woke Arkan distributed weapons, a shotgun and a Smith & Wesson .38. If the situation required it, Fabiani recalled Arkan promising them, with visible seriousness, that he would not think twice about shooting someone. He was not going to jail again.

2

On September 5, the day of the robbery, Katarina Osterholm and her colleague Monika Hedstrom were stationed at the glass service counters at the front of SE-Banken, doing nothing out of the ordinary, distributing and receiving money, according to police reports. It was just before noon and business was slow, with only a few customers on the floor. All that changed, of course, when the bank robbers arrived.

The three men in disguises crashed through the front entrance, waving "Wild West revolvers" and shouting, "Get down, lie down." Osterholm, as if waking from a daydream, started to say, "What's this?" but stopped short as a man launched himself over the glass and landed directly in front of her.

Osterholm would later tell police that she had never witnessed anything like this before. Although Hedstrom had experienced a bank robbery about a year earlier, she would explain that this one was much scarier. While the first one was "amateurish," she noted that the robbery on September 5 was distinct in that it was carried out in a "professional" way. The three men clearly knew what they were doing, she said. Another employee echoed that observation to investigators: "Maybe this sounds strange," a man named Kurt Andersson hypothesized. "But this seemed more prepared, more planned."

There were twelve witnesses that day. In their testimonies to the police Arkan was referred to repeatedly as "the tall" one with "lithe" movements who leaped over the glass. He had donned dark pants, a dark sweater, and brown leather shoes and gloves. Kostovski, witnesses said, headed toward the back of the bank. He wore a green jacket and a blue hat, with a scarf covering his face. At one point the scarf slipped down and Hedstrom observed his "slender face," which made her think that he was around thirty years old. Few would remember much about Fabiani, other than that he wore a blue scarf around his face and stood guard at the door with a revolver.

The robbery unfolded at a lighting clip. "Where's the money?" Arkan, "the tall" one, shouted in English at Hedstrom and Osterholm. He rummaged through Osterholm's cash drawer, stuffing packets of bills into a "red and black" plastic bag, pausing only to check for exploding dye packets. When he finished with her drawer, he went into her purse, and then over to Hedstrom's station. There was a trap there, but he didn't fall for it. "He took all the money," said Hedstrom, "but left the bundle [of money] that had been placed as so-called bait, where the numbers of the notes have been written down."

Soon three people walked into the bank, one man and two women. One of the women was Birgitta Ljungkvist. When she stepped through the door, she immediately saw that there was a problem. "The staff was lined up by the wall inside the counter with their hands above their heads," she recalled. She tried to leave, but was cut off. It was likely Fabiani, though she couldn't remember anything specific about the men because she "got so paralyzed when she saw the revolver." Waving his gun in her face, the man indicated for her to sit in a chair near the entrance. Like the rest before her, she raised her hands in the air, but he motioned for her to put them down. People on the street would look in and see her with her hands up, and he didn't want that. For the rest of the time Ljungkvist focused on the floor, "not daring to look at the robbers."

Meanwhile, on the second floor, employees were having lunch when the bank director strolled in and said he'd heard a "strange sound" coming from the service floor. Had anyone else noticed anything unusual? No one had. But being the bank director he needed to be sure, so he turned and walked out the door and headed down the stairs to see what was up, if anything.

It was, however, already too late. As the director made his way to the floor, the bank robbers were headed out the door. How long the robbery lasted was never documented in records. Few of the bank tellers had time to process what was going on, let alone act out or count elapsed time. As most of the witnesses noted, the thieves came at them in a whirling blur, bagged the money, and soon after, like ghosts, they disappeared.

3

Arkan and his men had in their possession about $10,000, by most standards a solid haul for 1979. As they raced off in their Alfa Romeo, the bills piled in bags beside them, they noticed a police car. Fabiani stomped down on the gas, sending the car lurching forward at a fast pace. They cut a corner, and then another. There it was still. They took another couple of turns. Pedal to the floor. Still with them. Adrenaline rushing and the street life losing shape, all three men began talking at once. As Fabiani later told interrogators, there was a "big panic."

Soon the guns came out, and shots were fired. It was the only way. Who fired—whether it was Arkan or Kostovski—no one would ever come clean on that point, but the strategy worked. Taking shots, the police veered off, giving Fabiani enough time to lose them. He sped up, cut another corner, then parked.

They ditched the car and split up, agreeing to regroup later at the central train station, though Fabiani wouldn't make it. As Fabiani loped along the downtown streets, the police materialized out of nowhere. At first, he ignored them, probably thinking they hadn't spotted him. Although they started to yell, he kept walking, head down, and then up, like some office jerk on his lunch break, just enjoying the day, lost in deep thought.

In the distance he spotted a pavilion and walked toward it. His escape hatch. When he got there he tried the front doors. Locked. At that point, the police arrived. They yelled again. He spun toward them, as if about to run or retaliate. Whatever his plan, it was over. They were right there, guns drawn. It was time to surrender.

Although Fabiani didn't have the money and claimed to investigators that he was just the door guy at the stickup, he did possess some interesting items: a Smith & Wesson .38 with four unfired cartridges and two spent cartridges, several phony Italian IDs, a stiletto, and a ferry ticket.

How about your pals? the police wanted to know.

That night his pals were plotting the country's greatest escape.

4

When you ask Swedish crime addicts about Arkan, some talk about a still on a bank's surveillance camera as the young bandit exited with a bag of cash. In that frozen image, Arkan's head is tilted upward, as if instinctively attracted to the celebrity of the camera's gaze, and on his face is a big grin. According to Walter Repo, the investigative journalist, the image earned Arkan a new moniker: the smiling bank robber.

Although I was never able to track down the video, I did find a photo of him escaping a Swedish bank with his loot. Whether or not the smiling freeze-frame of him really existed, I liked the idea. So apparently did a part of Sweden. While police issued bulletins warning that Arkan was "extremely dangerous," the myth of the smiling bank robber grew in the public mind, like an addictive television drama. In some circles, what the smiling

On September 5, 1979, Arkan and his two accomplices,
Carlo Fabiani and Slobodan Kostovski, robbed the Stockholm
bank SE-Banken. Arkan is allegedly the one with the bag of
cash.

bank robber did, where he did it, how much he took became a spectacle to
be talked about.

Culturally, there was something to this addiction. As a bank robber,
Arkan embodied the darker side of the age's pervasive hippie spirit, that
footloose, antiauthority, live-for-the-moment generation of twenty- and
thirty-year-olds who saw Jack Kerouac's *On the Road* as its bible. Not just in
Sweden, but all over the Western world. It was a time of self-indulgence, a
time when the pursuit of happiness trumped basic responsibilities,
whether they were political, judicial, societal, or familial. In Tom Wolfe's

coinage, the 1970s was the "Me Decade," and Arkan was the king of Me, doing whatever the hell he wanted, wherever he wanted, whenever he wanted.

Of course, when Arkan was robbing banks, it was years before he was associated with mass murder, long before the violence in Yugoslavia that would make him one of the world's most evil men. As far as people in Sweden were concerned, he was just a kid bank robber with a particularly notable smile. He made for a perverse sort of entertainment, not unlike other historical bad guys—John Dillinger, "Pretty Boy" Floyd, "Baby Face" Nelson, Billy the Kid, to name a few.

Drama always seemed to emanate from him. Like any great cliffhanger, he perpetually kept people wondering. When will he hit again? Will the police catch him? Who is this young man? What will he do next?

He wasn't just a fleeting curiosity either, here today, gone tomorrow. Not even close. He would maintain Sweden's interest through his blockbuster days of banditry, and then become a brutal warlord in Serbia's wars in Bosnia and Croatia, days that would earn him the sinister sheen. Nevertheless, it could be argued that it was in Sweden that his life of crime really took off, and Sweden would remember that, for better or for worse. Even after his assassination, some who grew up hearing about his criminal high jinks would even refuse to believe that he had, in fact, died. "I'd put money that he's still alive out there, somewhere," a Swede in his thirties told me. "A man like that doesn't die."

5

After the SE-Banken heist, Arkan and Kostovski withdrew to the Stockholm suburbs and waited to hear about their friend. Would he rat them out or suffer? They likely read the papers, listened to the radio, and watched television, hungry for any scrap of intelligence. Several days after the heist, word finally came: A hearing was scheduled for Fabiani at the City Court building.

The wheels began to turn, and the two criminals devised a plan. Ultimately, they decided to break him out. It was an insane idea, and later people familiar with the case would wonder why the men would ever have been willing to risk their freedom. What were they thinking? They had their money, what did they need with Fabiani?

Arkan wasn't exactly one to think about the odds against him. When the hearing opened on September 11, 1979, he and Kostovski climbed into a brown Ford sedan and headed downtown. They parked on a street next to the courthouse, and by the time they entered the building it was after 10:00 A.M. Walking through the halls, the men took note of the lax security. According to police reports, Fabiani's official proceeding was scheduled to take place on the second floor in the court's Twelfth Division.

The men sported fitted dark suits, starched white shirts, and polished black shoes. Arkan wore a gold pinkie ring embedded with sparkly diamonds. Although no one seemed to notice the loaded revolvers in their coats, people in the courtroom recalled their appearance. As one witness later recounted to the Swedish press, "They were so polished that they awoke my curiosity. Who were they?" The hearing in the courtroom at that moment was for a gambling ring, which made one man wonder if they were "big gamblers who had come to listen to the trial" or just "attorneys having a break from another proceeding."

Fabiani wasn't there, but the two men sat down anyway and waited to see what would happen. Several minutes passed and Fabiani still didn't come. Feeling anxious, Arkan turned to a man next to him. "Are there any more trials in the building?" he asked in perfect English.

The man looked at him, noticed the gold ring. "Of course," he said. "There are trials in the entire building."

Worrying that they'd miss him, Arkan and Kostovski rose quickly and left. They rushed through the building, searching room to room, until they finally located Fabiani in a waiting area. His hands were cuffed in iron, and four officers surrounded him.

Arkan and Kostovski shouted, "Get down!" "We'll kill you!" A shot rang out. One officer took a gun butt to the head. It was like a Hollywood action flick, the way the two men charged the room, guns blazing, not even thinking about the fact that they were just two men up against an entire building.

Reports indicate that there were a number of people present in the room that day, including attorneys and a judge, as well as some other offenders awaiting trial. An extra pistol was thrown to Fabiani, who, despite the handcuffs, snagged it. Before the officers could figure out what to do, the three had broken a window and were leaping out.

It was a seventeen-foot drop, according to most of the city newspapers, which plastered the story all over their front pages—and they dropped fast. The last person out fired a shot that grazed a guard's head.

On September 11, 1979, Arkan and Kostovski stormed the Stockholm courthouse and
freed their bank-robbing partner Fabiani, who was to be tried that day for their crime.
After firing several shots, the three men broke a second-floor window and jumped seven-
teen feet to the ground, before escaping in a car.

Then Arkan and his gang were gone. Poof, like that. When the dumbfounded people in the courtroom came back to life and ran to the window,
all they saw was a brown car speeding away, then vanishing into the busy
morning traffic.

6

The whole event made me wonder if this really even happened. I mean, how
could two men walk into a fully staffed courthouse, free a prisoner from his
guards, and then leap seventeen feet to the ground without any injury and
just drive off? It didn't make sense. It made me think of courthouses in
small American cities like Baltimore and Orlando. Could two men walk into

courthouses in those cities in the 1970s and break someone out like Arkan had? No way. I'd never heard of such a thing. Did someone dream this story up?

It's a question I confronted over and over in my search for the real story behind Arkan. No matter how many people I interviewed, I kept coming up against these legendary stories that may or may not be true. There were stories that stretched the human imagination, but there were also stories, I began to find, that were undoubtedly important to this master criminal's larger history—that mythical "origin story" that made Arkan so epic in people's minds.

What I began to sense was that Arkan was a lot like the superheroes and supervillains that inhabited the colorful pages of many of my childhood comic books, in which every character had a mysterious and, many times, implausible "origin story," that backstory that explained how he or she became the superhero or supervillain. "That sounds just like a movie," my friends back in America would always respond when I told them about Arkan.

And they were right: The stories did sound like some filmmaker had scripted them. Except when the stories were verifiably true. Like the breakout in Stockholm. That was true—unless the witnesses, the police, and all the local media had conspired to tell one vast lie. Though it didn't make any of his earlier wild feats easier to grasp, it did make me believe that what happened next wasn't so improbable.

7

Although the general elections in Sweden were days away in what was becoming a very tight race between three right-wing parties and their Social Democratic opponents, the conversation in Stockholm shifted abruptly to the breakout.

The police force swooped down over the city. Helicopters took to the skies. That day and night, dozens of officers went from house to house in an operation described as "vaccuming," hoping to turn up clues. By the end of the first day all they had found was the light-brown Ford Taunus, ditched several blocks from the courthouse.

Newspapers ran stories all week. A headline the day after in *Aftonbladet*, Stockholm's biggest daily, blared: SHOOTING DRAMA IN CITY COURT!

Included was a picture of the shattered courthouse window. Another paper described the escape as a "breakout in true mafia style," noting the perpetrators' speed and professionalism and the injured guards hauled away on stretchers.

Police officials were stunned. So was the public. Nothing like this had ever happened in the city before. What was going on?

There was some speculation that the men were involved in an international crime ring. A detective named Nils Linder worried that the "three men were planning a much bigger crime together," but couldn't say what.

By the third day, still no leads had surfaced, and the mood around the city had dimmed considerably. A big black headline in the *Aftonbladet* blared: ARE THEY TERRORISTS?

"There is something that isn't right here," suggested Detective Harry Gebestam. He wondered if the men had sprung Fabiani because he was "the brain of something."

Some conjectured that the three men were members of a militant leftist group from Italy known as the Red Brigades. The Red Brigades' stated mission was to create a revolutionary state through armed struggle, separate from the Western alliance. Founded in the 1970s, the group had been credited with over fourteen thousand acts of violence, including the kidnapping and death in 1978 of Italy's former prime minister Aldo Moro. Considering that Fabiani was from Italy, and that a number of bank robberies there had been carried out to fund the Red Brigades, the theory wasn't too far-fetched. Expanding on this, the *Aftonbladet* wondered if the men were planning an "action against some top politicians in Sweden."

It would be weeks before they heard from the men again. Druing this time, the city would stew and the men's celebrity would grow. "We actually fear that these men are planning a very serious crime," Linder told *Aftonbladet* toward the end of the first week, in a comment of accidental omniscience.

8

Meanwhile, Arkan and his men landed safely in a protected apartment somewhere in Stockholm, their ears still besieged by the raucous sound of alarms and police sirens. They didn't wait around there long. Just enough time to cut off Fabiani's wrist irons, give him a new set of clothes, and reboot their systems. Back in the street, they climbed into a silver Oldsmobile and fled for Gothenburg. When they arrived, the Olds was traded for a green Volvo, and that night, while Stockholm got turned upside down, they found refuge in the apartment of a young Swedish girl named Majbritt.

According to Fabiani, Arkan and Majbritt were more than just friends, though Arkan never said one way or another. While they crashed in the living room, Arkan and the girl, Fabiani said, "made love together." Although Majbritt didn't speak much to the others—mainly because of the language barrier, and because she was away at school during the day—she was good to the convicts. On occasion she brought home food and didn't charge Fabiani for any of the long-distance phone calls he made home to Italy. Whether or not Majbritt was aware of what the three men had been up to in Stockholm, or what their plans were for Gothenburg, is unclear. It was probable, however, that she knew about Arkan and his devilish past. How couldn't she? Unless she stayed clear of the papers that ran his picture and name. Still, in the short time they stayed with her, all the cash and weapons were kept out of her sight. As far as Fabiani and Kostovski knew, she was in the dark, and would stay that way.

After settling in, Arkan scarcely missed a beat. There is no record that he spoke to his wife, Agneta. Instead he had his eyes set on another bank, though Fabiani felt it was too risky. After days of debate, they agreed to hit a department store in the city called Nordiska Kompaniet (translated as Nordic Company), or NK. The store, which sprawled over four floors, sold luxury goods and saw three million shoppers annually. It would be the equivalent of robbing Bloomingdale's.

The crew spent several days monitoring the store, reports say. They noticed that a truck pulled up in the late morning, when the mall was closed, to fetch the store's profits from the day before. They made mental notes about how the transaction took place, the handful of people involved, the bags of money, and the security coverage. What became obvious was that the morning would be the best time to make a hit. The money was all in one place, and it could be done fast, with few people around.

So on September 21, ten days after the Stockholm breakout, Arkan, Fabiani, and Kostovski, armed with nightsticks and revolvers, broke into the mall. In a hallway, they fought through four staffers, including two guards. One woman ended up in the hospital with head injuries. The men couldn't be stopped. In less than five minutes, they were in and out. When they returned to Majbritt's apartment, they counted the take: 283,474 kronor, or about $42,000, which was divided three ways.

Before they had time to celebrate, the police found them. From a window, the men noticed cars pulling up to the apartment. Much commotion ensued, with stuff thrown into bags. Arkan took Majbritt to the side. There was a brief exchange, but nothing notable. As they stepped out the door the girl watched for a second, looking a little baffled by the uproar, before picking up some sheets and pillows that had been left in the living area and disappearing into her bedroom. She would never see Arkan and his crew again.

The reports don't say how they got away, but once outside they located a car and drove to an unnamed friend's house before traveling to Norway, and from there to the Netherlands, where they allegedly held up several jewelry shops. After that they parted ways, probably figuring that as a group they were now much too vulnerable.

Little else is known about Arkan's two friends. Like many others during that time, friendships were fleeting. You met someone, organized, did some jobs together, had some fun, and then moved on. As far as the question of why Arkan and Kostovski risked their skins to break Fabiani out, it would never be answered, though maybe the reason was a simple one: because they could.

In the end, they were probably better off with each other than without. Several weeks after going their separate ways, Fabiani was captured for a robbery in the Netherlands. The judge sentenced him to four years in prison. At some point Swedish investigators caught up with him. The interrogation they conducted illuminated the crew's crime spree that fall. His confession to those crimes would also send him back to Sweden three years later to serve out a seven-year sentence. What he did after those seven years in jail is a mystery. He would never be heard from again.

As for Kostovski, he, too, was arrested around the same time for armed robbery in the Netherlands, and sentenced to six years in prison—but he didn't stick around long. In 1981, he escaped, shuttled from hideout to hideout, and allegedly robbed a bank. Several months later, still in the Netherlands, he was recaptured and served out his sentence. When he came up for parole in 1988, he was extradited to Sweden for his crimes with Arkan, namely two armed robberies, the courtroom breakout, and two murder attempts. He'd spend eight years in prison there. Later he'd show up in Belgrade, where he'd continue to carry on with the underworld. Over the next decade, there would be more reported crimes, including an assassination charge.

Arkan didn't fare any better. That fall he was arrested in Amsterdam for three alleged armed robberies, including a downtown jewelry store. He'd tried to escape on a bicycle, but there were too many police officers around. The court sentenced him to seven years and, deciding not to take any chances, sent him to a high-security prison known as Bijlmerbajes. It was not a hopeful development. How could he be so damned careless? Suddenly, after all that had happened, after all the effort he had expended, it looked like his career was taking an unexpected turn toward the worst.

9

Bijlmerbajes possessed the glum appearance of a Moscow ghetto. It consisted of six drab apartment block–like towers that were surrounded by a thick concrete wall. Connecting the towers to one another was an underground tunnel, known as the Kalverstraat. When it first opened in 1978, the prison was considered progressive, with clean glass windows in almost every cell, giving the inmates copious natural light. When the windows started breaking, bars were added, and Bijlmerbajes became just like any other depressing high-security correctional facility in the world.

Arkan wasn't in prison very long before a Dutch magistrate named S. B. M. Voorhoeve turned up to talk about his crime life and the notorious breakout. With him were Y. M. Th. A. Fraser, described as his secretary, and a man named G. H. van Asperen. When the men sat down the smiling bank robber, by way of introducing himself, announced, "My friends call me Zeljko. However, I do change my name sometimes."

Then he began to lie. "I haven't been to Sweden since 1974," he told the men. In fact, in September 1979, when the robberies went down, he was vacationing in Italy and Yugoslavia. "I went with my wife and son to a nudist camp, in northern Yugoslavia, on the coast," he explained. "I don't remember the name, so I don't remember if it was called Pula or if it was close to Pula."

The fact that investigators had interviewed his wife, Agneta, seemed to humor him. "You should not pay attention to the explanations of my wife," he said. "The police have fooled her into talking. What she said was said under pressure and what she said isn't true." He added that he was now divorced from her, as if that was another reason not to believe her.

"What I know about the robberies," he told them, "I know from the newspaper. I heard from friends in Milan that Fabiani escaped from Stockholm, and so I called a girl in Sweden and asked her to send me a paper about the robbery."

So he knew Fabiani?

Sure, Arkan admitted. Fabiani was a friend, but he hadn't seen him since the Belgium prison breakout.

What about Kostovski?

Not a friend. In fact, all he knew about the guy was that he was "born in Yugoslavia in 1953."

At one point the interrogators reached into a bag and placed on the table a picture of the bank robbery in Stockholm. It showed the bank floor and men in masks. "I can't recognize anyone," Arkan responded, seemingly unfazed. "All of them are covered in masks. I wouldn't say Fabiani is one of them, but, if he says he is, then that's the case and you have to arrest him."

The young bandit's pronouncements sometimes veered into the territory of the absurd. "I have never used a mask, and also I have never pulled the neck of my sweatshirt over my face," he said earnestly. "Also, I don't have friends who have done this."

The investigators presented another picture, this one of Arkan's silver Oldsmobile. Fabiani had confessed to the police that it was used to escape to Gothenburg after the courtroom breakout. Did Arkan know anything about the car and its use in the crimes? "At some point I drove a silver gray Oldsmobile," he admitted. "I used this car for vacations in Yugoslavia and Italy, and then I went to Copenhagen via Munich, Hanover, and Hamburg." Then it was stolen from him, he said, although he couldn't remember where or when, but he certainly wasn't in Sweden with it in September.

Voorhoeve pointed out that Kostovski's fingerprints were all over the car. Impossible, said Arkan. "I have never been with Kostovski or Fabiani in the Oldsmobile." A couple of minutes later, he reconsidered the question, deciding to offer his own explanation. "That man leaves his fingerprints everywhere," he said about Kostovski. "If he has driven my car, he stole it. I have heard that he is a thief."

The verbal jujitsu persisted when the officer opened the subject of the ferry tickets bought in Copenhagen to transport the Oldsmobile to Oslo. Voorhoeve was in possession of those tickets. "That doesn't mean anything to me," said Arkan, flicking the man away like a flea. "Neither does the fact that I have been identified as the person who bought the ticket. You also say that there was a ticket for Fabiani to Oslo, but that doesn't mean anything to me either."

He was bulletproof. Or at least, he pretended to be. He was a good liar.

What about Majbritt? Did Arkan know her?

"I don't know Majbritt," he said, flatly. "And I don't know where she lives."

We found the ignition key to your Oldsmobile in her apartment, said the magistrate. How did it get there, if you don't know her?

"If someone found a key to the silver Oldsmobile in her apartment, then it has to be an extra key. As I have already said, I was not in Gothenburg."

Your clothes were there, too, the magistrate pointed out, as he pressed him to break. As evidence, more pictures were displayed. In addition, it seemed, the police had gotten confirmation from Agneta that the clothes belonged to Arkan and not someone else.

Preposterous, Arkan contended, batting him away again. "I don't recognize anything that belongs to me." He added, "I wouldn't pay much attention to my wife's explanation concerning this, for reasons I have already explained."

Like a professional boxer, he danced his way off the ropes, even when he was hit with evidence that would have knocked out any other man. The green Volvo? Arkan's fingerprints were inside the car. If he wasn't in Gothenburg, how was it possible that his fingerprints were in the car? This evidence seemed rock solid, but Arkan wouldn't budge, even at the cost of sounding completely unbelievable. "How my fingerprints can be in the Volvo, I don't understand," he said, as if the placement of his fingerprints in that car was the result of some inexplicable supernatural occurrence. Then, he offered lamely, "I have sat in many cars."

In the end, Arkan confessed to absolutely nothing. To underscore his innocence, he went one more step and retracted wholesale everything that he'd told the Swedish investigators who had visited him two years earlier in the Belgiam prison. "I actually confessed what I did in 1974," he told Voorhoeve and the two other men, "but the reason why I confessed was because my wife had just given birth and my wish was to go to her in Sweden, to be extradited there."

At last, he wanted the investigators to know that he considered himself a moral man, a man who had been, well, misinterpreted. "I have never committed violent acts," he explained at the tail end of the interview. "And I have no deaths to answer for. If I had, I would not have been able to sleep at night."

10

Arkan escaped from Bijlmerbajes in the spring of 1981. The circumstances of the break are vague, but evidently armed men outside helped him out of the complex. The men were rumored to be Yugoslav State Security. From there he fled to Switzerland where, apparently, Bern police arrested him. He escaped after a couple of hours or a couple of days, depending on whom you believed, and traveled to Germany, where he got into trouble again, but not before stories of his gangster life began trickling down through the layered network of Yugoslav émigrés. "I had heard about him," said Slavoljub Ninkovic, a Serb who was eking out a living as a professional gambler in Koln. "There were a lot of rumors flying around about him and what he was doing in Europe," he said. "We knew the stories."

It was around this time that the name and history of Arkan began to stick in people's minds. If you knew him, you knew him as Arkan. Not Zeljko. He slept on couches and at hotels, sometimes at a girl's house or apartment. He showed up at gambling parties dressed to the nines, with his gold watch and diamond-embedded rings catching the lights. He won and lost, but no matter what he always seemed to need money. The appetite for money drove him to rob more.

In Frankfurt, he hit a jewelry store. On his way out, he was shot. This was verified in a Gothenburg police report filed on July 14, 1982. "It is known that Raznatovic carried out a robbery in Frankfurt," the report read, "and that he was wounded in connection to the robbery and ended up in a hospital, which he later escaped."

How he escaped that hospital while under police protection, however, is stitched with what feels like some exaggeration. Milomir Marić, a Serbian journalist, recalled a version that seems to predominate. "Arkan woke up completely naked in the hospital. So he put on a sheet and went to the roof," Marić told me. "He jumped to the next roof. It was deep night. Then he went to the ledge, and dropped down to the ground. There, he waited in the bushes for someone to come. A guard finally appeared and he knocked him down, took the guy's clothes, and took off. Later, he went to meet his buddies, and borrowed some cash from them. With that money, he bought a two-foot knife, samurai style, I believe. Then he robbed a gold shop and left Germany."

He vanished after that. It was necessary to keep going, to save his future. He apparently did a pretty good job. Some of his pursuers, after talking to informants and finding nothing in some of Europe's most shady crevices, concluded that he had either retired from crime—or died. Swedish investigators harbored the darker thought. In their report, an investigator wrote: "According to an unverified rumor, Raznatovic died from the complications of gunshot wounds from the robbery in Frankfurt in 1981."

What they didn't know was that Arkan, relentlessly on the lookout for advancement, had already moved on from petty crimes and $25,000 bank heists to a wickeder pastime that paid much better.

8

HIT MAN

1

When Yugoslav intelligence contacted Arkan in the winter of 1979 for his first hit job, he was twenty-seven years old. His target was a Croatian nationalist planning an attack on Tito. For his day job, the man worked behind a reception desk at a hotel in downtown Zurich. Bozidar Spasic, a senior official at Yugoslav State Security, or UDBA, at the time, described the hit to me as the "famous one."

Spasic said, "Arkan walked in[to the hotel] and shot the guy in the head while standing all the way back at the front door." He paused for effect, and then added, "The guy was eating a plum and fell dead with the plum in his mouth."

I told him to stop right there. "A plum," I asked, incredulously. "He shot him with a plum in his mouth?"

Spasic nodded eagerly. He repeated the story and pointed to his open mouth as if he had something stuck in it. "True story," he said, running a hand through his metal-gray hair. "I know this."

I met Spasic at a drafty office in Kladovo, a remote village of about nine thousand people along the Danube River in eastern Serbia. Although people said that it would take me a couple of hours to get there by car from

Belgrade, the trip ended up being more like four hours, most of it through tiny villages and scarcely inhabited forest and mountains. Kladovo felt extremely far away from the rest of the world—perfect, I thought, for a former spy in hiding.

We sat on plastic school chairs. At one point my translator said Spasic was wondering if I was with the CIA. That wasn't an unusual suspicion in Serbia. All foreigners asking too many questions were viewed with suspicion, but Spasic was just being careful, like any former secret government operative.

Spasic worked for the Tito's UDBA, for some twenty-five years. Eight, he told me, were spent working exclusively for "special international operations," which was the country's force behind "the elimination of dissident emigrants." At the UDBA Spasic was privy to myriad confidential reports filed away in the agency's most private rooms. When memos arrived at the Belgrade headquarters, he read them. When secret operatives like Arkan called from abroad, he spoke to them on the agency's protected lines. Specifically, he claimed that he had helped over 129 criminals infiltrate Western Europe in the 1970s and 1980s, and he knew about the agency's hit jobs, which he repeatedly referred to as "certain acts" and "dirty jobs."

"Dirty jobs," I asked once. "You mean killing?"

"What else do you think?" he asked, as if it was the most idiotic question on earth.

Arkan committed his second hit in 1981, he told me, the same year that the Bulgarian secret police attempted to assassinate Pope John Paul II. Spasic couldn't remember the month, though he said that Arkan traveled to Brussels to kill a man planning to overthrow the Albanian government. "The communists didn't want this guy upsetting the status quo and sent in Arkan and Candyman [who had also become a Serb hit man] to knock him off," he explained.

Although Arkan was wanted in Belgium for escaping from prison there four years earlier, he apparently didn't think twice about going back for the job. "They walked up to the man on the street in broad daylight and shot the guy," said Spasic. "After that they went around the corner, picked up their suitcases, and went to a café across the street from the crime. It was crazy. They watched the police converge on the scene. Arkan, you know, enjoyed seeing his creations unfold."

I didn't know that. When Spasic or other former agents talked to me about the Yugoslavian spy outfit, the experience was similar to hearing an alternative script to *Lock, Stock and Two Smoking Barrels*—the insanity of the intrigues, the secret setups, the covertly dispatched hit man who slithers in and out of underworld safe houses, and the utter craziness of it all, with oddball details tossed in for fun.

Some Serbians in current and former government positions believe that Spasic exaggerates his place in the underworld while others insist that he knows exactly what he's talking about.

Most agree that in whatever he says there is some truth. Still, like many of the others who spoke to me about the hazy operations of the UDBA and who verified Arkan's hit-man adventures, Spasic seemed to revel in the shadowy myth of the agency, its criminal operatives, and the legend of Arkan. What I could tell for certain as we spoke was that Spasic knew the power of a spy story, and for him an adherence to exact truth was probably just as dull as it was bothersome. Nevertheless, he always assured me, "I was there. I know."

2

Although the internal workings of the UDBA were deliberately foggy, it was thought that most assassination orders came directly from Stane Dolanc, the chief of the UDBA and a member of the Yugoslav federal presidency council. A witness at the International Criminal Tribunal for the Former Yugoslavia (ICTY) later asserted that Dolanc "was the individual who, in coordination with the other ministers of internal affairs in the different republics, would make decisions as to whether the ultimate solution would be applied to certain individuals, that is to say, liquidation of those individuals."

Dolanc was tall and widely built, with a long sloped forehead and chin rolls that gave him the overall appearance of a Komodo dragon. He had serious eyes and exuded an intimidating cerebral intensity, especially when he tilted his ponderous head downward and peered at his interlocutor over the top of his chunky glasses. Although he was a hugely enigmatic man, there was one thing that everyone knew: He and the UDBA were extremely dangerous.

The agency occupied a sprawling battleship-gray building in downtown Belgrade with tiny windows along Kneza Milosa, one of the city's widest thoroughfares. Like any other state security outfit, the UDBA was vigilant about protecting its mysterious existence. Old files were reportedly burned or shredded and agency workers were strictly monitored. Generally, the ordinary person on the street was terrified of the organization, and getting too close was considered unhealthy, though that didn't stop people from trading conspiracy theories.

Founded immediately after Tito's takeover in 1945, the organization carried out some of the country's darkest deeds, from ethnic cleansing to blackmail to torture to assassination. Immediately following World War II, hundreds of thousands of citizens were deemed enemies of the state, including Nazi collaborators and nationalists. Many simply disappeared—thousands were killed.

The UDBA represented a branch of the federal ministry of interior, and over the years the organization inserted its tentacles into almost every aspect of Yugoslavian life—the streets, cafés, even homes—and none of the country's sixteen million people was safe. Informants were everywhere. So were the agents. "[The UDBA] knew how to spin intrigues and rumors, to spoil old friendships and make new ones, or speed up divorces and marriages in the interests of the state," wrote the Belgrade weekly *Vreme*. "Some people were broken, some careers were cut short, while others were promoted very quickly [and] gained fame, status, and recognition."

The UDBA was similar in philosophy and élan to the KGB and East Germany's Stasi: a clandestine cold war group meant to protect government power and to eliminate domestic dissent. Ideologically, it also wasn't too far off from Romania's terrifying Securitate, which possessed one of the Eastern bloc's largest secret police forces in proportion to its population. Under the diabolical regime of Nicolae Ceauşescu, the Securitate employed an estimated eleven thousand agents and a half-million informers to watch over some fifteen million Romanian citizens. Hundreds of thousands of the country's population were imprisoned for political reasons, and many were killed.

Dolanc ascended to power in the UDBA in the 1960s, replacing a Yugoslav war hero named Aleksander Rankovic, who had become too enamored with his state-given power. It was a tenuous moment for the country. By then enemies that the state had thought dead miraculously began reappearing, like a mold you'd scrubbed away. After a decade or more spent hiding among Western Europe's Yugoslav diaspora, the state enemies slipped back into their birth country. They arrived under trains, in cargo ships, and in cars in disguises. Emboldened by Yugoslavia's mounting economic woes—rising unemployment, increased inflation, and international debt—they blew up train stations, theaters, and seaside vacation spots. They called for the death of Yugoslavia. They called for an independent Croatia or an independent

Kosovo. Others demanded Tito's blood and democracy. In addition to the domestic attacks, the dissidents struck at Yugoslavian properties abroad—in Austria, France, Sweden, Germany, Canada, and America. For instance, Freedom for the Serbian Fatherland, one of Serbia's most notorious nationalist groups, bombed half a dozen Yugoslavian embassies and consulates in North America, while one of its founders, Nikola Kavaja, made repeated attempts on Tito's life.

To deal with the country's emerging terrorist problem, Dolanc organized a superhuman killing machine, not dissimilar from the organized death squads in other parts of the world. Brutal criminals were the preferred hires—armed bank robbers, murderers, drug traffickers, men who were naturally violent, skillful with a deadly weapon, and, most important, capable of murdering on command without a drop of guilt. To inspire the hired bad men, deals were struck.

In exchange for their death work, the criminals were provided fake passports, cover stories, international support, impunity for any external crimes, and refuge in Yugoslavia. In other words, if they joined the UDBA, they could rob, smuggle, traffic drugs, and do whatever the hell else they pleased in Western Europe and, when things got too hot, they could return home—scot free. There was one other advantage to this deal: By sending criminals abroad, crime fell at home.

Before Arkan started working for the spy group's killing force in the 1970s, Spasic told me that an earlier crew of hired criminals had included Ljuba Zemunac, known as the "Strong Man" because of his penchant for fistfights, and Djordje Bozovic Giska, a bank robber and murderer, considered the gentleman of the deadly force because he was a smooth talker. Other men mentioned in these underground circles were Jusuf Bulic Jusa, Andrija Lakonjic, and Rade Caldovic, known as Centa.

When Arkan came onboard—after his father allegedly brokered the relationship with Dolanc in hopes of saving his son a thread of dignity—Spasic said he stood out; he was perceived as a man of ruthless amorality, a view that he would confirm over and over again through the years. "He was important because [at this point] he'd stopped knowing the difference between good and evil," the former agent explained. "The others would pretend they didn't know, but for the most part they knew. . . . Arkan was pathological and prone to do things most other humans wouldn't think of. He would hurt you or kill you without thinking twice. That was important to the agency."

Most times Arkan, like the others, received instructions by telephone.

Except for a couple of grainy pictures or a foggy description of the target, he received very little information about a target; the intent seemingly was, the less you know the better. According to former operatives, Arkan was also provided with money, guns, knives, and safe houses. What he and the others always assumed was that the target was armed and dangerous and that absolutely anything could happen.

It's verifiable that between 1965 and 1990 over a hundred Yugoslavs were murdered abroad. Of these deaths, not surprisingly, few successful prosecutions took place. When an investigation did happen, plaintiffs and witnesses usually backed down. Like gangland killings today, it was difficult convincing people to overlook the very real possibility that they would be murdered if they came forward—or at least severely maimed. The thing was, there were few, if any, witness protection programs, so talking just didn't pay.

There was, however, one memorable UDBA-related case that appeared in court, and it didn't have promising results. In 1981, two West Germans and a Yugoslav were arrested in Germany for murdering a former UDBA agent who had defected from the security service. Yugoslav officials, of course, denied any relationship to the killers. Although German prosecutors claimed that the three killers were paid thousands of dollars for assassinating the former agent, the Yugoslavs responded that any violence taken against the man, though tragic, was probably conducted by rival émigré organizations, not by the UDBA. The case was never solved, and it's unclear if the three men even went to jail.

In time, the UDBA had operatives engaging in activities all over the world, not just in Europe. Police records from the period report nine UDBA-backed assassination attempts in North America, six in South America, and two each in both Australia and Africa. Although Arkan worked mainly for the agency in Europe, where he was most active as a criminal, there were stories of him traveling as far west as Toronto, New York City, and Chicago.

3

Arkan's new life as a government agent didn't stop him from carrying on with his old ways. If anything, the new hit-man jobs made him bolder. When he wasn't working for the spy agency, he did what he always did: traveled, gambled, robbed, and, according to some, even started seeing different girls.

He also began moving into the black market, specifically in Holland, where he allegedly slithered into Amsterdam and Rotterdam with a crew of Balkan tough guys, hungry for action that paid: prostitution, extortion, and drug trafficking. "They didn't go by a name," said Michel van Rijn, who was living in Holland then. "Only as the Yugos."

Van Rijn was one who would know these things. Internationally infamous for smuggling art to the West from the Balkans and Russia, van Rijn had also spent time as a forger, a thief, and an informant for Scotland Yard. He was handsome, with dark hair and a canned tan, and he favored expensive suits. In the early 1980s he spotted Arkan frequently in expensive restaurants around town, like the Oester Bar, flaunting his wanted status like a badge of honor. "As much as I disliked the guy, I've not seen anyone with bigger balls," van Rijn told me. "Arkan was on a death course. It was just a question of time."

Arkan himself didn't stick around in the cities for long stretches, said van Rijn, maybe a week here and another week there. In his absence, his men stayed on and grew the new business, making contacts, setting up smuggling networks, and organizing protection schemes—and the crew flourished. Because there was little, if any, organized crime in Holland at the time, van Rijn told me, the money the Yugos made was "mind-boggling."

The Yugos expanded rapidly throughout the country in the 1980s, bringing cigarettes, jeans, antitank missiles, and hit men to the land of social harmony and windmills. "They were absolutely fearless," said van Rijn. "They had no problem sacrificing someone if necessary. They came in with Arkan and quickly became the kings of the underworld."

Throughout the 1990s, the group would continue to grow, with prominent Yugoslav mafia arrests turning up in the press. Over time, Arkan's group would evolve into a much larger, more sophisticated Balkan gang, which would eventually control heroin flowing north out of Afghanistan (ironic given his personal stance on drugs), weapons smuggled through the Balkans, and prostitutes trafficked from Africa to the alleys of Amsterdam. In the ninties, as the Balkans broke into war, these networks would grow bigger and more profitable, radiating outward to other parts of Europe, including Sweden and Germany.

Reports from watchdog agencies suggest that Arkan likely coordinated his initial underworld deeds with the UDBA, as the secret agency was considered to be involved in similar underworld operations. Though Yugoslavia's ministry of interior largely subsidized UDBA operations, a portion

of its funds likely came from illegal dealings. Arms sales factored signifi-
cantly: In the 1970s, for instance, the Yugoslav army and secret service peddled weapons to Israel, even though Yugoslavia was officially on friendly
terms with Arab nations like Egypt.

4

When the UDBA contacted Arkan in the winter of 1982 for an assassination job in Stuttgart, Germany, he was thirty-one years old and one of the
most wanted men in Europe. The latest Interpol wanted poster showed him
dressed in a checkered Sunday beach shirt, with bushy brown hair and a
pale, smooth face that gave the impression of a Delta Phi pledge. After his
hospital escape, Germany had begun pushing Serbian law enforcement for
his capture, and he was also wanted in Italy, Holland, Belgium, Switzerland,
and Sweden. Increasingly, there were few places to hide, though Arkan
didn't seem to think much about that.

The Stuttgart assassination is the one job that most people I spoke to remembered and readily mentioned when they talked about Arkan's work for
the UDBA. Most agreed that it happened sometime in January. This time,
his target was an Albanian man who lived on the top floor of a ten-story
building.

At first the man wasn't home, but that wasn't cause for worry. Jobs like
this, Spasic told me, could stretch on for days, weeks even. It was impossible
to predict, and besides, Arkan's employers didn't offer that kind of intelligence. His job was to wait and not to think about the time. The concern was
the killing and how the killing would be done when the critical moment finally arrived. So Arkan did what he had to do: He climbed to the roof of the
building and waited for the man to come home.

On average, autumn temperatures at night in this hilly city in southwest-
ern Germany, known as much for its Mercedes and Porsche plants as its
Riesling vineyards, hovered around 25 to 30 degrees Fahrenheit. To fend off
the cold, he wore a black wool thief's hat. His clothes were deliberately tat-
tered and dirty, a costume the crime journalist Marko Lopusina described to
me as "looking like a hippie." Still, as he waited, staying warm must have
been a challenge, especially as the hours dragged on and on, and then the
days.

During the day he was limited in what he could do on the roof, especially where he could go, according to Spasic. What if someone spotted him? His mission would be ruined. Or worse, he would be killed. When it was fully night, he might walk in quiet circles to get his cold blood flowing again to diminish the knife-chill air. It's plausible that he also spent stretches working on his already taut body, push-ups and sit-ups, maybe shadow kickboxing: throwing rock-solid jabs and uppercuts at his invisible enemy's chest and head.

Before arriving, Spasic said that Arkan had obtained a sleeping bag and some other camping supplies, including canned food. As far as weapons, he possessed a machine gun and a pistol. Lopusina told me that he also had a grenade launcher. He had to be prepared. Inside his sleeping bag, his ears were pried open to the night, his entire being cognizant. Lopusina described this as his "nose for trouble" and others called it his "sixth sense." He had to be conscious of the traffic below him, car doors opening and shutting. At the time, the Stuttgart streets teemed with Yugoslavs, communist organizers, drug smugglers, gamblers, proselytizers, liars, prostitutes, intriguers of every stripe. Up there, as he lay still, night dragging on, he probably heard voices, the chatter of lovers stumbling home from the theater, a lost drunk mumbling nothing at all, and the apartment under him silent as a rock.

When the job was complete he was supposed to notify his superiors back in Belgrade. If the UDBA didn't hear from him that would mean he was probably dead. There was always a chance of dying. That was the dismal truth. Of all the Yugoslav assassins, people agreed, Arkan emerged as one of the most fearless and prolific—and lucky. No one seems to know exactly how many men Arkan killed for the state, though the most prominent number out there among insiders is five to ten. Marko Nicovic, a former Belgrade police chief, however, believed that the number was more like "over a dozen, maybe fifteen." As in any spy story, specifics are always an elusive thing.

Arkan's target was one of the Gervalla brothers, according to Spasic. Whether it was Jusuf or Bardhosh Gervalla was unclear. For several years, the two Kosovar Albanian émigrés had been organizing an uprising in Kosovo, which they insisted be elevated from a province to a full-fledged Yugoslav republic. Tito, of course, rejected this idea, and the fight had been going on, at least in spirit, for decades. (Incidentally, the Gervalla brothers were considered the forefathers of the Kosovo Liberation Army, and one month after their deaths, the LPRK, or Popular Movement for the Republic of Kosovo, was created at a secret meeting in Turkey.)

It was over two weeks before his target arrived. Spasic made a big deal about this. "He waited for fifteen days," he said. "That's the kind of man he was." Other sources would say he waited four days or seven days. "And then on the fifteenth day," Spasic went on, as if quoting from the Bible, "the terrorist came."

There was, however, a wrinkle. Vehicles pulled up to the curb outside the building and, instead of one man, a gang of men stepped out and made their way inside.

What was Arkan going to do? Spasic paused before he went on telling the story. He looked out the window at the late sunlight and smiled.

Arkan was one man, Spasic reminded me. One man. Nevertheless, he owed the agency. They had done a lot for him—and this target was important.

Of course, he knew what he had to do but decided to get confirmation first. The plan he had was apparently too grandiose to execute without talking to someone. So he took a chance, slinked pantherlike downstairs to the street, located a phone, and called the UDBA. The agency was available around the clock.

"There are ten guys," he reported to them over a closed line. "Should I kill them all?"

When Spasic recalled this scene to me, he laughed. "Can you believe that?" he asked as he repeated Arkan's question. No, I couldn't, but Spasic was reveling and didn't seem to hear me. "Should I kill them all?" The retired agent shook his head incredulously, raised his palms in the air, as if he were asking for applause. "Amazing," he said, before going on.

On the phone, the men at the UDBA asked Arkan if he was really serious.

"Yes," the young assassin replied emphatically. "Do you want me to kill them all? I can do it, if you want."

Spasic said that the UDBA talked it out, and then the answer came back. "No," they told Arkan, "that would be a big mess. Don't kill them all. Wait till he is on his own and kill him then."

Arkan agreed and hung up.

The waiting went on until finally, later in the night, Gervalla emerged alone from the apartment building. By then Arkan was standing near the man's car. He raised his machine gun and fired it into the Albanian's body.

Later, both Gervallas would turn up dead alongside Albanian journalist Kadri Zeka. The Stuttgart murders, like the others, would never be solved, according to Spasic, who would later be expelled from the secret police for his outspokenness—talking about what the agency did made him a liability.

(He would also pen his autobiography, *Lasica Koja Govori*, or *Weasel Who Speaks*.)

Over the years other versions of that night would emerge. Lopusina's version had Arkan taking all three men out in a car on the street. "He took his big gun, the grenade launcher, and fired it into the car," he told me. "The car exploded and he walked up to it and, to finish them off, he shot each of the three men in the mouth. This was a message: They will not speak again."

Either way, the quality and definitiveness of his work earned Arkan the admiration of Dolanc. "One Arkan," Dolanc supposedly said, "is worth more than the whole UDBA." Not unexpectedly, less than a year later, Dolanc reportedly helped orchestrate Arkan's escape from prison in Lugano, Switzerland.

When a Serbian reporter asked Arkan about the Gervalla assassination many years later, the hit man chuckled. What he said in response could have been said about his career with the UDBA. "I don't know what you're talking about," he responded. "I've never been to Stuttgart."

9

THE MAN ARKAN
DIDN'T KILL

A self-described Belgrade gangster named Rocky tipped me off to Nikola Kavaja. Arkan, I was told, had tried to assassinate Kavaja, but somehow Kavaja had managed to slip away. Much like Arkan, Kavaja's back-story had a certain Hollywood sheen to it: World War II prisoner, communist soldier, CIA hit man, hijacker, and now fugitive on the run. Because his life, much of it spent in the shadows, had taught him not to trust outsiders, he was fiercely private. Somehow Rocky convinced him to see me, so early one morning we were driving over to his apartment in central Belgrade.

There were concerns. On the way over Rocky warned me not to push him too much. "If he doesn't like you, you might have to worry," he said. Rocky was in his late twenties and wore a shiny black leather coat and jeans. He mentioned people tied to chairs going to the bottom of the Danube. As Rocky navigated the bombed-out city's exhaust-choked streets, I felt like I was suddenly living out an alternative version of the film *The Insider*, when the person playing Lowell Bergman of *60 Minutes* was blindfolded in Lebanon and driven in a jeep full of heavily armed men to interview the leader of the Syrian-backed Islamic paramilitary organization Hezbollah. "Just be careful," he instructed, as we pulled to the curb. "Know what I mean?"

Kavaja lived in a drab, communist-era high-rise, three flights up, and his front door was steel. Rocky walked in without knocking. The two-room apartment was sparsely furnished: a single mattress and dresser in one room, and a scratched-up wood desk, a couch, and a bench press in the other. The dirty white walls were cluttered with pictures of the people who figured most strongly in Kavaja's personal iconography: General Ratko Mladic, Saint Sava, Stalin, Jimmy Carter, and a young pinup who was his current girlfriend. Guns and old military gear provided further ornamentation, while a blue thermal blanket covered the street window.

Kavaja was standing in the second room. "Hallo," he said brusquely, squeezing my hand. He was seventy-three, but he looked no older than sixty. He adhered to a strict weight-training routine that got him up every weekday before the sun. He was squarely built and muscular, with white hair cut to a military trim line and a fighter's mashed-up nose. Except for the fine white thread of mustache, he was cleanly shaven. In his dress he favored black shirts and black pants, which he tucked into polished black combat boots.

He seemed to be in good spirits and, in heavily accented English, he asked about America, where he'd spent a lot of time early in his life, some of it in jail. "New York," he said. "How is life in New York?"

We hunkered down on beat-up wooden chairs at the center of the claustrophobically small room. There were two others sitting on a futon pushed into the corner. Both were in their twenties, with short hair and leather clothing. When I started to explain why I'd come, Kavaja quickly cut me off. "Write down my name," he said, pointing at my notepad. "*N-i-k-o-l-a K-a-v-a-j-a*. You can call me Nik."

"That's a start," I said.

"It's a long story," he said, wagging a stubby finger at an unmarked bottle of clear liquid on his desk. "Do you want some schnapps?"

"No thanks. I'm fine with water."

"Water's for pussies," he said.

I looked at the bottle, nodded. "Most of the time I'd agree. But 10:30 in the morning is a little early for me to be drinking shots of schnapps."

"It's a hello," he insisted. "You drink some schnapps with me. We drink together."

He snapped his fingers for one of the futon shadows to retrieve shot glasses from the galley kitchen in the back. Later I was told that the two men were Montenegrin criminals, who considered Kavaja a mentor. Maybe they were. Maybe they weren't. Belgrade was like that. Throughout the day, others would come and go, including a Serbian interior ministry official and his blond mistress, a distant cousin, and some older mobsters in track-suits.

"OK," Kavaja said, tipping his glass down his throat. He swallowed the drink, then poured another and downed that. I swallowed mine. It was infernal—sort of along the lines of rocket fuel, burning all the way down. "Now we start," he said, clearing his throat.

I asked him to talk to me about the year that Arkan came to kill him, but he swatted the question away. "We start at the beginning," he said. To understand why an assassin wanted him dead, I had to understand where he came from and why he had decided to kill Tito. "I was born in 1933," he said. He looked off across the room, placing his hand on his forehead, as if to retrieve that time. When World War II came to Yugoslavia, his family got sucked up by the invading Germans and thrown into work camps. After three years he emerged and killed his first man when he was twelve—he threw an injured German soldier into a well. When Tito took over the bullet-scarred country at the end of the war, the new leader imprisoned and killed thousands he deemed enemies of the government. Some of Kavaja's family went to jail and some were killed, including three brothers who had fought with Tito in the war. "That's where my life really started," he told me. "I hated Tito. And I became a member of a top-secret anticommunist group."

Kavaja joined the Yugoslav Air Force, but began carrying out a number of missions against the country, including dropping anti-Tito leaflets from his plane and then blowing up a military airfield. When Tito's police found out what he was doing, Kavaja tried to flee but got caught. He spent a stretch in a Third World–like prison, with bars for windows, thinking that he was going to die of hypothermia or starvation, but he managed to escape from a prisoner transport train and finally made his way to Germany.

He was twenty-two when, he said, the CIA hired him as a Cold War operative to fight against communism, which was spreading across the world like an evening shade. Soon after he began hunting Tito, an adventure that would turn him into one of Yugoslavia's most dangerous dissidents. "Killing Tito was a big mission," he said, as he sipped another glass of schnapps. "For almost a decade, I hunted him. I was never a traitor—I wanted to save my country. That's why I was good for this mission. I was ready to give my life for it. If I died one second after I killed Tito I wouldn't care. He killed my three brothers. He destroyed my country."

Before he went after Tito, he said, he bombed Yugoslav buses in Austria and a hotel in France, assassinated several East German agents, and fought with the French Foreign Legion in Algeria. When Tito toured North and South America in 1963, visiting with various leaders, Kavaja followed. Dressed as a Catholic priest, with a long black robe under which he hid his Colt .45 and .357 Magnum, Kavaja chased Tito from Brazil to Chile to Mexico, and then to Washington, but the leader eluded him. "I could never get a clear shot off at him," he said. "Or he came in a helicopter . . . and I didn't have missiles." Tito didn't return to the States until 1971, when he met Richard Nixon at Camp David. Kavaja claims he was there. Disguised as a Maryland state trooper, he took a sniper rifle, climbed a tree within eyeshot of the property, and waited for his chance. Tito "liked to take walks," said Kavaja. "It was beautiful, I thought. Who wouldn't take a walk? I waited all day and night."

"In the tree?" I asked. "You didn't sleep?"

Kavaja chuckled. "I couldn't kill him if I was asleep. You don't know anything about this kind of thing! Sleep! What a fucking joker!"

I wondered if Tito ever went for a walk there.

Kavaja shook his head, disbelievingly. "Never," he said. "After two days, he left. And that was it. Nothing. So I didn't get him."

Meanwhile, Kavaja was turning up on Yugoslav State Security's radar. By the late 1970s, Kavaja and a few others had also started a terrorist group, known as Srpski Oslobodilacki Pokret Otadzbine, or Serbian Liberation for the Fatherland (SOPO). The group organized bombings all over the world, including a Yugoslav embassy in Washington and the consulates in New York, Chicago, San Francisco, Ottawa, and Toronto. "At that point, state security wanted me dead," he said. "I knew that."

That's when Arkan came into play. "He was just a kid then," Kavaja said. "But I heard that he was their best guy and that they'd sent him after me." Before he got to Kavaja, one of Kavaja's friends and coconspirators was murdered. The man's daughter was murdered, too. Kavaja had a picture of the man on his wall, just above his desk. "Arkan could have killed them, but of course I can't say for sure. It was a small world. You heard things. And I heard this."

Arkan came looking for him in New York City in the late 1970s. According to Kavaja, Arkan came down through Toronto and started asking around the émigré circles in Manhattan and Queens. Kavaja got word of it from friends. "There's a man asking for you," they told him, but Kavaja, like Arkan, was a master escapist. If he wanted to be invisible, he was gone. How long Arkan stuck around New York, Kavaja didn't know, but from that point on he watched his back. "If someone wanted to assassinate me, I know how they'd do it," he said. "Because I was an assassin myself."

At that point Kavaja stopped to show off a gun, which had been holstered under his desk. The shadows on the futon nodded appreciatively. "See this?" he said, fingering the black barrel. "This is my best friend in all my life. It's a German gun from before World War II, made in 1938. A Luger 9 millimeter. Very good gun." I asked if it was loaded. "You are a silly man," he said, engaging the bullet and then pointing it at me. Everyone laughed, except me. "More schnapps," I said.

In the end, the FBI got to Kavaja before Arkan. On November 21, 1978, twenty agents ambushed him on Park Avenue and arrested him for the bombings. They picked up dozens of other SOPO members, including another leader named Priest. Six months later a judge found them guilty but delayed the sentencing a month. Kavaja got out on a quarter of a million dollars' bail, secured by a friend, and set off to hijack a plane. With bombs strapped to his legs and chest, he climbed aboard an American Airlines 727 heading from JFK to Chicago. "My plan was to land in Chicago," he said, "pick Priest up, and then fly to Belgrade and crash into the Communist Central Committee building."

When they touched down in Chicago, Priest, however, decided not to leave jail. Letting the passengers go free, Kavaja, according to the numerous media accounts of that day, took the plane back into the air with a small crew, stopped at JFK, where he switched to a 707, and then somewhere mid-Atlantic he had a crisis. "I started rethinking my plan. I was ready to die, but I didn't know where the Central Communist building was in Belgrade. I didn't want to kill regular civilians. That was never my job. I wanted to kill Tito and the biggest symbol of the Communist Party—not go down as the guy who killed innocent people. My friend betrayed me, and I lost the target."

Kavaja landed in Ireland, where he was arrested, and then sent back to the States to prison, first to Marion, in Illinois, and finally to Lompoc, in California, where he heard of Tito's death in 1980 and the end of communism shortly after. When he was released in the early 1990s, he traveled back to Belgrade. By then Arkan was a famous mob boss and warlord. No longer a communist, Arkan was a nationalist, like Kavaja. "He sent a message to my house," said Kavaja. "He wanted to talk, but I didn't want to. Who's this guy? My dick, I was going to talk to him. I wasn't scared that he was this big man. Look at me now. I'm alive. He isn't."

It was late afternoon when Kavaja finished his story. More schnapps was passed around. Although more than half the bottle was gone, Kavaja did not seem drunk. Others had arrived to hear the tail end of his story. One of the Montenegrin kids toyed with a pistol. Then Kavaja called some girls to come over. Talking of the past had begun to bore him. "I have beautiful young girls," he said, making curvaceous shapes with his hands. "Life is good, you see," he said, smiling, before picking up the phone.

I stuck around for another half hour or so and had a glass of schnapps as a "good-bye." I must say that I never felt afraid of the man, though he would tell me before I left that he killed more than seventeen people in his life. When I pressed him for details about the other deaths, he wouldn't elaborate. What he did say however, would haunt me for a long time after. "There are some questions that you do not ask," he said, as we stood at the door now, his dim apartment behind us. He looked directly into my eyes, lethally almost. He meant that prying was not always wise. That some stories were best left alone. It was advice that I would later regret ignoring.

PART II

THE WARLORD

10

MY FIXER MILAN AND OUR SEARCH FOR TRUTH AMONG SERBIA'S CRIME LORDS

1

The first time I traveled to Belgrade in search of Arkan, Milan Vukovic met me at the airport. I hired Milan to help me gain access to the mobster's world, which I'd heard was protected around the gloomy capital city by a lethal code of silence. Few spoke openly about Arkan, at least not to strangers, and especially not to American strangers. Milan was a fixer, someone who connects people who wouldn't normally meet, opens doors that wouldn't normally be opened. Milan knew criminals, government officials, and pop stars. He knew people in Arkan's orbit, and his job was to break the silence.

Milan picked me up in his rusted-out blue Alfa Romeo and we headed straight to the city, Eminem blaring on blown-out speakers. He was twenty-nine and as gaunt as an indie rocker, with bags under his eyes and short black hair, just like many male Serbs, cut high above the ears and glossy with gel. He wore a Houston Rockets jersey and bleached jeans and had the nervous intensity of someone who spent too much time playing *Grand Theft Auto*, talking about our quest as he drove, moving his hands at a hundred miles a minute, even as he passed cars on the highway, his door inches from oncoming traffic. "You look very nervous," he said, as he screeched down an exit ramp.

I had met Milan through a colleague who had employed him during the wars in the 1990s. He was fluent in English and Serbo-Croatian but, most important, he was known to be resourceful, practical, intelligent, and more than a little brave. Over the loud music Milan began to talk about Arkan. He compared the criminal's world to "a spider's web." It was an analogy that I would never forget. You make a wrong move, you get close in the wrong way, Milan told me as our car blasted into downtown Belgrade, and "the spider eats you."

2

Over the three years that I chased Arkan's legacy through the Balkans, Milan tracked down sources, arranged interviews, translated, and helped me navigate the sprawling spider's web. At night, depending on where we were in the country, we inhabited dingy hotels and borrowed flats. We became quick friends, two men bonding over an incredible fear of mortality. Part of Milan's job was watching my back—but he also had to keep an eye on his own. This all became apparent fast.

Days into that first trip we drove to a small out-of-the-way café to interview three underworlders who used to work and fight for Arkan. They were tattooed, as muscular as dockworkers, and one mentioned a pistol. Twenty minutes into the conversation the biggest one leaned over the table, put a thick finger in my face, and said in English, "Don't fuck around, we will be watching you." What that meant, he didn't say specifically, but back in the car Milan told me stories about those who "fuck around" with these people. Usually it involved a broken leg or arm or, worse, being carted off to a desolate place. The Serbs had a name for this place: *vukojebina,* or as Milan translated, "where the wolves fuck."

By employing Milan, I knew I was putting his skull on the line, but he knew this, too. Sometimes he was comfortable with it. Other times he wasn't. As a fixer, he had to constantly juggle my world and his own. He operated a vegetable stall at a local market and lived in a furniture-stuffed two-bedroom apartment in a dilapidated ten-story building in downtown Belgrade with his three-year-old daughter and his girlfriend. Occasionally, he worried out loud that Belgrade was "too small," and if word got around that he was asking too many questions about Arkan, "big trouble" would make its way to his house and to his family. "I like my life," he said to me one day. "Do you?"

11

CRUISING IN
THE PINK CADILLAC

1

When Arkan returned to Belgrade for good in the early 1980s, he piloted a pink Cadillac with a smooth leather steering wheel and a gleaming, surfboard hood. His very presence drew looks. The city hadn't seen him in over a decade. No longer a young street punk, he was now in his early thirties, around six feet tall, and as angular as a switchblade, with a solid face that looked like it had been shaped in a woodshop—eyes like nail heads and a brow hard enough to beat you with. His dark hair, once long and shaggy, was shorter and in retreat, and he favored white suits with shiny gold jewelry, a gold Rolex dangling from his wrist. There were also the guns. He almost always carried two, because he never knew. One was a double-action, blowback Walther PPK and the other a semiautomatic Colt .38, which friends referred to ominously as the "big gun."

People first began seeing him in 1981 and 1982 for odd stretches here and there, but it was in 1983 that he began to settle back into the city for good. Although his criminal empire would soon dominate most of Belgrade, prefiguring the terrific madness that would later swallow up the country as it shifted away from communism, there was little evidence of his immediate plans in those first years back. People, of course, had heard about his bank-robbing years and the sensational prison escapes, and they also had some inkling that he had killed people for the government, but what he was going to do now, few knew. "He came home with a lot of money, we knew that," said Vojislav Tufegdzic, a crime writer who cowrote the script of the cult gangster documentary *See You in the Obituaries*. "Other things were not as clear." His silence only encouraged gossip. "There were a lot of rumors," said Slavoljub Ninkovic, an old gambling buddy. "People had heard about him and wondered about his plans. But he didn't say much of anything. He was very quiet."

Seeing him behind the wheel of his pink Cadillac, people began to refer to him as 007. Some days, you'd see him cruising along one of the sprawling central city avenues, which were crammed with buildings of mixed Slavic and Turkish architecture, or stopped at an intersection, window ajar, radio going, simply enjoying the smell of chestnut trees. He was with friends, sometimes alone, or with a new girl around his arm. He haunted underground gambling holes and played cards or roulette. Other days and nights, with his Cadillac parked, he was hunkered down at one of the many outdoor cafés, where people wondered about the future of a dying country.

He was silent about his vision, what he would do. Until suddenly he wasn't. He made his first major public statement late in 1983. He did it one night when two police officers came looking for him at his mother's house, where he'd been staying on and off since he arrived home. By then his father and mother had divorced, and just his mother lived there. When the knock came at the door, Arkan didn't ask who it was. Although reports say that the officers were there to question him about a robbery in Zagreb, where thieves supposedly walked off with a bag of gold, it was later rumored that they were really dropping in to size him up, see who this guy was in the pink Cadillac and the white suit.

Whatever the reason, the officers got something they most likely didn't expect. The door swung open and Arkan greeted the officers with either one or two pistols aimed at their skulls. Welcome, boys! While one of the men managed to scramble away, Arkan blasted the other in the leg, which sent the man stumbling, sucking air. According to one version of the story, his gun was loaded with rubber bullets, while another version said the bullets were real. On the floor now, the officer dug into his coat for identification. Held it up. What's this? Arkan asked, knowing full well what it was. Then, according to law enforcement officials, Arkan, the new man in town, actually started laughing, laughing as if it was one of the most hilarious things he'd ever seen in the world, a cop begging for his life—because that's what it was.

After that Arkan should have jumped into his car and split town. That was the sane thing to do, but Arkan didn't always act sane. He was going to make a point, because that's what needed to be done. He stuck around and allowed himself to be locked up, though he wasn't in for long. The UDBA intervened and instructed the city police to let him go, which they did, reluctantly. Within two months Arkan was out, and word of how he shot the cops and got away with it quickly seeped into the streets. It was a critical moment. His point became obvious to anyone in that Eastern European city who was listening—and everyone was. Arkan was home for good, and he was going to do whatever the hell he wanted to do. He also had big plans. "Don't fuck with me," he seemed to say that night, standing over the shot cop on the ground. "This is my town now. Mine."

The big question now was: Was there anyone who could stop him?

2

By the early 1980s, a virus of change was quietly beginning to burn through Yugoslavia's cities and towns. The country had billions of dollars in international debt, unemployment was creeping up, so was inflation, and a specter of violence threatened the land. Dictators, crime bosses, and nationalistic killers loomed like thugs in cheap suits, waiting for the moment to pounce. "There were dark things at work," Milan St. Protic, former Serbian ambassador to the United States, told me. "But on the outside, life was still pretty good. People were living comfortably. There was social help, state-organized vacations, and all of that. People in general didn't know that they should be worrying." The dark things would come, but not yet.

The country quietly came undone, but people, happy or not, lived in the communist fog, because the fog was the only thing that they knew. At that moment Belgrade had become Yugoslavia's most populous city, with almost 1.5 million people. To squeeze all of the people in, monstrous ten- and twenty-story cement apartment blocks rose up, soldierlike, north of the Sava River, filling up almost every last square inch of New Belgrade. There were cars. Lots of them. Ladas and Mercedeses and public buses clogged the streets, creating traffic jams and pollution. There were new nightclubs and cafés and stores, some of which peddled the latest Western music and Hollywood movies like *Star Wars* and *Lost Boys*.

Old Belgrade, on the east side of the Sava River, was just as jammed up with people and activity, and there was talk about restarting construction on the city's largest Serbian Orthodox Church, the Temple of Saint Sava. Construction had first begun in 1935, but it had stalled because of the intervening years of war. It would take another twenty years to complete. From a dusty outcropping above the city, the church would climb 22 stories, with room for 10,000 people, 49 bells, and a 4,000-ton gold dome up there in the clouds, the penultimate symbol of a tragic and heavenly Serbian people on the rise.

Arkan approached the city like a man who hadn't eaten much of anything for decades but beans and water. Soon after the police shooting, he began to organize. Foot soldiers were recruited from his hometown and abroad. He taught these men the tricks he knew. Soon he was traveling around the city with a few tough guys in black leather coats. He plunged into extortion and stolen goods, mainly cigarettes and cars. He also reportedly expanded his organized crime networks in Sweden, Germany, and Holland and bought into a small casino on Sveti Stefan, a Montenegrin island on the Adriatic.

It wasn't long before he surfaced as the leader of an emerging, though small, Balkan underworld, with a refined sense of justice. When someone challenged his supremacy, he dispatched his thugs to issue threats. He ran protection schemes and began loan-sharking. Some people told me that he eventually received as much as $1,000 per month from each business he protected. Although his contract killings for the UDBA had slowed, the federal spy agency still protected him, which only elevated his place in the criminal underworld and allowed him to commit crimes with virtual impunity. When the Belgrade police tried to arrest him, they allegedly counted the minutes that went by before someone from the agency, in most cases director Stane Dolanc, stepped in on his behalf. It was a joke.

His love life was a little rocky. Several years had passed since he'd left Agneta, his Swedish wife, and it was assumed that he had little contact with his son, Michael, though their relationship would change in the future. Now girls came and went, like fireflies flickering on and off in his increasingly permanent midnight. Of these girls, people remember a Belgian woman and then a Belgrade actress, relationships that produced two children, both of whom are still alive.

Then there was Natalja Martinovic—a beautiful, tall, skinny twentysomething with sandy hair, from Montenegro. In his circles she was considered an intellectual, having studied literature and philosophy at the university. When she started coming around with Arkan, riding shotgun in one of his expensive cars, people joked that she was out of his league. Privately, his friends worried she'd change him.

"It was an odd mix," Vladan Dinic told me. Dinic was a family friend and publisher of the tabloid *Svedok*. "But he fell in love with her. And I think she fell for him. Maybe she liked that he was a tough guy. You know how girls are. And he liked that she was a kind of homebody. Secretly, I think, he really wanted to settle down. But he could never do that. That just wasn't Arkan."

3

Newly minted Belgrade narcotics cop Marko Nicovic couldn't have known how the decision to go after Arkan would change his life. It was 1983. Nicovic was a tall, broad man with a knife-chiseled face, a thick mane of black hair, expressive eyebrows, and a carriage like a baron. At thirty-six, with six years of police work already under his belt, the first stretch in homicide, he did most of his work undercover, posing as a big-time drug buyer, donning snazzy suits or dark trench coats as he chased cocaine, opium, and hashish, which traveled east to west along a notorious Balkan route.

Although Yugoslavia had a reputation for strong drug control, south Serbia, especially around Kosovo, was known to be an intractable gray spot. There, hard-core traffickers carted in truckloads of product from Istanbul, packed it up in the middle of the night, and then shipped it off to Trieste, where it was distributed to Western Europe.

Like Arkan, Nicovic had big dreams. He had his eyes set on rising in the cop world, which meant he had to take on big cases and not back down when big criminals made their way into town. The fact that his arms and legs were lethal protected him in his dangerous line of work. Nicovic was an eighth-level black belt in karate—but not just any black belt. As he liked to boast, he was "one of the only white men in the world to hold an honorary place in the Japanese Karate Federation."

The young cop worked out of city headquarters downtown—a lusterless monster of a building where your feet and voice echo through the long, cavernous stone halls. Stacks of files littered his desk. In no time he emerged as a go-to man, always taking on more cases. He was a language whiz—fluent in English, French, German, Italian, and Spanish, and a little Japanese—and having trained for police work in Greece and America, his superiors relied on him to focus on international investigations, which meant almost every major drug ring was his game—and that included Arkan—but Arkan would not be easy. As almost every city cop knew, it wasn't as much about catching him as it was about getting charges that would stick—and then keeping him in jail.

Nicovic took his job seriously. Even with Tito in the ground and the old communist leader's iron fist gone, law enforcement continued to maintain a strong presence. Like most of the other city cops, Nicovic was proud of his role in reducing crime. In the 1980s, the city's most common offenses were passport forgery, assault, and robbery, with drugs creeping up into the mix but mostly as a hardly seen peripheral force. Of the eighteen or twenty murders that occurred in and around Belgrade in those early years, 90 percent were solved, according to Nicovic. One of Nicovic's biggest cases before landing in narcotics involved the arrest of two Armenian assassins responsible for the 1983 murder of Galip Balkar, Turkey's ambassador to Yugoslavia.

Police, unlike many of the other government jobs, like steel production or car making, were paid on time every month (Nicovic made about $700 a month) and their positions were respected. Although the cops had a solid rule over everyday civil life in Belgrade, the one group that sometimes made it difficult for them to operate was their counterparts at the federal level, the secret police. Given that the secret police watched out for Arkan, getting him was going to be complicated, even for a cop who had an appetite for thorny, high-intensity takedowns.

Nicovic didn't care about easy tasks or hard tasks. He didn't seem to be one to differentiate. He was stubborn and aggressive, and if he set his mind on something he kept his mind on it until it was done, whatever the consequences. When it came to criminals, he was determined to send a message. "It was not fun for them to get arrested," he explained to me. In fact, if necessary—and usually it was necessary—he and his men made the experience "physically painful" for criminals. He wouldn't say exactly what that meant, chuckling instead.

A 1975 University of Belgrade law school graduate, Nicovic possessed a deeply analytical mind. As he watched Arkan cruise the city in his fancy cars, quickly aggregating muscle and riches not only in the drug world but also in other rackets, he puzzled through questions. Who was this man?

What were his ambitions? He watched him extend his razor-sharp tentacles and force them into the hind parts of Belgrade. The trick, if there was one, was to get him when he wasn't looking, or to convince people watching him that he was more of a detriment to the city than an ally. Nicovic looked at the young man like a scientist examining a slide of a previously unseen germ. It was ugly, the germ's future, he speculated.

When he spoke about the task of dealing with Arkan to me, he wasn't flashy or hyperbolic. He didn't brag about his place in Arkan's story, like many did. He knew he was expected to be cinematic—because he's the master cop pitted against the master criminal—but he wasn't excited about it. Though the decision to go after the man would bring him close to death, it was his duty, and talking about it in any other way seemed to make him a little uncomfortable. Nicovic told me simply, "Catching him . . . It was my job."

4

When evening darkness spread across the city, the mobsters began arriving at Amadeus, a downtown nightclub tucked away in the basement of a nondescript concrete building. They drove luxury cars—Mercedes, BMW, Audi, etc. The men were dressed fashionably gangster—Arkan in his polished black shoes and tailored white suit, accompanied by a white scarf in the winter. The mobsters had faces that meant business, and they came in ones and twos and threes, many with scantily dressed girls slung across their bulky arms.

Every wannabe or big-time gangster required a hangout. Amadeus was Arkan's joint. He'd opened the nightclub with two men he knew could keep secrets—Candyman, the state security operative, and Dragan "Tapi" Malesevic, a realist painter who doubled as the country's most adept passport forger. At the time, Nicovic described the trio as "the top mafia guys in the city."

Arkan had a reserved table in a corner. As the club speakers pulsated and lights flickered around him, he sat with his back to the wall and watched the room. Still a teetotaler, he drank nonalcoholic beverages and frowned on smoking. Drinking and drugs, he lectured sometimes, made you unreasonable, which was the last thing you could be in his line of work. Unreasonableness got you caught—or killed.

One night blurred into another. There were lots of late nights, but night was the best time to work. This was 1983 and 1984. His street soldiers came and went, taking orders as he sketched out plans. It was important that the music was loud. It was important that no one heard him or his men, because you never knew who was listening. When he wasn't talking business, he talked about Europe, how he'd traveled in Sweden or Italy or Holland, though he was short on details about what he had done and with whom. In rare moments of emotion, for instance, on Tapi's birthday, he fired his PPK into the ceiling.

While people waited to get into Amadeus, others sought out less exclusive clubs. Nightlife was boiling over in Belgrade and new places sprouted up every couple of months. There was lots of new music, and in particular people were energized about Novi Val, or New Wave. America had bands like the Cure, the Smiths, New Order, and Depeche Mode; Yugoslavia had acts like Azra, Ekatarina Velika, and Elektricni Orgazam. New Wave was the zeitgeist, and some of the band members and clubgoers dressed as if the world was coming to an end—Sprockets-like black clothes, sleeveless shirts, punker hair, and eye shadow.

In Belgrade the music was more than just dressing up, getting drunk, and dancing all night. Sure, people liked to do all that, just as they did everywhere else in the world, but the music meant something, too. You could hear urgency in the chorus lines, a staccato cry out that was sometimes rebellious and sometimes liberating, but other times gloomy. The music spoke of the times, of the increasing darkness and uncertainty rumbling just underneath life in the rapidly decaying communist country.

Occasionally, the music referenced the country's new generation of gangsters. For instance, the popular rock band Ribja Corba, or Fish Soup, gave voice in particular to Arkan's mobbed-up approach to business. In its mid-1980s hit "Don't Go Walking Down My Street," the band sang about a gun acquired in the underworld and warned: "I will use a bullet on you with pleasure. So don't go walking down my street."

The song was a boast and a direct challenge, one that police officer Nicovic took personally. One night as the band played on and the night turned dizzy, Nicovic was actually sneaking down Arkan's street, setting up for a direct confrontation. "He wanted to make that club a business," he told me, "but we decided to destroy that possibility."

5

Everyone knew Branko Savkovic. Around Belgrade, people called him Zika Zivac, or Zika the Nerve. The Nerve, who worked for Arkan, earned his nickname for his physical dominance and fearlessness. In fact, the rock band Fish Soup had a famous pop ballad mythologizing one of his criminal attributes, his tree-like strength. "He was born with a miracle gift," the band sang. "He can kill with one right fist."

When rumors started going around in 1985 that the Nerve was working on a drug deal for Arkan, Nicovic imagined his first break on the case. He pressed his street informants for more information, urged them to dig deeper. Taking out the Nerve would send a message and cripple Arkan's burgeoning empire, which was creeping across Europe. As intelligence came back in fragments, Nicovic puzzled things together.

Early sources indicated that the deal involved several pounds of heroin, but soon that number doubled and quadrupled, and soon it had reached twenty-two pounds with a street value of about $8 million, hardly small change in the 1980s.

Still, Nicovic didn't move to make any arrests. He was patient and kept asking his sources for more. Soon there was a Turkish connection uncovered in town. Nicovic contacted police officials in Turkey, where the drugs had originated, and then started calling around West Germany, where he thought the haul was headed. Then the hard work paid off.

After four months, the Nerve made his move. He packed up a Volkswagen Golf with the twenty-two pounds of heroin and steered it out of town. He crossed borders until he made it to Germany, where he probably thought he was home free, but in Stuttgart, the game was over, and undercover German police intercepted the Nerve. There is no doubt he was irked. What the fuck is this? Who are you guys?

The Germans probably just laughed. Looks like you got something you shouldn't have, hey, buddy?

The local court slapped the Nerve with a ten-year sentence. Back in Belgrade, Nicovic arrested the Turkish connection with another ten pounds. "It was a big success for us," Nicovic told me.

Although he didn't get Arkan, not this time anyway, it had to have been a damaging blow. Who could afford to lose that kind of money? Arkan was still rising, and a strike like that had to hurt.

Instead of celebrating the successful operation, Nicovic decided to turn up the heat some more on Arkan's world. Instead of going home at night, he rounded up a few men and began showing up at Arkan's club. "We'd walk into Amadeus, switch on all the lights in the middle of the dancing, and ask for everyone's documents," he said. " 'OK, who has the guns? Hand 'em over.' "

There, at his corner table, Nicovic would find Arkan sitting conspicuously in a dapper suit, sipping his nonalcholic beverage, surrounded by men with guns. There was nothing the mobster could do about the raid but shake his head and think about revenge.

The cops body searched the subterranean crowd, emptied pockets, confiscated pistols and contraband. Sometimes, just to make a point, Nicovic and his men threw sucker punches, mashed faces into walls. "We wanted to make it very painful for them to operate," said Nicovic.

It wasn't just one or two nights. It was every night, Nicovic and his men coming back, again and again, a storm that wouldn't quit. By the end of the first month, the Belgrade cop with an appetite for mobster blood felt like he was making progress. "The guests had had enough of it," he said. "They stopped going there."

6

When Arkan wanted to forget about all of that, he headed to the gambling tables, and these days he began gambling a lot. He sought out games in hotel rooms and private apartments, places protected by armed men and police payoffs. Usually, it was late at night, long after Amadeus had shut down and most were sleeping. He played baccarat, poker, and roulette, and bet large sums of money as if the payoff would save him.

Slavoljub Ninkovic knew about these endless gambling-fueled nights. He met Arkan for the first time in the fall of 1983, after a five-year poker bender in Germany, where he'd worked a string of dead-end jobs to fund his addiction. "We became fast friends," he said about Arkan. The two played high-stakes games, with $1,000 antes. "You didn't have $1,000 in your pocket, you didn't play," he said.

The more the stakes, the less Arkan thought about things going on outside the room—Nicovic, the Nerve, Amadeus, or what to do next. The games were in Belgrade, and then they were in Croatia and Montenegro, and they dragged on for days, but you wouldn't know that at the table, where the world slipped away. At the table Arkan was a kind of sphinx, Ninkovic said. You never knew what he was thinking. "He didn't show much emotion at all," he told me. "He didn't even raise his voice, like all the others who were always yelling about things."

Except when he lost. There were good nights and bad ones. If Arkan won, Ninkovic said, he demanded payment immediately. If he lost, well, that's where things could get dangerous. As the stories go, on particularly bad nights—and there were some pretty bad ones—Arkan would withdraw his trusted PPK from the inside pocket of his suit jacket and aim it at the dealer. You see this? Beautiful, isn't it? The metal nose of the gun glinting in the artificial light. Ninkovic said that was enough for the house to erase his debt, though he could never go back to the place again.

There were weeks where it seemed Arkan was living off NoDoz, popping pills whenever his eyes began to slant or his head felt heavy. His gambling became almost pathological. Once Ninkovic remembered leaving a game in Belgrade around 4:00 A.M., getting into Arkan's silver BMW sedan, a new car, and traveling five hours to Zagreb, Croatia's capital, for another full session of cards. "I wanted to go to home and sleep," said Ninkovic. "But Arkan kept driving. He wouldn't let me out."

The game in Zagreb was a defining one. When they pulled into the city, the sun was just rising over the buildings. The game was held in a hotel suite. About fifteen other players showed up, most of them from the underworld. Ninkovic didn't remember much of that day, except one hand. "There was a father and son there," he said. "The son was up against Arkan on this hand, and he says to the father, 'What do you think I should do? Should I fold or keep playing?' They were Gypsies. The father can't believe the question. He shakes his head and says, 'When you robbed that train in Italy, you weren't afraid, and now you're afraid to play the game.' That was the kind of game it was." Arkan won the hand and walked away that day with over $100,000. "This was how life was back then," he told me. "You could call it more than a little wild."

7

Before everything turned to hell, Arkan attempted to negotiate a truce with Nicovic. He showed up at police headquarters and made phone calls. "I got something for you," he told the police officer.

One day it was a Rolex.

Another day: "I have a nice car for you, Marko."

Nicovic shook his head, laughed at the man's audacity. Not a chance.

"OK, Marko," Arkan said, laughing at the audacity of an honest man. "I tried."

Then Arkan went out and turned over the city: He got in a fistfight with a traffic cop and threatened to kill some officers at the airport when they wanted to stop him from driving his trucks on the tarmac. He blew red lights, flashed his gun in public places, smoked the speed limit, and threatened police some more.

Nicovic fought with the UDBA about taking Arkan down, but the spy agency kept putting up roadblocks. Over and over they told him to get lost. Arkan was still one of theirs, but Nicovic wouldn't go away. He kept pushing. Because that was how he worked.

Soon the UDBA was having its own second thoughts about Arkan. As the spymaster Spasic admitted to me, "We began to see that he was getting out of control. We knew we had to do something."

The chief concern, Spasic told me, was an obvious one. Arkan's aversion to order was threatening to uproot the generally civil city, but there was also something else bubbling under this issue, something that actually raised more flags than the first. It was a question of master and slave. What if Arkan got too big? What if one day the agency could no longer control the man they had created? It was a perfectly plausible notion. The fact was, Arkan had become a master criminal, and if he turned on them, if he decided that he no longer needed to respond to their demands, it would be terrible for everyone and potentially disastrous. The feeling was that he needed to be cut down.

On several occasions the agency met with Arkan and talked things out. Subtle threats were issued.

You're causing us problems, they told him. Do you know that?

We created you. Not the other way around.

Don't you understand—there are rules, and you don't make them.

Do you want to disappear?

When he announced that he was marrying his girlfriend Natalia, the news gave the agency some hope that he would settle down. At the least, marriage would distract him a little, mitigate whatever monster was building up inside while they figured out what to do with him.

The date of the marriage is unknown, though most agree it happened in the early 1980s. Those who knew about the wedding described it as a small affair, with hints of criminal ambition. According to Vojislav Tufegdzic, the Serbian crime writer, everything at the ceremony and party after was festooned in white. Same with all the guests, "like the *Godfather* movie," Tufegdzic told me.

Not long after, the couple had a child, then three more. Observers noted an attentive and playful father. Arkan, most said, was extremely proud of fatherhood. He spent a great deal of time with his kids, at home and strolling through the city streets. "He was proud of his children," said Ninkovic. "He was a good father." At night, people saw him less at clubs and fancy restaurants. Ninkovic said that he even slowed down his gambling habit. It got people wondering, especially at the UDBA, if he was over his rebellious years, which had started decades ago with his father. Was he becoming a middle-class family man? Did he have a real job lined up? Had he changed?

The answer came in the spring of 1986. One soggy April night, as the rest of the country shook their heads over the Soviet nuclear meltdown at Chernobyl, Arkan turned up at a private casino located on the eleventh floor of a twenty-story high-rise in New Belgrade. After a long stretch of roulette and craps, the losses began to pile up. By the end, he had lost "tens of thousands" or "hundreds of thousands," depending on who you ask. He didn't demand his money back, as he'd done on other occasions, instead, he stormed out of the room, and when he got into the elevator he pulled his gun and smashed it into a man's face. "Just for a look," Nicovic recalled. "The guy asked, 'What floor?' and Arkan pulled his gun and hit him."

Nicovic couldn't overlook this one, even if it cost him his badge. He arrested Arkan on charges of possession of a deadly weapon and assault, and told the prison guards to ignore the secret police if they came for the prisoner. "Don't even think of letting them take him," he instructed the guards. He put his job on the line, because, in the end, what was the point of being a police officer if you couldn't stop the city's biggest threat?

While Arkan awaited trial, Nicovic worked quickly to gather evidence against him and dispatched men to search his house. As he expected, the search turned up a jackpot—an arsenal of weapons, identification cards from several different countries, eleven passports from various Western European countries and one for the United States, a diplomatic passport, and six "press passports."

Nevertheless, Arkan wasn't going to go down quietly. When he appeared at the first district court in Belgrade, he had one last trick up his sleeve. Standing in front of the judge, he reached into his coat pocket, pulled out his wallet, and extracted a card, which he presented to the court. "I work for the federal police," he told the court casually. "Here's my ID."

It was an audacious move. Before that he had not talked publicly about his relationship with the UDBA, and most of the stories people in the city knew about the agency's very hush-hush relationship with criminals was rumor. Arkan changed that with a few words, and then he admitted that he had some weapons. "I have guns, around twelve," he said. "Where I got them, it doesn't matter."

Still, the judge seemed undaunted by the admission, and issued him a sentence of eight months. Arkan's alleged response: "A bad year makes the eagle spend his winter with the chickens."

"Not just the winter," the judge added, as Arkan was hauled off in metal cuffs, "but the spring, too."

To Nicovic's surprise, Spasic and the secret police decided not to bail out their top agent. They would let him suffer. To drive home the point, Dolanc, the agency head, dispatched Spasic to the jail to end their almost decade-long connection.

Spasic expected him to be angry, and he braced himself for the worst, but the worst didn't happen. In fact, what happened, according to Spasic, was, if anything, extremely unusual. "He comes out swaggering like some rap star, waving at guys, slapping high fives," Spasic said later. "I told him I came with a message and explained that our relationship was over. But he just laughed."

He didn't stop blabbering behind bars. He sent threatening letters to Nicovic. "I will kill you." But he didn't try to escape. When he got out, he emerged hardened, with more contacts, feeling the tug of his destiny.

He set to work building a seven-story marble edifice for his home, sort of a monument to himself. A fortress! The location he picked was a one-plus-acre plot in Dedijne, one of the city's most exclusive neighborhoods, home to diplomats and government officials. Across the street was the Red Star soccer stadium.

Before the house was complete, he opened a high-priced ice cream store on the back side and called it Ari, a nickname of his. He hired attractive women, dressed them in skimpy clothes, and sent them out to wait on the thirty-five or so tables that spread across the sidewalk in the summer months. It was likely a criminal front, but no one really knew what to make of the place, except that it was outrageously expensive. A banana split, for instance, cost around $30, as did a fruit plate.

Ari, like Amadeus (which had now been shut down), became mainly an underworld hangout. The clientele included burly guys in long leather coats with pistols tucked into their waistbands and generously proportioned molls in too-tight clothes attached to their sides like additional ammunition. Occasionally, others dropped by to gawk, as if it were some sideshow. Alhough politicians and police close to him began to describe Arkan as a "simple sweetshop owner," Nicovic knew better and kept watching for another break.

In 1987, Nicovic made chief of narcotics, and the next year he moved up to head criminal investigator. By 1991, he was promoted again to chief of Belgrade police, a position that he'd always coveted, but when he got there, he couldn't do his job. The city was falling apart. Politics got in his way. Blood was in the air. Dictators and gangsters were becoming kings, with Arkan the biggest king of all. "I don't know how many he killed to get where he got," said Nicovic. "But it was a lot."

The top cop never arrested Arkan again. "He became too strong," Nicovic told me. "He knew top police, top politicians. He traveled around with grenades and machine guns, bodyguards and three jeeps with his armed men. Eventually, I gave up chasing him. Decided it wasn't worth it." In 1992, as Belgrade became a black hell of murder and mobsters, Nicovic retired. "I left the police and went to represent corporate accounts and banks," he said. "After the war, even the president was afraid of Arkan."

12

LORD OF THE
SOCCER WARRIORS

1

The icy shadow of communism was melting away from the world in 1989. With the Cold War almost over, Eastern Europe was severing ties with the decrepit mother ship of the Soviet Union. The fall of the Berlin wall was followed by the rise of the rebel playwright Vaclav Havel in Czechoslovakia and the victory of Lech Walesa, a former electrician and Nobel Prize winner in Poland.

The revolution in Yugoslavia was different. Tito had ruled over the fifteen million citizens in the federation's six republics with an iron fist and a secret police force. Even in economically rough times, the country, with all of its ethnic rivalries, always seemed to hum along in a sort of white-shirted orderliness, but when the iron ruler died of heart failure (brought on by surgery to his leg) in 1980 and communism began to erode, a void opened up. Unlike other emerging postcommunist countries, Yugoslavia didn't move quickly enough to build the political and economic infrastructure needed for a working transitional government, let alone a free-market democracy. So the dangerous decline began.

By 1989, real income had fallen by more than 30 percent and unemployment hovered around 20 percent, with wages frozen. The country ac-

Red Star fans at a game in 2006. During the war in 1990s, Arkan recruited these fans for his paramilitary group, the Tigers.

tually owed more than $21 billion in debt, a staggering amount that had been wasted on outdated industry left over from the Yugoslavian experiment of self-management. Inflation had climbed to 2,686 percent, and by 1990 things were so desperate that state banks had "frozen" all hard currency, robbing ordinary folks of any money they might have saved up for a future.

Of all the problems, ethnic rivalries were most disturbing. Once illegal and with violations punished by prison time and sometimes death, ethnic hatred creeped back into cities and villages like a bad cold. There were whispers of "those damned Nazi Croats" and "those bastard Serbs with chips on their shoulders." Without Tito's iron fist, the government seemed powerless and, as a result, its people were fast tilting toward an unknowable abyss.

Oddly, few outside the country saw it coming. The ones who did simply ignored it. Yugoslavia was just too insignificant geopolitically, and diplomatic energy was needed to help along bigger countries like the Soviet Union and Germany. George F. Kennan, however, was one voice of reason.

He was the United States ambassador to Yugoslavia from 1961 to 1963. Although he'd been out of the job for decades by the summer of 1989, he noticed currents that others didn't and sent a warning to Warren Zimmerman, the new U.S. ambassador to the country. "Today, with the Cold War ending, people think Yugoslavia isn't in a position to do any damage. I think they're wrong," he said. "I think events in Yugoslavia are going to turn violent and to confront the Western countries, especially the United States, with one of their biggest foreign policy problems of the next few years."

It wasn't only Yugoslavia presaging a scary era of bedlam. Signs of anarchy were emerging in other blind spots: Mafia fiefs flourished in a handful of the former Soviet republics; guerrilla armies sprang up in Albania; and Romania's dictator, Nicolae Ceauşescu, was assassinated. As Strobe Talbott, the future deputy secretary of state under Clinton, expressed in a speech to the National Press Club, "During a nearly half-century-long struggle, we were concerned about the spread of the communist order. . . . [After] the cold war, we faced a very different threat—the spread of postcommunist disorder."

The pronouncement sounded biblical, and it, kind of, was. Hell was coming. While world leaders looked elsewhere, Yugoslavia inched toward the most extreme embodiment of any biblical nightmare. Disorder swept over the country, like a fiery apocalypse, creating a bloody and chaotic world that had no name.

It was against this backdrop that Arkan began plotting out a disturbing play of power, murder, and riches.

2

On an icy winter night in 1989, Arkan came striding through the door at Red Star's Marakana soccer stadium, wearing a black suit, mobbed up with gold, looking very serious. In a back office, one hundred of the team's most devoted soccer fans had convened. As the fans watched the self-made Al Capone move through the room with visible importance, few knew that their lives were about to be in danger.

Red Star was the most popular team in Serbia, and the team's most adamant fans poured every single molecule of their bodies and souls into the sport, as if it were the only thing keeping them alive. War was constant for these superfans, who numbered in the thousands, and Arkan knew this when he showed up on the night he was to be crowned their leader.

In the history of hooligans, Red Star fans were considered weapons of mass destruction. They battled fans from other teams—with fists, bayonets, iron bars, and Louisville sluggers, a kind of warfare modeled after the English soccer thugs, whom Margaret Thatcher once deemed a "disgrace to civilization." Red Star fans took English hooliganism a hundred miles north of sanity. They intimidated their own players, visiting locker rooms when someone underperformed. "Do you want a broken leg?" Coaches were frequently threatened for bad tactical decisions on the field, or, when the losses started piling up, the officials were roughed up in back alleys.

Red Star fans were loose-lipped, smash-mouth brawlers, a contrast to the less extroverted presence of Arkan. At home games the fans jammed into the north end of Marakana stadium, sporting red tracksuits and white Nikes with red swooshes and plenty of gold jewelry—necklaces, earrings, pinkie rings. During matches, the north end was one angry red sea. Above them, flares and fireworks lit the sky. When they weren't beating people up they drank, smoked, and sang. If they hadn't knocked out some poor fool's teeth from the other team before the game, they'd do it after. "Axes in hand," they sang, "and a knife in the teeth/there'll be blood tonight."

Some claimed almost three quarters of Belgrade supported Red Star. "We were so powerful," a fan named Sloba Markovic told me, "you wouldn't even believe it." Sloba and his brutish brothers were pleased with the fear they inspired and proud of the distinguished place they held in Serbia's world of athletics. Fan leaders were even paid for their work and had office space at the stadium, where they choreographed "activities" and kept an eye on the team.

It was the usual hooligan stuff, until the country took its bad turn and a suicidal-seeming gloom began to seep in. The new world without Tito was killing them. Many of them newly jobless, the men felt stripped of their manhood, and it made them feel like they could murder, if that was what it took to get their lives back on track.

Naturally, they began channeling their anger at the stadium. Along with the physical stuff, they added new chants. At first the chants echoed the economic and social isolation, the feelings of dispossession, but soon the fans were placing blame and drawing lines in the sand. Someone had to pay for their broken world. Although Tito had put a deep freeze on ethnic hatred, that freeze was quickly melting away, especially at Red Star stadium, and the air was tense. Croats had to pay. Bosnian Muslims had to pay. We are no longer brothers, the Serbs at Red Star decided. You are not like us. We are not like you. All of you should die. When they played teams across the country, they hoisted placards that read SERBIA, NO YUGOSLAVIA and ONLY UNITY SAVES SERBS. This is where the face of the ethnic war showed before it really began. The fans threw three-fingered Serbian salutes and called for the death of Yugoslavia. "Down with Croatia," they sang.

Arkan must have sensed the fans were evolving into killers. He spent much time observing the men's growing anger at their place in the world, sometimes chanting with them in the stands, other times watching from across the street at his personal fortress, which was nearing completion. When it was finished he would be able to watch games from a top-floor balcony and, according to city lore, be able to access a secret room in the stadium from a secret bunker off his subterranean poolroom.

Back at Red Star that winter night, Arkan cut an ominous figure. The fans who didn't know him personally knew him by reputation. Darkly handsome, he was then the boss of Belgrade, having knocked off competitors, embarrassed a police chief, and intimidated every single government official who crossed him. It was not every day that you saw a man like this so close up. If you had, it wouldn't have been favorable to your health—unless you liked the loaded barrel of a .45 Magnum in your eye.

Sloba was twenty, didn't have a job, or a steady girlfriend, and lived with his parents in a too small Belgrade apartment. Same story with a lot of the other Red Star brotherhood. As Arkan strutted in, Sloba remembered the frozen silence that came over the room like a squall. What was going on? the men seemed to think, but no one asked questions. "He was like a god," said a fan who called himself Curly. "We immediately respected him."

As for what Arkan said, Sloba didn't recall him saying anything particularly notable. He introduced himself as a fan, obsessed with the Red Star soccer team and explained that he was taking over the club. He would lead all of them. Very little else was said, according to Sloba. When the mobster finished he gave a wave—or maybe it was a Serbian salute, the sign paramilitaries gave before killing their victims—and then he was gone.

When Sloba walked out of the meeting, it was freezing cold, the heart of another bitter Belgrade winter. The wind tore up the street, kicking up dust and trash. There was the smell of snow. He lit a cigarette, inhaling deeply. What he remembered about that moment was that he had a sense that he was about to become a part of something bigger than his shrunken, emasculated world, and he liked that. "I knew there was going to be change," he told me. "We all did." He was not scared, though he probably should have been.

Not long after the swearing in as president of the Red Star fan club, Arkan moved into a dingy room in the back of the stadium. It was an unremarkable space with a couple of office chairs, a couch, and a dirty window that looked out at a practice field. In the months that followed, surrounded by new and old disciples, he began secretly turning the fans into professional warriors. Once soccer fanatics, some of the men were about to become known as sworn members of the most murderous paramilitary gang in the Balkan wars, participating in what many human rights activists would later describe as genocide.

3

The ascendancy of Arkan from mob boss to warlord would most definitely not have been possible without the rise of Slobodan Milosevic. Early on the Serbian president recognized that criminals, if placed in the right positions, could be useful to him in accumulating and enforcing power. It was in fact Milosevic who, through political maneuvering, put Arkan in charge of Red Star, a move that revealed the malevolent designs the president had for his country's journey forward.

The story of Milosevic, which eventually becomes the story of Arkan, begins like this: The future dictator and destroyer of Serbia was born in 1941 in the tiny town of Pozarevac, fifty miles from Belgrade. He was always a little chubby and tended to wear clothes that looked too big. Death came to him early and brutally. His father, an Eastern Orthodox priest, shot himself in the head when Milosevic was a child. Years later his uncle did the same, and then his mother, a schoolteacher, hung herself.

Over the years he'd carry around those ghosts but had no real-life confidantes, apart from his high school sweetheart, Mirjana Markovic, a professor of Marxist theory whom he'd later marry. Except for power and the occasional cigar, he didn't seem to enjoy much. No extravagant homes, no busty mistresses, no vintage cars, not even a bowl of jelly beans.

He went to law school in 1960 and ended up with the national bank, Beobanka, which brought him to New York City. In 1982, he began his political climb when he joined the Communist Party. He was visibly ambitious. After being promoted to leader of the Belgrade Committee of Communists in 1986, the urge for power consumed him like a nuclear storm. As the Soviet Union, once Yugoslavia's savior and ally, crumbled, Milosevic sensed the end of his country and knew exactly what he would have to do. Yugoslavia, as people knew it, would have to die.

Milosevic didn't need to invent an ideology of annihilation for the country. In 1986, scholars of the Serbian Academy of Arts and Science did that for him. They wrote an incendiary paper suggesting that the five sister republics were cheating Serbia, and that only the Serbs had a right to live within Serbia's exclusive borders. Covertly circulated, it quickly became the unofficial platform for Milosevic's nationalism and the Serbian march to war.

Playing the nationalist card was a risky move, with scores of unknown—and lethal—consequences. Yet Milosevic figured that there was no other choice. He wanted power to be his alone, not shared. If the country moved toward democracy, that would be even worse for him. The kind of power he craved came at a cost. It meant dividing a people and creating an atmosphere of hate, and taking that hate and making it his own tool. That was dangerous. If he made a mistake, it would surely mean rebellion—or his own death.

Nevertheless, he was undaunted. Milosevic was a unique creature. He didn't seem to be a man who put much consideration into mortality. The suicides of his family members had hardened him to death and danger. In that way, he was a survivor, though a twisted one. Peter Maass, in his eloquent book about the Bosnian war, *Love Thy Neighbor,* dubbed him Mr. Suicide. This was where Milosevic lined up with Arkan. Specifically, both men knew about danger and death and survival and how the three notions intersected. In the end, the thing about these men, what connected them most, was that they were tied not to life, it seemed, but to the expectation of death, and what that death would bring to them in terms of local, national, and international domination. They were men tied to annihilation.

Milosevic's speech in the Serbian province of Kosovo on April 24, 1987, changed everything for the former banker—and for Yugoslavia. Looking back, it would be perceived as one of the first steps toward the death of Yugoslavia. Like Jerusalem for many Jews, Kosovo is the spiritual heart of the Serbian people. When men get a few shots of slivovitz in their heads, it isn't improbable that they will start talking about their terrible history and Kosovo's place in it. "We are a heavenly people," the Serbs say. Or in their language: *nebeski narod.* The feeling had its origin in 1389, when the Serbs were preparing to battle the Turks at Kosovo Polje, or the Field of Blackbirds in Kosovo. On the night before the battle an angel visited a Serb known as Prince Lazar. The angel offered him a choice between an earthly or a heavenly kingdom. As the story goes, he chose the heavenly

one, which resulted in the defeat of his troops and his ceremonious be-
heading.

Five hundred years of Turkish domination and repression of the Serbs
followed. If you ask around Serbia, most will tell you that those five hundred years were dark, dark ages. Serbs were tortured, killed, and treated like
third-class citizens. There was nothing much they could do about it: The
Turks not only outnumbered them but outgunned them.

Although the Field of Blackbirds would haunt the Serbian people cease-
lessly, it would also define them. In opting for a heavenly kingdom, Lazar inserted the Serb race into one of the key principles of Christianity: Die now,
sacrifice your lives, be victims, and you will be resurrected.

The idea of victimhood was impressed onto the Serbian DNA. God
would not forget such a sacrifice. Being heavenly people allowed them to
endure. They knew they would eventually have their day and their land. The
only question was when.

On the day that Milosevic spoke the words that would alter the course of
history, local Serbs had been complaining of Albanian hostility. At the time,
Kosovo was 90 percent ethnic Albanian, though it was home to many of the
Serbs' most significant monasteries. While Milosevic met with officials in a
municipal building, a crowd of Serbs began to surround the place. Local
police tried to beat them back, swinging nightsticks, but the crowd pressed
forward. They wanted protection. They wanted freedom. They wanted the
land to be their own and no one else's.

Hearing the screams, Milosevic stepped out onto a balcony. His people
jostled below. This was his moment of truth. Like a man waking from a
slumber, he suddenly perceived his destiny. The aspiring politician raised
his beefy hands, chopped the air out of the way like a boxer, angled his bulldog face forward, and shouted with meaning, "Nobody will ever beat you
again. No one!" The words resonated with all besieged Serbs. This was just
the beginning.

He returned to Belgrade, a colossus now with an enormous appetite.
Two years later he became president of Serbia, replacing his mentor and
friend Ivan Stambolic. He worked his message of nationalism into the state
media organs, slashing away at the old communist myths. He deemed Tito
and his regime evil and said that the former leader had held back the Serbs,
reduced them to nothing. We are a heavenly people. We deserve our day in
history. We have been victims for too long. Our time is now.

Like Hitler, Milosevic warned that enemies surrounded them, a message
of fear that seeped into the Serbian people like a germ. Mention was made

of the history of the Turks, then of the Austrians who came after the Turks. There was talk of the thousands killed during World War I, when Serbia fought with the Allies against Germany and Austria. There was a noticeable theme of Serbs as victims. Allusions were made to the Serbs, Gypsies, and Jews murdered in death camps by the Nazi-backed Croats known as Ustache during World War II. The silence about these crimes throughout Tito's reign could no longer be ignored. There was paranoid talk, too, of Muslim warriors, or mujahideen, and he talked of a "Greater Serbia." He said all of this subtly at first, and then got bolder as the country headed into economic and political free fall.

His power skyrocketed. Serbs responded to his message, just as he envisioned, especially the Red Star fans, but the fans had to be watched. He appreciated their animal force, liked their boiling nationalism, and perceived them to be natural warriors for his Greater Serbia. He knew that if they were left alone they were ticking time bombs. The fans were getting to be increasingly political and were joining several different Serb parties—some for Milosevic, others favoring his ultranationalist rivals. With their influence on the Serbian public, the question was how to get to them and make them entirely his own.

In 1989, Milosevic's head of State Security, Jovica Stanisic, was a member of the Red Star board. Stanisic, who would later be tried for war crimes at The Hague, drafted Arkan to take over the fan club. It made sense. Only a strong man would be able to tame the hooligans.

There had to be a deal, and the terms of the deal would become abundantly clear only in time: Milosevic would get his devoted followers and Arkan would get to expand his mob empire.

It was a telling moment for Arkan. Once a foot soldier for Tito, a communist, he was now switching sides. Going to work for Milosevic (who was a communist turned nationalist) meant joining the movement that was once his mortal enemy.

Few, however, would ever know much about Milosevic's direct relationship with Arkan. No recorded conversations exist between the two men, and the president would always deny any associations, even when questioned about it at The Hague. There is, however, one curious picture of the two at a funeral for a state security official in the spring of 1997. In it, Arkan, dressed in a black suit, leers over the shoulder of the unknowing Milosevic, as if about to kill. At the least, it is a creepy foreshadowing of the cruel days to come.

That was later. In the late eighties, in its internal communications, Red Star deemed Arkan a "savior." After that first winter night in 1989 when he

At the funeral of the Deputy Minister of the Interior Radovan Stojicic, a. k. a. the Hulk, who was assassinated in the spring of 1997. This is the only picture ever taken of Arkan and Serbian president Slobodan Milosevic together.

was crowned their leader, he began to unite the club's fans under the name Delije, a word that translates roughly as "Heroes" or "Rebels." Anyone who deviated from his rules was punished. "I insisted on discipline from the very beginning," he said to a reporter once. "You know these guys—they're noisy, they like to drink, to joke. I stopped all that in one go. I made them cut their hair, shave regularly, not drink. And so it began, the way it should."

4

It actually began on May 13, 1990. The first wave of Red Star fans began piling into Zagreb around seven in the morning, just as a yellow sun arced over the eastern part of Croatia's capital city. Sloba Markovic had traveled by overnight train, as had a couple hundred other brother fans. Red Star was playing Dinamo, and by game time, in the afternoon, there would be close to three thousand more Delije. As the train rolled through the city Sloba and others chanted pro-Serb songs. "Slobodan, send us lettuce," they sang, "there will be meat when we slaughter the Croats."

Arkan had spent months preparing the Delije for this day, which some would call the "day that ended Yugoslavia." He trained them in specialized street fighting, promoted new pronationalist songs, talked of the time they would have to defend themselves, but it wasn't just Arkan and his men. The country was turning rotten. Nationalism had by now thoroughly infected Serbia, and it spread like a fever throughout the rest of Yugoslavia, dividing neighbors, friends, and families along ethnic lines.

Slovenia was talking secession, and early in May, Croatia had elected the ultranationalist Franjo Tudjman as president. Tudjman was just as nihilistic as Milosevic. A silver-haired man with big square glasses and a perpetual scowl, Tudjman was a former communist army general. He was also a writer of odd historical books. One of his earliest was a roughly two thousand-page history of guerrilla warfare, though his most divisive was *Wastelands of History*, which questioned the Holocaust and suggested that the Serbs had inflated the number of their people killed during World War II in Croatian death camps. Instead of 500,000 to 800,000 slaughtered, Tudjman felt the number was more like 30,000.

Tudjman was imprisoned twice in the communist days for his anti-Yugoslav rhetoric, but when Tito died he became a rising force, launching his ultranationalist Croatian Democratic Union (HDZ). In the spring of 1990, on the campaign trail, he embraced the history of the Ustache, the Nazi-backed Croats who had expelled and murdered the Serbs during World War II, and then glibly announced one afternoon that he was happy that his wife was "neither Serb nor Jewish." After his election, his national-ism grew sharper, and Serbs immediately suffered. Serbs living in Croatia were downgraded in the Croatian constitution, dismissed from the local workforce, and forced to sign loyalty oaths. Tudjman's message was ab-solute: Serbs were not equal.

Red Star fans were no doubt thinking about bashing in Tudjman's head as they marched into Zagreb. At the train station, the Heroes clashed with Dinamo's "Bad Blue Boys" and then again, in the city streets, and finally at Maksimir stadium. Like the Bloods and the Crips, their colors defined them, the Heroes in red, the Dinamo fans in blue. Fists, flares, and metal bars were the weapons of choice. It was so startling because, more than anything, it was the first time that ethnic violence had so publicly reared its head in the country in almost half a century. In retrospect, history would see this day as Arkan's first war offense.

At the stadium. Sloba and the other Heroes ripped down signs and up-rooted seats and sent them flying. "We will kill Tudjman," they yelled, and then broke into song. "We are the fans from proud Serbia," they chanted. "Slobo [Milosevic], you Serb, Serbia stands behind you; come out on the benches, greet the Serbian race; from Kosovo to Knin, Serb is united with Serb."

Arkan arrived at the stadium with the Red Star players and took up a spot on the sidelines. In archived videos he wears a light-brown double-breasted suit with a white button-down shirt, and black shoes. There is a scene of him on the field looking up at his boys as they begin their march of terror. At this point, like an orchestra conductor, Arkan had to do little now to expedite his grand plan, except to watch.

The Dinamo fans fought back with rocks, and about ten minutes into the soccer game the fence separating the two sides collapsed, allowing the brawl to spill out onto the field. "We went to clean them up," Sloba told me. It would come out later that the Dinamo fans, just as hungry for blood, had used acid to melt through the fence.

At first the police did little to interfere, which led to speculation that the officers were pro-Serb. In fact, one Dinamo player spotted a police officer beating a Zagreb fan and decided to intervene. It's a scene that everyone mentions when they talk about the battle. The player, Zvonimir Boban, didn't just break it up. He took a running start and drop-kicked the officer.

Meanwhile, an old video of the melee captured Arkan moving about the battle-torn field, taking it all in. Later, he is seen protecting the Red Star coach, pushing him through a mob of fighters; then, a helicopter arrives to bail out the players. After an hour the battle is over, leaving more than a hundred people injured.

Although next year Red Star would go on to win the celebrated European Champions' Cup, it wouldn't change what happened on May 13, 1990. "We couldn't think of anything else after that day," said Markovic. "The real war was coming. We knew this."

What did real war mean? It meant the death of Yugoslavia. It also meant a new life for Arkan.

13

THE TIGERS

1

As Yugoslavia grew more divided, inching closer to direct conflict, Arkan grew more serious. He recognized that war would offer him greatness, and people noticed a change in him. Old layers were peeled away, replaced with new ones. He gambled less, spent fewer nights prowling the streets, and traded in the pink Cadillac for a Chevrolet Suburban with blacked-out windows. "He became different," said his old gambling buddy Ninkovic. "But he still had the charisma that drew people to him." He began calling secret early morning meetings at his sweetshop with local crime figures and Red Star soccer thugs. Dozens came. "Hard times are coming, boys!" he shouted at dusky faces. He explained that he was organizing a private army to fight for Serbia. "Our enemies are upon us," he warned.

Men who attended these first gatherings say he exuded a statesmanlike weightiness, stalking the shop floor, using his hands to express himself, like a man with a vision burning a hole in the top of his head. "He was a very convincing man," one man told me. "We believed in him immediately." The sounds of Serbian nationalism tinged his now fiery talk. He reminded the men how the Serbian people, his people, had been beaten up for centuries. He named the Turks, which he called the *mujadeen,* or dogs, the Austrians, and the Nazi Croats. He declared that he wasn't going to take it anymore. Sometimes he grabbed a couple of machine guns from atop a table and jabbed them into the air. The men loved that and pledged their support. "It is only a matter of time," he shouted to them one morning. "We must be ready, boys!"

Arkan transformed his sweetshop and mansion into the headquarters of his new army. Inside he hung gigantic paintings of gory World War I battle scenes, a war notable in that the Serbs beat back the much larger Austrian empire. On some occasions, one former soldier told me, Arkan slipped into a World War I military outfit, as if to suggest to his recruits that his task was as grand as the older Serbian freedom fighters. Outwardly, his message seemed to be: I am a Serb patriot who is going to save the country from its invaders. Inwardly, however, his ambitions were much more monstrous.

In general, the soldiers who went to these early meetings and who later worked and fought for Arkan did not speak to me using their real names. They feared retribution for talking. Talking could get you killed, they told me, even years after Arkan's death and years after the war. Killed by old friends or old enemies. The men also worried that talking would draw unwanted attention to them from the war crimes tribunal at The Hague. "My name is not important," one of Arkan's former goons told me. "The only thing that is important is the truth."

The truth was that there was no war yet, but war planning consumed Arkan. He dispatched a small group of men in SUVs with smoke-tinted windows and jeeps to recruit teenagers from the gritty city streets. Young criminals were always looking for work that would elevate them. The tougher ones were notable for the ugly scars on their arms, legs, and stomachs, straight and jagged lines carved with their own hands using store-bought razor blades. The scars were a fad at the time for local thugs, like all Diesel clothes, and were meant as a sign: Don't fuck with me. Arkan met with these recruits at his mansion, sometimes in groups, sometimes alone. He told them he would contact them when the time was right, and he didn't give them a chance to say no. Arkan also toured prisons, with permission from the Serbian government. Like a quick-eyed scout, he personally selected murderers and bank robbers, and when the day came they would be released to him.

Hush-hush conferences were held with government officials, specifically with Interior Minister Radmilo Bogdanovic, and also with Jovica Stanisic and Franko Simatovic, known as Frankie, Milosevic's handpicked agents at the Interior Ministry's Sluzba Dravne Bezbednosti (SDB), or the Serbian State Security Service. When Yugoslavia blew apart once and for all, the SDB would fully replace the federal state security agency, UDBA, headed by Arkan's old boss, Stane Dolanc. The new agency, not unlike its previous incarnation under Tito, would not always be used for constitutional purposes, of course. Instead, it would serve President Milosevic's political and criminal ambitions, settling accounts with rivals, carrying out political and personal assassinations, operating as an instrument to earn money, and, most important, directing the war for Greater Serbia.

The official Serbian men made quiet promises to Arkan about the future, knowing that the mobster never forgot anything. They knew broken promises meant a snub nose in your face, a fact of life that haunted men who betrayed Arkan. Sitting across the table from him, the gangster was articulate and calm, unless something came up that he didn't like, and then, according to old friends, he shouted or swore or slapped faces. Whatever anger his actions inspired, there was nothing the official men could do. If Serbia was going to have to fight for land, they needed him, just as they were going to need the other wannabe warlords making plans for murder and profit in other rooms, in other parts of the city. Over time the SDB would provide Arkan with equipment, weapons, and transport, and pay him millions of dollars, which would apparently arrive at his bases in sacks. The government would also help facilitate extensive smuggling operations, taking kickbacks from him to fill up their own personal coffers.

It wasn't long before Serbia's war plans began leaking out to the rest of the world. As Marshall Harris, the U.S. State Department's former Bosnia desk officer, told CNN, "It was clear that Milosevic and the people around him were determined to carve out a greater Serbia, and to expand their territory at Bosnia's expense and at Croatia's expense, and that the way they were going to do that was to purge that territory of non-Serbs." But no one intervened. No one told Milosevic to step down. No one raised a finger. Not yet, anyway.

Arkan's wife, Natalia, however, attempted to interfere. According to most that were familiar with the relationship at the time, Natalia was unexcited about her husband's private army, and it was the cause of much tension. Why did he have to get involved? He was thirty-eight, had four children with her, not to mention the other two in Belgrade and another in Sweden. She urged him to back off, to think about his family, but he wouldn't. How could he let go of something that felt so potententially life altering? Even the love of a woman would not stop him.

The first group of soldiers officially swore allegiance to Arkan and Serbia's war on October 11, 1990, just as rumors intensified that Slovenia, Croatia, and Bosnia were leaving the Yugoslav federation. On that day a couple dozen men traveled in armed trucks to a nearby church in Velika Plana called Pokajnica, which translates roughly to Church of Regret. The church was constructed out of logs cut from the local woods in 1818 and dedicated to the tragic death of Karadjorde, the leader of the first Serbian insurrection against the Ottoman empire in 1817. The symbolism was obvious: Arkan was about to become the Serb-saving warlord. "It was a beautiful day," one former soldier told me. "We were going to do something important."

The men signed written statements swearing to the Orthodox Church, and then were baptized. Although Arkan also had exhibited very little religious interest until then, aligning himself with the Orthodox Church was an important move, and it would differentiate his army from the insufferable Catholic Croats and Bosnian Muslims. Arkan also had had the men tested for drugs and warned that there would be "serious" consequences for soldiers who "fucked up" and acted like "drunk Chetnik army guys." There was no room for error. "We are a heavenly people," he told his future army.

Sonja Biskero, the director of the Helsinki committee of Human Rights in Serbia, described the first swearing in as "a godfather moment." Biskero worked out of an overcrowded apartment in downtown Belgrade, crammed with books, reports, and dossiers. She spent countless hours during the war years deciphering, among other things, the unsettling rise of Arkan, trying to figure out what he'd done, what he would do, what it all meant. "What was odd about him," she began to see, was "that he established a fatherly relationship with all of his men. Like the godfather in a mafia structure. They were all afraid of him. Every single one of them. He would go to their funerals and pay their wages, and if they died he'd give their families money every month. There was no one else like him."

Officially, he called his men the Serbian Volunteer Guard, but later that name morphed into the Tigers. As the story goes, the name came to Arkan after he acquired a real live tiger and made it his pet and mascot. Though he told some friends and journalists that he'd stolen the animal from a Croatian zoo, it is more likely that it came from the Belgrade zoo. With the new tiger, his private army vision suddenly became complete. Once Delije soccer fans and common street thugs, they were now something else.

Yet, the Tigers almost never happened. When Arkan's enemies arrested him, everything spiraled.

2

On November 29, 1990, around 2:30 A.M., five armed men slipped into the tiny Croatian river town of Dvor na Uni looking for action. They were undercover until their cover was blown when a roving police car appeared and flashed their vehicle to the side of the road.

Doors opened. Flashlights came out. Presumably the officers asked the occupants of the vehicle what they were up to at so late an hour: You don't look like you're here for a tour.

The armed men probably tried not to sweat it. Just passing through. Curiosity, you know.

This late?

Late?

Flashlights illuminated the rogue vehicle. We're going to have to take a quick look. You understand, right?

The police hardly had to look before the flashlights lit up a stockpile of weapons, apparently enough weaponry to arm a platoon of guerrilla soldiers: submachine guns outfitted with silencers, hand grenades, special revolvers, forty-shot pistols, CS gas canisters, rocket launchers, and four hundred rounds of 9 mm ammunition.

The men were the Serbian Volunteer Guard, directed by Arkan, one of the car's passengers. A paper in Zagreb would later describe Arkan as carrying so many guns that "the weapons were dropping out of his pockets." Interestingly, the Heckler and Koch submachine guns were engraved with the Yugoslav army's coat of arms, a clue to what the job was all about.

The work had started in earnest months before, possibly as early as July. Arkan and his core group, with the support of the SDB, had been moving artillery, ammunition, and other military equipment into strategic locations in Serb-dominated swaths of Croatia and Bosnia, where local Serb groups numbering from two men to one hundred were being armed and prepared for an uprising. Jerko Doko, then Bosnia's minister of defense, testified at The Hague that these local units eventually received as much as 51,000 firearms, 400 heavy artillery pieces, 800 mortars, and 200 tanks.

Arkan attempted to sweet-talk the police, of course. He explained that they were in Dvor na Uni out of "pure curiosity." Just down the road, for example, there was a beautiful river. That must have elicited some laughs, though it convinced no one. Arkan and his men were cuffed and booked. Later they were charged with conspiracy to assassinate the newly elected president Tudjman and conspiracy to plot an armed rebellion in the Krajina region of western Croatia, where the population was primarily Serb.

Arkan and his men were sent directly to jail in Zagreb, and months passed before anything happened. Back home, people wondered if the city mob boss would ever return. The secret police wrung their hands. Had Houdini lost his touch? "When he went to jail, everything stopped for us," said Sloba Markovic, who had sworn allegiance to Arkan at the Church of Regret. "He was the king. So we had to wait."

In late April 1991, Arkan and his four-man crew were brought to trial. In terms of public interest, it was an O. J. Simpson–like event, with newspapers and television covering it from start to finish. His youngish mug was plastered on every tabloid cover. Although still handsome, his face had grown pudgier over the years, his neck thicker, and his eyes roiled from sleeplessness and nerves. His hair also looked to be thinning and in retreat. One of the most memorable pictures caught him sitting in the packed courtroom in a light-colored suit with his hands in his lap, clasped as if locked by cuffs. Three police officers surround him, his shoulders are slouched, and his glum look is best described as that of a schoolboy who, after being scolded, has been sent to the corner to consider his bad behavior.

Finally, after forty-two days of court proceedings and seven months of custody, the men were convicted of plotting an armed insurrection and sentenced to twenty months. For a moment, things looked grim. However, a few days later the tempo changed. On June 14, Arkan and his men were mysteriously released. Why? No one knows for sure, but there were plenty of theories. One speculated that Arkan's Tigers kidnapped Tudjman's daughter, who was living outside of Belgrade at the time, and an under-the-table trade was made. Another suggested that Tudjman was paid one million German marks. Still, the truth of his release didn't really matter. What mattered was that the Croats had made a profound mistake. Though they didn't know it at the time, setting him free on that summer day would eventually cost their country a great deal of terror and death.

3

When Crazy Horse arrived to pick up Arkan at the Zagreb prison, he immediately sensed trouble—"something didn't smell right" was how he put it to me years later. His nose was twitching all over his face. "I knew something was going on," he said, pointing at his nose, then at his eyes.

It was an early June afternoon when Crazy showed up for the rendezvous, though I could not verify many of the details he would go on to describe, except that he had been there. Retired from his criminal life years earlier, after returning to Belgrade from Italy, he still considered Arkan a close friend; history like theirs was binding. "We don't forget those old times," Crazy said.

Pulling into the prison parking lot, he perceived an unusual number of police cars and ambulances. Then there was the skinny man, partly obscured by a tree. What was he doing there? As he drew closer, the man's face came into view. It took a minute to register in his brain, but then it did. He knew the man, and one of his first thoughts was, there's going to be "big trouble."

The skinny man was Miro Baresic. In 1971, Baresic, a Ustache terrorist, had killed the Yugoslav ambassador to Sweden, Vladimir Rolovic. He was a famously bold operator, almost as bold as Arkan. According to Swedish newspapers at the time, Baresic had forced his gun into Rolovic's mouth and fired one shot into his brain. Two more shots followed. Though he was captured and imprisoned, Ustache terrorists hijacked a Swedish jet a year after his trial and negotiated his release. First, Baresic fled to Spain, then to Paraguay, where he joined the death squads of dictator Alfredo Stroessner. Later, Baresic was arrested again, this time by the FBI, and returned to prison in Sweden, where he languished for eighteen years until released.

Then he was on the prowl again, and Arkan seemed to be his latest target. Crazy was sure of this. Why else would he be there?

So Crazy devised the costume idea. He went into the city and bought a wig and a Hawaiian shirt and snuck them into the prison. "Put these on," he told Arkan before they had time to catch up. "We have to move fast."

Arkan didn't ask questions, Crazy said. Old friends didn't have to talk to understand. The two were back at their old tricks, just like in Italy. Arkan slipped into the disguise, and the men went out the back door and got into Crazy's car. No one saw them. At least, that's what they hoped.

They headed to the airport, but on the highway, the situation threatened to come undone. Arkan couldn't sit still. He kept turning around to see if there were pursuers. He swore he saw someone. "Drive faster," he yelled. "Drive faster. They're going to kill me."

Then they got lost. Somehow Crazy made a wrong turn and the car was suddenly heading for downtown Zagreb. "Turn around!" Arkan screamed. "Turn around, we're going the wrong way!"

Finally they made it, and freedom was in view. A private plane waited, its engine roaring, with no other suspicious cars around. If Baresic had tried to tail them, he was gone, and Arkan absconded to Belgrade, where his friends and soldiers waited. "It was a big party when he got home," said Ninkovic. People flooded his mansion, and soon there was blasting music shaking the concrete walls. Although most said that he was exultant that night, which soon melted into morning, he also seemed a little distracted by bigger events, that were minutes from unfolding.

4

Finally, the war came. About a week later headlines announced that Slovenia was officially seceding from Yugoslavia and Milosevic sent in the Yugoslav army, or JNA, which fought a ten-day battle before allowing the country to go. Soon after, Arkan watched on television as Croatia announced its decision to leave the federation. Although the plan had been in the works for months, Croatia's move, unlike Slovenia's, would not end peacefully or fast.

President Tudjman had been provoking Croatia's Serb minority of six hundred thousand ever since he stepped into office. In addition to demoting the Serbs, he'd adopted a new flag with a coat of arms that looked an awful lot like the Ustache badges worn during the mass Serb killings in World War II. More recently, Serbs were turning up dead or missing, Serb houses were being burned, and there was rarely justice. Milosevic's state-run media was all over these crimes and wondered how Serbs living in an independent Croatia would survive under Tudjman. Who would protect them? Milosevic, who seemed to increasingly model his wickedness on old Johnny Quest cartoons, used his media organs to hype an imminent genocide. There was much talk of Ustache killings, gas chambers, and baby-killing Croat armies. There was also talk about religions that couldn't get along, specifically about the Croats, who were predominantly Catholic, and how they intended to eradicate the Orthodox Christian Serbs.

By July 1991, things were getting noticeably bloody. Milosevic and his secret police unleashed armed rebellions in three key chunks of Croatia, known collectively as the Krajina, or military zone, beginning in Knin, the grimy nowhere mountain town that straddled an important rail post connecting Zagreb to the southern coast. Newspapers began reporting deaths, and "war" was being used to describe the worsening situation. A month later, after more deaths on both sides, Milosevic enlisted the Yugoslav army to augment local nationalist Serbs, and began to forcibly expel Croats from Serb-dominated Croatia. This began the quest for Greater Serbia.

Civil war would gobble up the country from 1991 to 1995, first in Croatia, and then in Bosnia, making it the deadliest event in Europe since World War II. Soon after Milosevic maneuvered the Yugoslav army into the battle-front, brutal crews of volunteer killers wielding jackknives, pistols, and rifles followed. Of these, few would perpetrate more crimes and benefit from those crimes more than Arkan.

When Arkan headed to the front sometime in August, the soon-to-be warlord had reportedly signed up over three thousand men for his private army, including his brother-in-law, Aleksandar. Although the main group numbered between 500 and 1,000, the Tigers, according to some official reports, would grow at times to as many as 9,000, a large part of them coming from weekend warriors, refugees, and Red Star football fans, the fierce fan club Arkan had nurtured.

Before he left for combat that summer, Arkan allegedly dashed off a quick message to his enemies in Croatia. "You will never catch me alive," he promised them. What he didn't say, but should have said, was, I'm coming back to take what's mine. There's nothing you can do to stop me now.

14

WHAT I LEARNED
AT RED STAR STADIUM

Curly couldn't goddamn believe it. It was late one fall afternoon in 2004, Belgrade was covered in a mess of fallen leaves. I sat on a black faux-leather couch at his desk in a dingy office at the rear of Red Star stadium, where he now commanded the team's notorious hooligans, the same men that Arkan had once lead. "Who the fuck are you?" he asked, giving me a grim look, and then shaking his head at four of his beefy followers sitting and standing around me.

I explained that I had come to talk about the Red Star fan club, which was partly true, and then, as an aside, I mentioned Arkan. No one liked to talk about Arkan, especially Red Star fans, though many considered him a kind of godfather. Curly shook his head, clenched a fist. "I should take this American asshole outside right now," he said to his men.

The four others laughed, looked at me, and then looked at Curly, as if waiting for their cue. Milan, my fixer, shifted in his seat, glanced at me as if to say, maybe coming here wasn't such a good idea after all. I watched Curly pace behind his desk.

The room had a few framed posters of the Red Star soccer team on the peeling white walls, and a grimy window that looked out at a grass and dirt practice field. It was the same room that Arkan had once occupied. Curly sported a ratty Red Star sweatshirt and blue jeans. He was probably in his midforties, stringy but muscular, with hands that couldn't keep still, and flinty eyes. The four others were in their twenties, wore either too big leather coats or red and white Nike sweat suits. Two of them sipped beer out of plastic cups, faces red from drinking, and noses mashed like they'd been broken one too many times.

"You fucking bombed our city," Curly said suddenly, leaning over the desk, which was cluttered with newspaper clippings, crumpled paper, and a bottle of whiskey. It had been five years since the international force had bombed Belgrade to stop Milosevic from killing in Kosovo, and just under four years since Arkan had died, but Curly said it as if it had happened just yesterday. His face grew red, and for a second it felt like he was going to lunge at me. "You bombed our city and now you're here asking me questions about Commander? Commander was a patriot."

I started to say that I hadn't had anything to do with the bombing, but that didn't matter. His boys were starting to close in around me. The weekend before they'd tangled with their local fan-club rivals, the Partisans, and sent one guy to the hospital with a broken leg. Their weapon of choice: metal bars. There was one bar against the far wall. Milan began fiddling with his belt nervously, and then started to make an excuse to go. Curly chopped the air with his hands like a kung fu man. "Do you know a fucking thing about our life?"

I got the history question a lot in Serbia. When you spend enough time in the country, ask about the war, what it meant, and how it started, you get an earful about stuff that had happened centuries ago, as if centuries ago was just the other day. "I should beat the shit out of this American fucker right now," Curly repeated to his boys. Then he turned to me. "What do you think?" he asked.

"About what?"

"About what I said."

I hedged. I said I agreed it was bad that America had bombed them, though it wasn't only America. Then I said that it was not my fault. I shrugged, looked at my trail shoes.

Curly just shook his head, waiting to make a decision about his fists.

The thing about Serbia is that time always seems to collapse. It's true that the Serbs were an unlucky bunch, which was what Curly was getting at. That bad luck went back far in time. After the Field of Blackbirds slaughter in Kosovo, there was of course the five hundred years of Turkish rule. There were other invaders after that. After a twenty-year-old Serb assassinated Archduke Franz Ferdinand of Austria and his wife, Sophie, sparking World War I, the Austrians drove the Serbian army from their country. Hundreds of thousands retreated into the mountains, where thousands died of exhaustion and starvation before they reached safety on the Adriatic. Four years of exile followed before the Serbs fought back, and World War I ended with a spark of redemption. The Kingdom of Serbs, Croats, and Slovenes was born, a creation of the Treaty of Versailles, and there was even a Serb king, though the king didn't last long. The Croats complained of being discriminated against, imprisoned arbitrarily, and murdered. Some of that was true. In 1939, the country split up over World War II and the Serb king was gone. The Germans bombed Belgrade and backed the Croat Ustache leader Ante Pavelic, and life again became a nightmare for the Serbs: many were killed.

When you get to talking about World War II, there is no avoiding mention of Jasenovac. Jasenovac was a Croatian-built extermination camp for Serbs, Jews, and Gypsies, considered the third most prolific murder camp in recent history, after Auschwitz and Treblinka. A network of five camps and three subcamps, Jasenovac sprawled across 150 miles of rolling land along the Sava River, southeast of Zagreb. It was in operation from 1941 to 1945. Killing was unimaginably cruel there. One of the more sadistic guards, according to local legend, invented a knife called the Srbosjek, or Serb-cutter, which was basically a small, curved blade attached to a leather, open-fingered glove, meant for rapid slaughter. The exact body count at Jasenovac is unknown, but some Serbian accounts run as high as 700,000, though most put the number at around 100,000. When Curly asked me if I knew a fucking thing about his life, he was clearly referring to this ugly, ugly history. He's right: it was gruesome, it was sick, it was heartbreaking, it was all of that. Today there is a memorial on the site of Jasenovac, a wide-open field with a colossal concrete monument shaped like the petals of a flower opening up to the sky.

After World War II, Tito tried to unite the country and crush its bloody history. He told the Yugoslav people to forget everything that had happened in the past, as if amnesia was something that could be self-imposed, as if Serbs could forget that they were owed, that they were a heavenly people. Orthodox Serbs were forced to live peacefully with Catholic Croats, and time passed as history slipped away. The painful days actually did recede and became lost like a tide. Many people got on with their lives, put the old days behind them. Until Tito died. Then ten thousand tons of history came pounding back.

Some pundits and journalists say that it was all of this ugly history that started the Balkan wars in 1991—a bunch of people who couldn't put their past behind them. Others say it was two psychopathic politicians hungry for power—namely, Milosevic and Tudjman—who exploited the history enough to turn people against one another. In reality it was probably a little of both. The people had the history, and Milosevic and Tudjman manipulated it, made them feel as if there was no other choice but to fight.

When the war came, some left the country, others protested, while many of Curly's men joined the Tigers. Curly suggested that he went to war, too, but he wouldn't talk about it. Nor would he say anything about Arkan. In the absence of an explanation, he lifted his right arm and flashed me the three-fingered Serbian salute, which was a thumb gun, with the middle finger. "Do you know what this is?" he asked.

"Holy Trinity," I said.

He stared at me blankly. During the war the Tigers would flash that sign standing over dead Croats and Muslims.

That's what the war seemed to be about to Curly and other nationalists. They were God's people. After all these years, centuries, it was now their time to be on top. Greater Serbia was as much about heaven as it was about an ancient historical claim.

Still, there was one thing that I had trouble getting my head around. If the Serbs were a heavenly people, I couldn't help but wonder if that heaven, when Milosevic came into power, had suddenly been overrun by the devil.

Our meeting was finished. "This is not a friendly place for you," Curly warned.

Milan and I rose to leave.

As Curly and his men watched us go, their laughter echoed through the long stone hallways.

15

WAR!

1

In the summer of 1991, well after midnight, a unit of the Tigers pushed into the Croatian town of Tenja. They were heavily armed and dressed in black, just slinking and indistinct shapes, their booted feet creeping grim reaper–like through the high summer grass of the eastern Slavonian countryside. Some ex-Tigers told me that it was August, others insisted it was as early as July. The town of 6,800, just a skip over the northeastern Serb border and once ethnically mixed, had been under siege for months now. People had been murdering each other, and the killing was still going on. Now the Tigers had come to put an end to it, decide who would stay, who would go, and who would die. People always had to die, especially when the Tigers came to town.

The Tigers I spoke to said that Tenja was one of the gang's first jobs for the Serbian government. Inside an abandoned house along the town's main strip, the men put down their machine guns, rocket launchers, and other equipment and made plans, a former Tiger who called himself Mr. X told me. They peered out of broken windows, hunting snipers, Croat fighters, refugees—any sign of enemy movement. Nothing. The dirt road was shrouded in shadow. An hour's drive from Belgrade, the town, which sustained itself mostly from farming things like peppers and corn, felt like another world. "We waited for a long time," said Mr. X. "At least it felt like a long time."

When the battle came, it sneaked up on them, as it sometimes did. Just as the sun swelled over the denuded treeline, machine guns roared, Croat fighters poured into the streets, and then a grenade landed on the first floor of the house. One Tiger, seeing that the pin had been pulled, glanced at his comrades before announcing, "Guys, I'm leaving," and then tackled it. He was killed instantly in the explosion, but that act of sacrifice saved the rest.

Arkan communicated with the men by radio. Is everything all right? Mr. X didn't know at first. When he looked down, he saw that he had shrapnel in his leg, and then a sniper from somewhere killed another of his men. "I kept thinking, like Arkan told us, cool your brain, cool your brain down," Mr. X told me. "We didn't know that there were going to be so many Croats."

Soon more Tigers arrived, and they swarmed the town, firing rounds at sniper roosts, rolling grenades into basement hideouts, and chanting fighting words over a megaphone as if it were a sporting event. Call the cops? We are the cops! They took over rapidly and hurried door to door, looking for weapons, asking about ethnicity. Are you Serb? Ustache? Croats who had remained were evicted. Men, women, children—it didn't matter. If you had a weapon, you were shot. Houses were pillaged, then burned. Soon the Croat fighters had either disappeared into the woods or been killed.

When Arkan materialized, he was driving a T-80 Russian tank, which the Tigers had pilfered earlier from a nearby Croatian army base. He drove the tank down the main strip, treads kicking up dust and stones, and blew up a few Croat buildings. "We cleaned up," Mr. X boasted. "That was it." TVs, refrigerators, stereos, anything that was valuable got packed up into the backs of trucks and carted away, though Arkan would always say that it wasn't the Tigers doing this but other Serb paramilitary men. Whatever the truth, the men in black were scary in their speed and execution, the way they appeared out of nowhere and completely dominated a place like a force-seven hurricane.

Arkan, the warlord, was finally born. He was not like other men around him. He was a man possessed by the prospect of dominating people and places, and he had finally found the perfect situation that would allow him do those things. What this meant exactly for the region would take some time to understand, but if there was anyone who had a sense of the warlord's future, it was Dobrivoje Radovanovic, who had interviewed and analyzed Arkan as a juvenile delinquent almost twenty years earlier. "Until the war, Arkan was just an ordinary criminal, good but still just a bank robber," said Radovanovic, who was now director of Belgrade's Institute for Criminal Research. "But when the war started, Arkan flourished. In a world where anything was possible, he became a god of his own destiny, the ultimate taskmaster. He could control everything, and he did—with impunity."

2

Arkan plunged headfirst into the emerging conflict, as if it were the most natural place for him to be—driving tanks, shouting orders, chanting battle songs, firing guns whenever he wanted, killing at will, as if he were in a first-person shooter game. The baby-faced commander led his Tigers through Croatia and later Bosnia, from 1991 to 1995, in a wrecking train of privately owned satellite-equipped SUVs, jeeps, and tanks, some of their hoods and doors emblazoned with a scowling tiger, murdering and thieving under the banner of Serbian nationalism.

There were specific things that made his Tigers stick out: Their faces were always shaved; they wore their hair short, and they dressed in black or camouflage uniforms, with bulletproof vests and black woolen balaclavas, with slits for eyes, known as *fantomka,* or phantom mask; on their hands, when it was cold, they wore black gloves cut off at the knuckles; Tiger patches were sewn onto upper arms or stitched into hats, with the words *"Arkanove Delije,"* which translated roughly to, "Arkan's Heroes," just like the Red Star fan club. They also packed fierce weaponry—automatic rifles, submachine guns, antitank launching grenades, grenades, long "Rambo-style" knives, and ropes "for choking people."

The Tigers operated quasi-independently, not dissimilarly from the Salvadoran death squads a decade earlier, though everyone was almost certain that Milosevic controlled them. In fact, documents demonstrate that kill-and-cleanse orders came down from the SDB. As the warlord's personal secretary later testified at The Hague war crimes tribunal, "Arkan did not fall from the sky. His units would never have been able to act in the way they did had they not been an integral part of the state security of Serbia."

Still, Arkan maintained exclusive control over his own men, dictating what they did and didn't do. Power radiated from him, and his standing on the battlefield was reportedly above all commanders in the Yugoslav army, which was by now almost fully controlled by Milosevic. Although he

The Tigers, ready for war.

sometimes had backup from the official army, the feeling was that he could do virtually whatever he wanted during the war, as long it was not against Serbs.

The Tigers were not alone as a paramilitary outfit. Over five years of war there were at least 83 other groups operating in the territories of the former Yugoslavia—56 of them in support of Serbia and self-proclaimed Serbian republics, 13 for Croatia, and 14 for Bosnia. Most acted locally, with operations focused on a single county, or *opstina*. All—Serb, Bosnian Muslim, and Croat volunteer groups—did their share of illegal killing. Typically, the local thugs worked in conjunction with bigger, more organized outfits until the town was broken down and cleansed ethnically. After the town was secured, the bigger outfits moved on to other counties while the local thugs took over the town's command, some even muscling into political positions such as mayor.

Arkan operated with these other Serb volunteer forces, though he seemed to do it reluctantly. Team play didn't appeal to him, especially when it meant working with men who weren't up to his amphetamine version of warring. Secrecy also seemed to be an issue in his warring tactics: what he did, how he fought, and what happened when the fighting ended. In general, he perceived the other Serb irregulars with maximum disdain, as if they carried bad odors. Some of their leaders, he believed, approached the theater of war in an oftentimes improvisatory and ad hoc manner, like a pickup basketball game. Not only that, most of the infantry guys he thought were "rugged, messy, unshaven, and drunk," according to Marko Lopusina's book about the warlord. All that was no surprise, considering that some 80 percent of the Serb irregulars were thought to be jailbirds.

The Serbian government saw its policy of sending locked-up criminals to the front lines as "reform." When Arkan got his prisoners, he disciplined them and made them understand that if they screwed up it was easy to make them disappear. For the criminals not under Arkan, however, the idea of reform was a joke. The front lines were probably a dream come true, a paradise lost or a real world version of *Pirates of the Caribbean*. The criminal fighters drank, killed, raped, and thieved—things many of them had done before they were thrown in jail. There was even a group of fighters who dressed in fur hats, wore big curved knives across their chests, and had full beards as if they'd just emerged from a cave atop the highest mountain. These men were known as Chetniks, the nickname of an ancient Serbian guerrilla organization that had opposed Ottoman rule.

Still, the Serb army wasn't exactly steam pressed and sober either. Many didn't even want to fight, after having been basically forced into duty at gunpoint. There was a significant population that didn't believe in the war, didn't know what the whole conflict was about, or would just have rather been somewhere else, perhaps with a girl in a comfortable bed, or sipping plum brandy with friends. There was a good chance that some had even participated in the massive protests on March 9, 1991, in Belgrade, where tens of thousands took to the streets to express anger about Milosevic's hold on political and economic power. While over three hundred thousand educated young men and women eventually fled the country to escape what more and more seemed like a death trap, the unlucky ones got sucked into the ranks of the JNA and sent to the front, where they were paid slave wages, some as low as $7 a month, and fed slave meals of bread and water.

By comparison, the Tigers were paid up to $1,000 a month (part from Arkan, part from the secret police), plus whatever they could filch.

Arkan broke his elite Tigers down into strike, combat, and operative companies, ranging between forty and sixty men, similar to an army platoon. Typically, his men were the first to arrive in a town and the first to leave. As Serbian General Andrija Biorcevic explained a few months into the war, "We surround a village, [Arkan's] men go in and kill anybody who refuses to surrender." In the Serbian tabloid *Svet,* one Serbian paramilitary, Rade Leskovac, dreamily recalled those first days of cleansing, killing, and wreaking havoc with the warlord. "Always now in my dreams about what once was, I see a dusty village road and the Serbian flag carried by Raznatovic and his boys together with the Star supporters' flag. They always trumpeted their way through villages, shouting one after another, 'Arkan, Arkan.'"

The Tigers fought in Borovo Selo, Borovo Naselje, and Luzac. The list goes on, though some of the list is not all that clear. According to documents from the International Criminal Tribunal for the Former Yugoslavia, Arkan and his troops would eventually wage war in twenty-eight counties throughout Croatia and Bosnia. But if you went by witness accounts that circulated during and after the war, that number was four or five times larger. In fact, some reports indicated that Arkan and his men fought in dozens and dozens of battles, sometimes simultaneously. Although it is a physical impossibility to fight in three and four cities at once, the war was full of exaggerations, and later on, as Arkan rose in celebrity, there would be sightings of the warlord in the field when he was actually sipping tea at the Belgrade Hyatt.

The facts of his battle sites notwithstanding, wherever he actually fought, the focused methods of his fighting were legion. For Arkan, the rules of engagement were necessarily relaxed, if altogether nonexistent. Rules of engagement are standing orders that restrict the objectives of soldiers, identifying what is or isn't an appropriate kill target, according to tactical aims and rules imposed by international law. Arkan, according to observers from the UN, killed whoever he deemed dangerous or got in his way. He had a methodology to his killing and cleansing, which was refined and tweaked over the later months and years, but looked something like this: The process started with relentless shelling from tanks, from airplanes, from sniper roosts; then the Tigers (with JNA and other paramilitary imitators as support) announced themselves; fighting-age men in the town fled through cornfields, through streambeds, and hid in the trunks of cars; those caught were killed; women, children, and the elderly were pushed out of town or sent to camps; sometimes civilians were raped or beaten or shot; religious artifacts and other traces of the ethnic group were burned, defaced, or erased; soon the stealing began; trucks and vans and buses arrived to cart off the booty, which was sold in Belgrade and abroad.

Some were happy to see Arkan and his masked men, especially Serbs who had spent months fighting off equally horrifying Croatian gangs. The fact is: He did save Serbian lives. In those early days of bloodshed, one Serb recalled to a *Vreme* journalist his being surrounded by enemy fighters: "I was writing a farewell letter, I was hungry and in pain. They were no longer shooting at us, but somewhere in the distance. Shooting grew distant. Then Arkan and his Tigers entered the village. I was ashamed. I had shit in my pants from fear, although I'm a Serb. All of us were grateful to him. That man saved us. He is crazy. He is a tsar. He is God. He is Popeye."

Most people, however, panicked. There were so many stories in that first year of war. None too far-fetched. Throats of non-Serbs were slit. "Rape rooms and mutilation chambers" were organized at hotels, with areas devoted to "vaginal and oral attacks." Children were tied with rope and crushed under tank treads. Corpses were disfigured with butcher knives and left in the streets to rot in the fall sun. Some people just plain vanished. One day they were there, the next they were gone forever. In Dalj, for instance, a protected witness later testified at the war crimes tribunal how Arkan emptied the prison of around eighty Croatian inmates. They were never seen again, except for two men who bargained with the warlord for their lives, paying him "one or two million German marks."

Stories like this inspired some Western diplomats to start employing the phrase "ethnic cleansing" as a way of describing the situation. The point of ethnic cleansing, though a watered-down descriptive, is to drive a specific ethnic group out of a territory controlled by another ethnic group. So a town or village once inhabited by many kinds of people was now home to only one kind—Serbs. It got sticky when people began to wonder if this was the same as genocide, or wondered if it could become genocide. The intention of genocide was something more sinister than ethnic cleansing: to not only drive a group of people out of a particular place or region, but also to destroy them completely, rub them off the face of the earth. The world was always reluctant to employ the term genocide, because it meant that explicit action had to be taken, according to signatories to the UN convention on genocide, and action wasn't always easy, especially when it came to overly cautious Western politicians. The reluctance of international justice, of course, had been seen before. There was a debate about genocide during the rule of the Khmer Rouge in Cambodia, and later over Iraq gassing the

Kurds, and then in Rwanda. When the debate turned to the former Yugo-slavia, Arkan's name invariably came up, too. Was Arkan perpetrating geno-cide for Milosevic? Was the intention of this man and his soldiers not only to move bodies out of the Serb-targeted villages and towns, but also to wipe out non-Serbs altogether?

Of course, it is impossible to confirm all of the stories about Arkan in Croatia, or for that matter most stories during the war. Hyperbole was com-mon on both sides of the battlefield, even though thousands of people were killed, but what's true is that, as the war unfolded, people began to be-lieve those stories, apocryphal or not. They passed them around to other towns and villages with a devotion that bordered on the religious. After Arkan took a city, people in that conquered city called friends and relatives in other cities and warned them to leave before the Tigers arrived in them. "Arkan is a crazy man," one Croat said to me. "He and his men have no god." This was the psychological component to the war: Be inventive and cruel enough in your killing, and the ordinary stories will mutate into sen-sational stories, and people, fearing your wrath, will leave town before you even arrive. At one point, the Croatian national TV network, HRT, claimed that Arkan's "beasts roasted Croatian children and then ate them." Out of all the stories during the war, though, the one that the Croats no doubt wanted to believe was the news that Arkan had been captured in Vukovar.

16

THE DANGERS
OUT THERE

Milan didn't agree with everything that Arkan did as a warlord, but he didn't completely disagree either. Although he couldn't morally square all of Arkan's murderous activities, he believed that Arkan was a Serb patriot who fought hard for the dignity of his people and country. It was a dirty war, he said. And it wasn't only the Serbs who perpetrated evil. The Croats and the Bosnian Muslims engaged in their own fair share of atrocities against the Serbs. They burned homes, tortured, and killed. Milan wasn't saying that this fact absolved Arkan from any of his crimes in the war. In fact, he conceded that he was probably a war criminal, as the international tribunal's indictment suggested. What he was actually getting at was different: Although Arkan committed crimes, he also protected the Serb populations in Croatia and Bosnia when others didn't. It was for this that a huge part of the population of Serbia adored him—and still do. It was for this that Milan sometimes felt more than a little conflicted as he worked for me. We argued about it sometimes, and he'd say, "But there are so many sides to the story." Plus, he would declare, "you are not a Serb, so you will never understand." Although he would never admit it, sometimes I could see in Milan's eyes that he wondered if he was betraying his world, his people.

When his mind got knotted up over our work, Milan often quoted American pop songs as a way of expressing himself. One afternoon, as we walked away from Arkan's men, he sang despondently, "This day is killing me softly." If we were late for a meeting or just needed to go someplace fast, he crooned, "Let's hit the road, Jack." He also had interesting locutions, most evident during nervous episodes when he'd mutter things like, "I'm having mental problems" or "They are fucking me around."

Milan tried to keep most of what he did away from his young girlfriend, believing—rightly so—that she would lose sleep if she knew how deep he was getting into Arkan's world. I worried, but the worry wasn't completely new terrain for Milan. He, like most of the fixers in Belgrade, had been involved in the region's wars. Back in the early 1990s Milan worked with some of the most important international media, including the *London Times*. Milan, like many of the other fixers, was not a professional. He didn't go through any sort of official schooling. Instead, he fell into the job because there were no other jobs during the war. The economy was tanking, inflation had gone berserk. People were poor. The war fixers took risks, but the risks were worth it financially.

When the fighting ended, most fixers were forced to take up work that paid dirt. They worked at fruit stands. They drove taxis, and some, like Milan, opened small shops or cafés that teetered precariously on the edge of solvency. They were always hungry for money, because nothing paid like the war. When I came around the first time and asked him to help with my research, Milan was happy to have the extra money. He had debts to pay. His girlfriend wanted a second car and renovations at home. His daughter needed after-school English lessons, dance class fees, and a computer. He was dealing with a lot. "God is spitting on me," he said of his situation.

His second thoughts began when the phone calls started coming late at night. The first ones were hang-ups. Then threats came. One morning Milan reported that a young criminal named Zoran had called at around midnight. "Last night that fucker Zoran called me and started to scream on me," he told me over the phone. "He was calling me pussy, shit, and so on. He said he will come tomorrow in my shop to slap me over my face, and I answered I can't wait until tomorrow."

So Milan met Zoran at a bar in New Belgrade, about twenty minutes away from his home. "Of course pussy was there with two big dudes and some chick," he told me. "Conflict continued, and he pulled a gun, and said, " 'You want to keep your knees,' and I said to go out and to fight like a man. Then he told me that he killed so many persons in his life and that I should go out and forget him and his phone numbers." Milan came out unharmed, but the message was clear: We were getting too close to the spider. Back off before something serious happened.

Milan agonized, letting out a storm of emotion that had been building up for a long time. It was worse than the war, he fretted, because, if you were on the wrong side then, at least you weren't the only target. We were alone. Milan didn't sleep much. He got headaches. Soon his girlfriend came to him. She urged him to "stop hanging around with mass murderers."

During my trips, I suffered similar concerns. At times I was sure that we were being watched or that someone out there was looking for us. Twice I considered escaping the city, and made late-night inquiries about changing my plane ticket. Was there room on tomorrow's flight to London? I grew paranoid. Meeting locations were changed at the last minute to make sure no one was setting us up for a beating. I hardly slept. My stomach hurt constantly. Some nights, at my rented flat in central Belgrade, I triple-locked the door and barricaded myself in with furniture. I had a small bag packed near the window, holding my passport, cash, and a change of clothes. It was two floors down, but if someone got in, I could make the jump and get away. I carried a schedule of trains heading out of Belgrade to Greece and Hungary. I was always ready to leave, but at the same time, I wasn't. Truth is, I eventually became addicted to the dangers out there, and, though he probably wouldn't admit it, so did Milan.

17

CAMP ERDUT

Whenever Arkan's men withdrew from the battlefied, they shifted northeast to the captured town of Erdut. Their camp sat on a particularly foggy stretch of the Danube, in northeastern Croatia, just over the Serbian border, and was secretly financed by the SDB. Abandoned low-slung concrete buildings had been transformed into barracks and stocked with pricey high-tech weaponry and training tools. A dirt and grass soccer field had become an obstacle course and firing range. One building was an office, another a chow hall and kitchen. The food wasn't even that bad, considering the jail-grade stuff served to the Yugoslav army. Coca-Cola flowed freely, and there were chicken and pork dishes, also, on special occasions, steak. Next door was a deserted winery, and when the wind was right, the air smelled of stale grapes. Sometimes Arkan's pet tiger lumbered around the campgrounds, as if he owned the place. At the front gate, made out of stone, armed men in balaclavas watched for intruders.

Training went on around the clock. Soldiers in black or green could be seen sparing, crawling on their stomachs, running through tire trails, doing marching steps, chanting Tigers fight songs, or emptying rounds of assault rifles and machine guns. There were morale talks, where Arkan stood in front of the men like a football coach and told them things like, We are Tigers, do you know what that means? Soldiers were instructed on the strategies of ethnic cleansing, and Arkan shipped in specialists to discuss the psychology of death, because there were lots of dead people where they were headed.

The days were always hard and long. Soldiers who were there told me that wake-up was at 5:30 A.M., and by 6:00 A.M. the men had made their beds, dressed to perfection in their blacks or greens, and were standing in front of Arkan or one of his commanding officers. By 6:30, the day had started, and the men were running with full equipment up and down the dusty local roads. Even the ones who had gone through military training before described the daily sessions as "grueling" and "unlike anything I've ever seen or done or heard of." Through these sessions Arkan continued his metamorphosis into a warlord: His men now called him Commander, a name that would stick with him even after death. "I train them all day," Arkan liked to say. "And sometimes at night." Or as he told CNN when the news channel visited his camp early in the war, "Before they fight, they train and train and train. Then they are real soldiers."

Fall came and went. Temperatures dropped down into the teens and winds like steel fists drove across the river. Snow fell. Some days the gloom was such that it felt like evening all day long. Arkan never appeared to be bothered much by the dark cold. In videos taken of him then in the snow-covered camp, his face is always focused, his shoulders relaxed and his eyes fixed, like a man caught middream.

No matter how hard the training, the preparation never ended for Arkan. At night he toiled over maps. Unlike his soldiers, he inhabited a single room, which was ornamented with diagrams of Greater Serbia. Bent over them, he made calculations, just as he had during his bank-robbing days, a math of cause and effect. If X, then Y. If not Y, then Z. As the days and months passed, his vision of the conflict took a fuller shape in his head. With it was a mental blueprint of his future, one which he had been pursuing since boyhood.

According to one former soldier, he had only one diversion—a personal radio. No one else was allowed to have such a thing, of course. Occasionally, as he worked through the night in his room, Tigers remembered at different times songs by Bob Dylan, U2, and Simple Minds drifting quietly through the cold midnight rooms. "I don't think he ever slept," one Tiger told me. "It was kind of scary."

People from state security visited regularly, doling out instructions on towns to be sacked and making money exchanges. The appearance of the men was immensely troubling—and telling, as it provided persuasive evidence of the connection between Milosevic and his dreaded instruments of ethnic cleansing. Jovica Stanisic, the head of the Serbian State Security Service, who was later charged as a war criminal, popped in now and again. So did Radmilo Bogdanovic, minister of internal affairs. As did Radovan Stojicic, known as Badza, or the Hulk. The Hulk headed up the so-called Territorial Defense of Eastern Slavonia. Later he was promoted to be Serbia's deputy minister of the interior, where he reportedly got mixed up with high-powered criminals in arms- and drug-dealing schemes, which lead to his assassination in 1997 in a Belgrade pizzeria.

New recruits arrived at the camp weekly in jeeps and buses. They came from all over Serbia. Some were Serb refugees, arrested and sent there by local police and forced to act as backup for the Tigers. In this hellish world the refugees were considered expendable scum, dispatched to walk through minefields or to dig frontline trenches as mortars rained down around them. There were always stories about the refugees who resisted—stories of men being stripped naked and tied to trees along the river until they were broken down. In the winter it was freezing, and in the summer their naked bodies were exposed, like fruit, to the swarming mosquitoes that soldiers always complained were as big as birds. There were other stories, too. "People there were punished by having to bark like dogs. They were tied with chains to doghouses, and people had to bark," one refugee recalled later. "Once Arkan addressed us and said: 'Listen here, does anyone want to give me a blow job?' No one dared say a word."

At one point, Arkan reportedly arranged a direct bus service from Frankfurt, Germany, for "weekend warriors," though I could never confirm this. According to UN investigators, the program reportedly grew by word of mouth.

When new recruits arrived they were tested for drugs, sworn in, baptized, and required to give up all personal identification—license, photo IDs, anything that would connect them to the Serbian government on the battlefield. Most of the new recruits were young, some with the manner of skilled fighters. Others seemed more like semiliterate hooligans, the sort of criminal that hailed from the underworld of Eastern Europe.

Arkan also continued to enroll convicted criminals. It was no surprise that some of his commanding officers were underworld partners, with Bible-sized police files. Among others, there was a convicted murderer, a hired assassin, and a bank robber. The idea of having all of these criminals seemed to delight him, and he often boasted about them. For instance, one day he escorted a man named Captain Dragan Vasiljkovic through the camp's sleeping quarters. Dragan, who would later be charged by Croatian courts for war crimes, ruled over a band of Serb warriors called Kninjas, or Red Berets. At one room, Arkan paused. "You see this room," he told Dragan, wagging his finger in the doorway. "This room contains two hundred and fifty years in prison." Meaning that the men had committed crimes with sentences that, if served, added up to 250 years.

Whenever I asked former Tigers about their worst memory of Erdut, I usually got the same answer: punishment. Like any strong mob boss, Arkan gained a reputation for ruthlessness, and if you fucked up at Erdut, you paid for it—in a world of hurt. Soldiers who disobeyed received fifty to one hundred lashes—on their backs or on their legs. Zuti, a former officer of the Tigers, explained to the Serbian newspaper *Vreme,* "We used a truncheon called an 'Ustashe-thumper.' It was a thick electrical cable. When that hits you, brother, it drives your liver or stomach up to your brain."

Drinking, former soldiers told me, carried a more extreme penalty. If you were caught with a bottle or wine on your breath, the offender was hoisted up a flagpole in the training yard, lashed upside down, and then forced to run off the buzz, a trek that could take place in the middle of a freezing winter night and go on for dozens of ice-packed miles. "You know I insist on discipline," he told his Tigers many times.

Ruzica Mandic, a member of the ministry of defense of Krajina, the Serb-occupied region of Croatia, worked in a compound fifty yards from Arkan's camp. At night the countryside was quiet except for the crickets— and Arkan. He was always swearing, his voice carrying bansheelike across the countryside. Fuck. Fuck. Fuck. Some nights it went on past midnight, Mandic told me. About what, she didn't know. During the day she witnessed soldiers training in the Danube. Some of them didn't even look like they could swim, their dark heads bobbing up and down, disappearing in a fast-moving current. More than once, she wondered, when will one of them drown? Throughout the war, she also witnessed trucks weighted down with supplies rolling in daily and full trucks leaving—probably with contraband. From the start she knew something wasn't right with the warlord. Like others around her, she told me, she knew "this wasn't just about the war."

Not all of the men who came to Erdut ended up being cut out for Arkan's brutish world. Some had signed up out of curiosity, others for the adventure, as one would sign up for Outward Bound. These men, while they probably believed in the Serbian cause, didn't want to kill or be killed. Which was to say that not all of the Tigers were bad, or intended to be bad. The situation related to the bigger war question of why regular people allowed themselves to be controlled by something that was evil. A handful of the unhappy soldiers made attempts to escape, though it was probably one of the most dangerous things to do. These men took off in the middle of the night or in the middle of a battle. While the lucky ones got away and disappeared for a long time, heading for Western Europe, America, or Australia, the unlucky ones were caught and dealt with accordingly.

There was one deserter whom a few of the former Tigers talked about. Arkan appeared with the man one morning before about a hundred other soldiers standing in formation. Shouting, Arkan explained that the man had attempted to leave his brothers behind the night before. He condemned the crime, and then instructed another soldier to beat the man fifty times with a baseball bat. Bones cracked like popcorn. When the beating was complete, the man collapsed into a bloodied and lifeless heap in the dirt. "This is what happens to people who cause trouble," he warned the rest of the Tigers, before thundering away. The man was never seen again, and the message was clear: If you make me look bad, if you betray my empire, my dream, you'll have trouble. I can kill you.

No one dwelled on this stuff for very long, though. You couldn't. A lot of bad things happened at the camp and in the war, and if you invested too much thought in it you'd simply lose your mind. Plus, the war was moving too fast to sit around thinking, former Tigers told me. As Arkan said whenever they were about to head into battle, "You have to keep your head cool, boys. Otherwise, you're going to get yourself killed."

18

VUKOVAR: I KILLED TWENTY-FOUR USTACHE!

1

The Danube River cuts through Croatia's fertile eastern region of Slavonia, its banks rife with vegetation, nourishing corn and pepper farms and a run of small villages and cities, with names like Erdut, Borovo Selo, and Vukovar. These are a few of the ones swallowed up by the war. Among them, Vukovar is the largest, farthest downstream, and it spreads out across the river's western shore. Before the war Serbs represented a slim percentage of the city's fifty thousand people. Mixed marriages weren't uncommon, and generally people, whether Catholic or Orthodox, got along. There was a fresh market, churches, schools, and a big hospital. To outsiders the city was prosperous, with a solid middle class from the region's oil and farming industries, and suburbanlike two-story houses lined up along the dusty streets like rows of teeth. In the warmer months families lulled along the slow-moving river, picnicking and fishing, doing what families do when work is done. When the war came all that changed.

By September 1991 the same sad story playing out in much of Croatia was playing out in Vukovar. Croats turned on Serbs and Serbs turned on Croats. On both sides there were disappearances, burned houses, and firebombed shops. Newspapers chronicled the fear. People armed themselves, and Tudjman's own army was in Vukovar. The Serbs fled across the Danube, packing everything into barges and ferries. Soon Milosevic sent in the JNA.

Vukovar, however, was a key ingredient to the Suicide Man's Greater Serbia, a grandiose territory known as the Krajina that Milosevic imagined would eventually stretch west from Serbia's northernmost border through Slavonia, and then shoehorn along the Croatian coast, a part of the country that bordered Bosnia, ending somewhere around Dubrovnik, the prize of the Dalmatian coast.

Vukovar, however, wasn't the easy fight every nationalist Serb figured it would be. In fact, it was probably one of the bloodiest battles in the first stretch of the war. It was also one of the most revealing when it came to how the war would unfold over the next four years. Although the JNA's tanks and infantry had completely infiltrated the city's suburbs after two months of bombardment, the ten thousand-man force couldn't break the thousand or so Croat soldiers camped out in the exploded buildings at the city's dying center. Despite its astonishing firepower, the Yugoslav army, which had then become synonymous with the Serb army, was an uninspired force. Its daily desertion rate crept higher, disorder reigned, and there were soldiers who wouldn't even get out of their armored trucks anymore. One Yugoslav soldier was so enraged and scared about the ensuing battle that he hijacked a tank and piloted it back home to Belgrade.

In Vukovar, the balance only shifted to the Serbs after: (1) the UN Security Council imposed an arms embargo on all Yugoslavian republics, closing off any gun shipments to Croatia and giving an immediate advantage to Milosevic, who controlled both the Yugoslav army and all of its weapons; and (2) when Serb paramilitaries, armed to the teeth, began piling into the city by the thousands.

Which brings up an important point about the Serb paramilitaries: Vukovar was probably one of the first full-scale clashes that exposed how much Milosevic, in the absence of a devoted army, would have to rely on his paramilitaries to wage and win his diabolical war for land. After the JNA surrounded a town, put up roadblocks, and shelled it to pieces from a distance, the paramilitary crews—rarely the JNA—rushed the town and "mopped up." It was a simple process that would be repeated hundreds of times over the next four years, but it was a process that, in the face of a passionless JNA, would have been impossible without the paramilitaries. Without the paramilitaries it would have been a much different war, one surely with less death and destruction, a war that might not have really gotten off the ground.

This, of course, was not the case.

The Tigers entered central Vukovar on November 2, 1991. While the Yugoslav army bombed from gunboats positioned in the Danube, the Tigers cut through the front lines of snipers and landmines. As they sprinted through blown-up streets, their combat boots crunched rubble. Roads, hardly visible anymore, were covered in chunks of brick, roof tiling, and mountains of plaster dust, which blew around in the fall wind like a snow-storm. The Tigers arrived mostly on foot from the nearby woods and corn-fields, appearing out of nowhere like ghosts, firing machine guns and shoulder rockets, and swinging knives. They wore green camouflage and black ski masks. Fires burned in the somber light, the air reeked of cordite, charcoal, and burning flesh. Most buildings were so chewed up by bombs and bullets that they were no longer inhabitable. Toward the city center the Tigers hunkered down in abandoned Croatian houses, organized, and then fanned out across the hellish landscape as other Serb paramilitaries did the same.

Except for scale, it wasn't very different than Arkan's earlier battles, un-til the rumor of his capture began burbling over walkie-talkies and station radios. Looking back on it, the timing of the abduction was so perfect in its myth-making potential that it almost seemed staged to help his celebrity along. According to legend it happened like this: In a heated flash of vio-lence, with rockets tracing the air, bullets whizzing everywhere, and bodies falling, Arkan ducked for cover. When he rose he found that his crew had disappeared and that, thanks to an ever-shifting combat zone, he was now behind enemy lines. How it happened is unclear. Maybe guns chased him there. Or maybe he simply miscalculated his position. He was lost and alone and, soon enough, his enemies got him, and the airwaves were crack-ling with the word that the Croats had taken control of their first major hostage.

Meanwhile, night swallowed the war zone, and then there was no more word about him anymore. No one had any intelligence—not the Tigers, not the JNA, nor any of the other Serb groups.

Had they killed him?

A sense of doom quickly enveloped the Serb side, the fog of war gone very bad. There were conversations about how Arkan would never make it out. There was probably talk about how the Croats would soon be dragging his mutilated corpse to Zagreb, the capital city, where it would surely be put on public display, like a hard-fought-for trophy, like what Achilles did to the Trojan prince Hector. Arkan had mocked them and now it was their turn to have some fun.

As the hours passed the reality of his demise began to sink into the Serb front and the troops sagged. Morning arrived, and the sun climbed over the steaming ruins.

Suddenly Arkan appeared. Like a resurrection.

General Tomislav Simovic was one of the first to see him at JNA's forward operating base. As Simovic would later recall, in a scene worthy of Thomas Bulfinch's *Age of Fable,* Arkan stomped right into the Serb barracks "without a trace of fatigue, as if nothing had happened." With him, Arkan carried "a sniper gun across his shoulder and a bloody Ustasche hat hanging on it." That day he explained to his men and Simovic how he had single-handedly taken on the enemy. "I killed twenty-four Ustache!" Arkan bragged.

True or not, it was a good story, and it would advance him. He wasn't just some leader who gave orders but a commander who fought and was willing to die. Nationalist Serbs loved that about him, even if it was a big lie.

2

Vukovar fell on November 17, 1991. All told, the siege had gone on for eighty-seven days. Hardly anything in sight was left undamaged. Bullets and bombs had chewed up or destroyed most buildings. The air was full of a blizzardy dust, and dead cats, dogs, and corpses of adults and children were strewn about as if they'd been picked up, hacked away at with kitchen knives, and thrown. Over 2,000 people were dead, with tens of thousands of refugees. Of the 50,000 people who once called the city home, only 10,000 remained, most of them Serbs, because Vukovar was now a Serb town.

Arkan stuck around to "mop up." There were still Croats to address. There were prisoners at the Velepromet storehouse and suspected terrorists hiding at a hospital. Bogdan Vujic, who belonged to the JNA's military intelligence at the time, remembered puddles of blood on the storehouse's concrete floor. "I saw lots of prisoners in a room with bloody heads, many of them with their ears or noses cut off," he said, adding that paramilitaries were robbing the wounded. He said that he put forty detainees on a bus to a prison camp in Serbia. That was what they were instructed to do with prisoners of war. Arkan, who arrived shortly after the bus had gone, had different plans. Upset that the Croats had been taken away, he demanded that they be returned. He told Vujic that he was going to deal with the "criminals," including a woman, he said, who had killed fifty Serbian children. "I was worried about this," Vujic said, "because wherever Arkan came, there were consequences." Although the prisoners didn't return to the storehouse, their bus was intercepted and they were murdered.

The most gruesome case of slaughter was left for the city's main hospital. By November 18, about three hundred Croats had taken refuge there—wounded soldiers, families, and staff. There were also Croatian troops dressed like doctors. All of them believed that they would be evacuated, following an agreement made with the JNA. Of course there are no such things as promises during war, especially a war where men like Arkan ruled.

That night, or the night after, most of the hospital people were bused about three miles to a desolate strip of land known as Ovcara Farm, not far from a power plant, where around 250 were immediately put to death. Later an excavator was dispatched to cover the fresh corpses with dirt, and the covered dirt was then smoothed with steamrollers. Though everyone in the area knew what was under that earth, it would be almost two years before the bodies were uncovered.

Arkan would always deny his involvement in the Vukovar hospital massacre, though one of his soldiers bragged about the act to the Croatian magazine *Globus.* "We summarily executed three hundred prisoners," the soldier said. "We have a people's court here, you shoot and that's it." If the soldier was really who he said he was, Arkan was indeed involved; Tigers did not do anything during the war without Arkan's orders. It was more than an unspoken rule; if a Tiger acted alone, especially at this level, he would have been just as dead as the hundreds of others in that man-made pit at Ovcara Farm. Like one of his ex-soldiers said, "You do something in violation of the commander, he fucks your mother."

Eventually, Defense Secretary George Robertson of the United Kingdom would claim that a UN-led investigation found that the warlord had in fact played a critical role. Although he was never indicted for the bloodbath—the war crimes tribunal charged three JNA officers after his assassination—questions would always loom about what he did and didn't do.

19

BECAUSE WAR PAYS

1

Arkan wasn't only in the war for the killing and expansion of Serbia, of course. Sure, he always said that—that he went to war to defend his people and his land—but this was more than partly a ruse. When he wasn't fighting, documents show, his men were roving the landscape of bullets and fallen bodies, looting homes and businesses, and then selling off everything on the black market.

Black market possibilities abounded during the war, and money oozed out of the land, especially after the United States and the Europeans decided to impose the first wave of trade sanctions on Serbia. Fewer products were available, so prices shot up. The numbers were mind-boggling. Whole communities were pillaged, and local gangsters and warlords traded on the front lines. Through the wars in Croatia and Bosnia, it is estimated that over a billion dollars in goods were stolen and resold.

Arkan and his men were said to profit most. Soon after the war started they began making hundreds of thousands of dollars, maybe even millions. The way they worked was simple. Imagine being able to walk into a city of thirty thousand or fifty thousand and take whatever you wanted. That's what they did. Like a bunch of demented kids on a free shopping spree in a toy store. As one man recalled in *The Los Angeles Times,* "When they entered a . . . house, a couple of the Tigers would head for the kitchen and start moving out kitchen appliances. Others would go for the television and the VCR. Somebody else would start digging in the garden, looking for buried jewelry. You could always recognize Arkan's men. They had dirty fingernails from digging."

There was so much to take. In Vukovar, Arkan's men apparently pillaged a tire plant and a shoe factory and shipped everything out in trucks and vans. Cash and gold were stuffed into bags and luxury cars driven away. One Belgrade journalist who traveled with Arkan for several weeks watched him repeatedly drive his white Pajero jeep in and out of eastern Croatia. "He was supervising as his men drove truck after truck of plunder across the Danube into Serbia. They were taking blankets, tires, shoes, and whiskey." In Sarajevo, the capital of Bosnia, five thousand brand-new Volkswagen Golfs were hauled away from one factory, a take valued at 90 million German marks. Arkan's Tigers supposedly resold some of them in Bulgaria and Belarus.

Arkan didn't work alone on these plundering adventures—not at first, anyway. At the beginning, before he became untouchable, he shared cash booty with the SDB. Evidence of that appeared for the first time in a secret Serbian government document dated November 19, 1991. In it, there were details about what Arkan should do with a portion of his Vukovar spoils. "For the needs of the unit, keep 2,500,000 German Marks and 15 kilograms of gold," the confidential document read. "[And] 3,876,000 dollars, 430,600 Swiss francs and 38 kilograms of gold will be taken by our agents."

The document came from Sector V of Milosevic's Interior Ministry. The most elite group within the ministry, Sector V handled intelligence and counterintelligence and supplied weapons and training materials for most of the militias. Although Milosevic had grown his domestic police force to about 130,000 to enforce his rule, Sector V was reportedly only a dozen or so men headed by the chief of Serbian state security, Jovica Stanisic, who was also Arkan's superior and friend. Few knew anything about the group, and it was meant to stay that way, especially with men like Arkan working for them.

"From the beginning, Milosevic wanted his people in the SDB to be channels for Greater Serbia," an agent named Cedomir Mihailovic told the war crimes tribunal years later, although there is some dispute about his claims. Mihailovic, whose badge number was MUP 2675, worked with the secret services from 1991 to September 1994, until he fled Serbia and went into hiding, for fear of being killed.

"Unlike the army," he said, "this was Milosevic's handpicked apparatus and he wanted the minimum of people to know. By using paramilitary groups, the appearance of disorder could be maintained."

Of course, Arkan wasn't the only one experimenting in this new entrepreneurial underground. War profiteers—from paramilitary leaders to street criminals—were popping up all over the place, like a fast-moving germ infecting the land. They were the new Kapitalists, and they had unique skills—they could break your neck, fake a customs form, hijack a Mercedes, blow up a shop, start a front company, murder a best friend, or run for parliament. The only entry requirement was that you had to pay state security its obligatory tax, but that was petty cash compared to the hundreds of thousands many began packing away in offshore bank accounts.

Still, not everyone in the dying beast of Yugoslavia agreed with the corruption. Specifically, resentment in the Yugoslav army began to boil up, with a special anger reserved for Arkan. Out of all the other burgeoning war profiteers, some among the rank and file viewed the baby-faced butcher's rise as particularly troubling. Part of it was envy, no doubt, but there were also those who really didn't buy into the dirtiness of the war. They had integrity, if there was such a character trait still left in the region, and for the greater part they felt that they were fighting by combat rules set down years ago in the Geneva Conventions. Why could Arkan do whatever he wanted? some wondered. Why was he fighting this war anyway? He wasn't a military man. He wasn't even in the military. Not ever. Sure, his father was a military man, but Arkan hated his father, and he hated what his father stood for. What was that about? The subliminal sentiment was that the warlord had to be stopped before he made everyone else look bad.

One officer took a bold stand. Lieutenant Colonel Milan Eremija, a morale officer of the Yugoslav army Guards Division, composed a memorandum warning the Serbian government about Arkan. In that internal army memo, which was later mentioned at Milosevic's trial at The Hague, the lieutenant colonel cited atrocities committed by paramilitary commandos, including the time when Croat prisoners in Lovas were forced to walk across a minefield. In his opinon, Eremija wrote, Arkan's primary motive in the war was "robbery and the inhuman treatment of Croatian civilians." Toward the end of the memo, the lieutenant colonel urged Serbian officials to disarm and disband Arkan's group, along with a couple of others, including the White Eagles. In particular, he wrote, "authorities of the Republic of Serbia must participate in the campaign."

That was a pretty big shot across Arkan's bow, not to mention more than a little courageous for someone to challenge a man who had already killed so many people, including his own. Nevertheless, the grievance largely fell on deaf ears. There was just too much at stake for Serbia at that moment, and Arkan had become more necessary than ever.

2

By the end of 1991, after a series of unsuccessful cease-fires brokered by international diplomats, talk had moved to UN military intervention, and the general feeling in the world was that Serbia had to be stopped.

In response, pressure to complete what he had started quickly consumed Milosevic, and urgent messages were sent to his army and volunteer commandos at the front lines. Whatever you started, finish it. Drive forward. Fast. Kill, loot, do whatever you have to do, but secure our turf before the UN guys move in.

The one thing that Milosevic had going for him was that the international community was known to be slow to act. On military action, President George H. W. Bush deferred to the Europeans, and the Europeans began to wring their hands. Milosevic had time, and he used it.

The war for Greater Serbia kicked up a few notches in speed. The Tigers fought in Laslovo, Bogdanovce, Tordince, Erestinovo, and Osijek, Croatia's third-largest city, which Arkan predicted would fall faster than Vukovar. "We moved from one town to the next without hardly any time to rest," a Tiger named Trax recalled. "We'd storm the towns, do what we needed to do, take over the police station and the government buildings, and once all that was under the control of our people, we'd move on to the next town. A lot of people were killed, including my own friends."

The sped-up war had consequences. A dozen or so Tigers died, and Arkan, more than anyone, mourned them. As commander and self-proclaimed godfather, he administered last rites and paid for every burial. The pain he felt for the fallen men even extended beyond the grave. When the bereaved families needed financial assistance, he stepped in as surrogate father and husband, wrote checks, and arranged for housing and food. The only thing the fallen were denied, it seemed, was a proper obituary. Some things had to be kept secret. Forever. "We weren't allowed to place an obituary saying where they had died, where they had been killed," Arkan's personal secretary told The Hague tribunal years later. "All we could say was [that] they had died defending Serb lands."

The death of Natalia's brother was a different situation altogether. The others weren't direct family. When Aleksandar died in Croatia, Arkan had some intense explaining to do to his wife. She had been against the war business from the start, not just slightly but viscerally, entirely. Suddenly her brother was dead, and there was nothing Arkan could do about it, even if he did organize a grand good-bye.

Natalia was understandably devastated. After the funeral a chilly darkness consumed the married couple. I heard that days passed in which they hardly spoke. Blame was being processed. "I don't know if she [Natalia] blamed him for bringing him—Aleksandar—to the front lines, but their marriage started to fall apart after he died," said Vladan Dinic, publisher of *Svedok* and friend of the Raznatovic family. "They grew very distant. It wasn't a good time."

Natalia wanted Arkan to stay in Belgrade, and people said that she renewed her case against the war. "His mother always supported him, but Natalia kept telling him to come home," said Slavoljub Ninkovic, Arkan's old gambling partner. "She was afraid, especially after her brother died."

Nevertheless, war was where Arkan belonged, and he soon headed back to the trenches. Still, soldiers noted that he didn't appear to be completely himself. "He didn't seem to think much about his life," said Sloba Markovic, the former Red Star hooligan. Markovic told me about a few jeep rides he took with Arkan through the war zone not long after Aleksandar's death. With Serbian fight songs blaring on the radio, the two men ripped across minefields without looking. On a curvy mountain pass, with the nose of their jeep inches from the cliff's lip, Arkan stomped down on the gas. "Every corner he was on two wheels," Sloba recalled. "Once we went from Bijeljina to Knin. It's usually an eight-hour drive, but we did it in five. I thought I was losing my mind in the war, but I nearly lost my mind on that drive." Sloba paused, thought for a moment, and then added, "I think he [Arkan] was absolutely crazy."

3

The war in Croatia finally decelerated in late December. After six months of concentrated fighting, ten thousand people were dead, hundreds of thousands had moved away, tens of thousands of homes had been destroyed, and the Serbs controlled one third of the country. Cyrus Vance, a UN mediator and secretary of state for Jimmy Carter, brokered a cease-fire. The deal required the JNA to withdraw fully and the insertion of thousands of peacekeepers into Serbian-held Croatia. Not surpsingly, Milosevic agreed to the deal. Even though local skirmishes would continue on and off for the next four years, the Serbian president had accomplished his task. He'd achieved the partitioning of Croatia into Serbian and Croatian territories, and Croatia's borders had been redrawn. He had his land, and now the international community was going to protect it—at least until the Croats took it back in 1995.

The Croatian adventure was also good for Arkan, but for a different reason. Croatia was a test drive to make certain that his Tigers could perform, and they had done so successfully—murdered, thieved, and cleansed. Not only were hundreds of thousands of dollars now flowing into the commander's war chest, millions more were being worked on in the captured countryside. One thing was perfectly clear: The war stuff was eons easier than robbing banks. No one had done anything to stop him: not the United States, not England, not Germany, nor any of the Western countries. Not a finger raised.

Excluding the loss of his brother-in-law, Arkan seemed to be so positive about his new warlord role that he reportedly slapped a brand-new license plate on his SUV. It read VUKOVAR—an unabashed celebration of his first major military campaign, and also a promise of how things would go in the future—and the future was coming fast. Although the JNA withdrew from its stolen land and allowed the peacekeepers to move in, Arkan kept his army in Erdut in eastern Croatia. With the exception of doing some last-minute mopping up in Croatia in defiance of the cease-fire, he mainly stayed put, sharpened his knives, polished his guns, practiced complicated boxing kicks, trained his men, all the while avoiding his marital woes. He watched the news reports and talked to his state security contacts and counted the days until the battle in Bosnia-Herzegovina. Bosnia, as everyone would soon learn, would be different. In Bosnia, Arkan would perfect the war machine that had kicked out truckloads of dollars. The rules would be simple. Just like they were in Croatia. Non-Serbs would have to get out of his way—or die.

20

MEETING THE TIGERS

I met two of Arkan's former Tigers one fall afternoon in 2005 at a café, just around the corner from Saint Sava, Belgrade's largest Orthodox church. The café was a single-story concrete building painted mustard yellow, with tables set up outside. Both men refused to give their names, though one was the man who liked to call himself Mr. X. Before arriving, Milan had warned me that the men were probably armed. "I think they're in the protection business now," Milan said to me, employing a euphemism for the mob. "You never know with these guys."

Mr. X was the larger of the two, and he had a prominent tiger face tattooed across his muscular bicep in honor of his days killing non-Serbs. "You like that?" he asked me, flexing. He wore faded jeans and a tight blue shirt with the word DEFENDER stitched across his thick chest. As he spoke, a map of veins strained around his temples and forehead. Steroids were clearly a part of his workout diet. Although it was a mild autumn day, dribbles of sweat beaded his forehead and his military-shorn hair glimmered with gel. The second Tiger, who didn't say much of anything, wore a track-suit and sunglasses and mostly kept his eyes locked on Mr. X's Range Rover parked haphazardly on the sidewalk, as if expecting a drive-by shooting.

Mr. X talked about his first days as a Tiger, his training, and the fight in Teja, Croatia, that nearly got him killed. "I had gunpowder in my blood," he said, explaining his reason for joining the war. "My grandfather was in World War II. I was made for war. Some people are made for lawyering. Some for doctors. I was made to be a soldier. But not just any soldier: a soldier in the Tigers. That was a very special unit."

For about thirty minutes the conversation went smoothly—until Mr. X stopped abruptly. Something had occurred to him. His hand went to his forehead, as if searching for some lost detail, and then his eyes narrowed and his face tightened. He whispered something to his partner in the track-suit, and his partner shook his head. Mr. X leaned across the table toward me, both arms flexing. He asked me, "Do you know the *GQ* journalist who wrote that story about Ceca [Arkan's wife]?" I shrugged. Why? I wondered, feigning ignorance.

He slumped back in his chair, rubbed his fists, and then said he wanted to talk to that journalist to "settle some business." He didn't like the story. He hated it, in fact.

Mr. X looked at his partner, then looked at Milan, and then his eyes locked on mine again. He was looking for me to give something up. Did he know that I had written the story? The piece had portrayed Arkan as a war criminal and asked if Ceca had knowingly benefited from the war.

I felt sick in my stomach and thought of making an excuse to go to the bathroom. How did I get myself into this mess? I thought of home in New York. My head and chest began to sweat. Of all the moments, this was a turning point in my travels for the book. For a second, I wondered, had Milan set me up?

Milan, who knew about the GQ story, looked at me and then at Mr. X, who muttered something in Serbian. I worried about what Milan was saying. Turning to me, Mr. X said, "We have people in United States. We have people all over the world."

I took this as a clear threat. Milan was trying not to appear nervous, but his left leg was moving and I could tell at that point that he had no idea what was going on. He was just as freaked out as I was, and I imagined him think-ing, "This is fucking killing me softly."

Milan hadn't set me up. He was too good of a man for that, but what was keeping him from giving me up now? Consider his situation: If he lied to the Tigers, they could find out later. Belgrade was small. They had guns. They were in protection. As Tigers, they had killed before, so what would stop them from killing again?

Milan didn't budge. He was brave and, in a good way, more than a little crazy. Which is what made him so good at the job. He said that the *GQ* jour-nalist was a fucking American asshole for that story. I readily agreed, emit-ted a wooden laugh, and shook my head in disbelief. I wanted to cry. I felt like I was going to vomit all over the table. We assured the Tigers that our story about Arkan would be different. We nodded, smiled some more, and tried to act normal.

That killed it. We didn't talk about anything special after that. The fall weather. Red Star. Mr. X's Range Rover. Wasn't it nice? Soon Milan nudged my leg and made eyes, suggesting that it was time to go. After ten minutes, he made an excuse to leave—we had to pick up his girlfriend, but we'd call later—of course, we never called the two again.

After that, we drove around the city for an hour or so, just talking, thrown off by what had happened, maybe also trying to forget. We wondered if they really knew I was the one who had written the story. Was this a missile across our bow? Milan didn't know. He didn't say much. It was better not to think about it. It would be like this for over two years. We kept messing with the mass murderers, toying with the spider's web—and then worrying that they would eventually catch up. Because they always did. As deep night crept over Belgrade, Milan sang, "This world is killing me softly."

All I could think was: They know who I am. Our time is running out here. I had tracked Arkan's life through Europe and back to Belgrade, but still needed to understand what had happened in the war and how the world, as Yugoslavia knew it, had changed forever. Quitting now would mean my project was incomplete. I couldn't leave what I was searching for, because I knew I had not yet found it.

21

MY NAME IS TRAX; ARKAN MADE ME DO IT

1

Trax didn't want to die. He was thinking this even before he got the call from Arkan. The war talk was everywhere: on the radio, on the television, on the streets, and in the bars. You couldn't get away from it. He was twenty years old and, as he watched others his age leave the country or go into hiding in the city, he kept wondering, "Am I going to get called to fight, am I going to die?"

His war order came in March 1991. It wasn't from Arkan. Not yet. This one came from the Yugoslav army. They needed him and they needed him now. What could he say? So he slipped into a pair of black military-issued combat boots, picked up his orders, and trudged from his small Belgrade apartment to the Slovenian border, where the Serbs were intent on keeping the country from seceding from Yugoslavia.

Trax was tall and gaunt, with buzzed dirty blond hair and a tough-guy face, with a scar that traveled the length of his right cheek. His teeth were stained yellow from a two-pack-a-day habit, and he had a long, bent-up nose. For four months he sat along the Slovenian border, with a few thousand others, waiting to move, but was mostly bored and wondering how the hell he had gotten himself into this mess.

When Slovenia finally announced its intent to officially separate from Yugoslavia on June 25, 1991, the army ordered Trax and the other soldiers to attack. Trax proved to be intelligent and fast on his feet, and he was a good shot, which made him stand out. The war, which wasn't much of a war, lasted for ten days, with less than sixty casualties before the Yugoslavian government decided to let Slovenia go and sent Trax and the other soldiers home.

Trax humped it back to Belgrade, exhausted from sleeping on thin cots and eating empty meals consisting of little more than bread and water. He needed rest. On the TV he watched the Serbs ramp up to the war with Croatia, and then the war itself, playing out nightly like a sporting event that he didn't even like. The army was talking about sending him back, and he didn't want to go. He didn't even fucking care. What war? He hated the tall boots and the cold tents and the absence of good-looking girls. All he wanted to do was stay home, listen to his electronica music, be with his mother, ride his motorcycle, and find a way to make a damned living.

Trax started thinking seriously of hightailing it out of there. Enough was enough. He'd spent his teens on and off in petty crime, doing some robbing and stealing some cars, but he'd always nursed a flickering idea of better things. Every third or fourth person was unemployed in Belgrade, but like all of his buddies, Trax didn't have enough money to get out of the country and start over somewhere else. Besides, he didn't want to leave his family behind.

When the carnage finally petered out in Croatia, he felt a little relief. Then talk started about a conflict in Bosnia, and he revisited the idea of hiding.

Then Arkan sent for him, and all Trax could think was, Why the hell does this happen to me? The fact was: He couldn't ignore a call from Arkan. The other fact was: Trax, whether he liked it or not, was headed back to war, this time as a Tiger.

What Trax didn't know as he set out one morning to visit the warlord's Belgrade headquarters was that warring with Arkan would change him. When I spoke to Trax, he told me that Arkan would introduce him to things that most people wouldn't ever set eyes on in their lives, things that people would never want to know, scary things that would keep him awake at night many years after everything had happened. "You don't even want to know," he said, but I did.

2

Bosnia-Herzegovina is a brutal land. Mostly landlocked, except for a six-mile stretch along the Adriatic, it is encased by Serbia and Croatia and reaches across the ragged Dinaric Alps. In the mountain areas the winters feel a lot like the Arctic—unpredictable, cold, and snowpacked. In 1984, the mountains were home to the winter Olympics in Sarajevo. Westerners know the white weather as beautiful from ABC's daily coverage of ski jumping and downhill racing. Bosnians live it. Snowstorms regularly come out of nowhere, charging down the rugged mountainsides with below-zero temperatures and gale-force winds.

Bosnian Muslims used the icy cover of the winter of 1991 and 1992 to begin pulling away from Yugoslavia—just like Croatia and Slovenia had already done. To them the mother country was a rump state now, derisively known as "Serboslavia." In December there had been a lot of quiet political maneuvering, but by late February 1992 Bosnia, led by the moderate Muslim Alija Izetbegovic, had organized a referendum on independence. Although Bosnian Serbs, under the spell of Milosevic, decided to boycott the vote, 65 percent of the republic went to the polls and 98 percent of those said that they were prepeared to leave the Yugoslav federation.

The decision to secede caused lots of problems. Holdout Serbs complained that they were being railroaded into a new state and accused their opponents of rights violations. Who did the Bosnian Muslims think they were, forcing them to leave Yugoslavia? A man named Radovan Karadzic, a former psychiatrist and self-described poet, stepped up to lead the Bosnian Serbs. Almost immediately, Karadzic, whose most distinctive characteristic is his winglike sweep of raccoon-striped hair, demanded a separate Republic of Serbia inside of Bosnia. With Milosevic's tacit support, he began to make plans to stake out his people's rightful piece of land.

In no time, the Belgrade media machine rumbled alive, spinning out lies: Bosnian Muslims are terrorists, mujahideen; they diet on skinned babies; they aim to kill your fathers and impregnate your wives; and they are going to burn down every Serbian Orthodox church. It was the Field of Blackbirds all over again. The Turks are coming! Something had to be done, warned Karadzic and Milosevic. In Bosnia, Milosevic made the same argument he had for Croatia—the Serbs needed protection. Arkan readily agreed. In Erdut he began referring to Muslims as "wild dogs." The Serbs, he declared, were up "against the wild dogs."

In Bosnia, religion became the most prominent divider, which was strange considering the republic's history. Since World War II the Bosnian people had lived in a pluralistic society. Of the 4.4 million in Bosnia, 44 percent were Muslim, 31 percent were Serbs, and 17 percent were Croats. They all spoke the same language, intermarriage was commonplace, and for the most part people seemed to get along. Casting the Bosniacs, a medieval term for Bosnian Muslims, as terrorists didn't make immediate sense.

Bosniacs weren't your average Muslims. Many of them didn't even give a damn about Allah. They didn't kneel and pray five times a day, they ate pork, drank whiskey, caroused with multiple women, some behind the backs of their wives. I traveled all over Bosnia and saw only one woman in a head scarf. Most of the Muslims I encountered looked like every other white European. They could have just as easily been from Switzerland or Germany. Some even had blue eyes and blond hair, not unlike surfers in southern California.

The fact about Bosniacs was that most didn't even come from the Middle East. Much of the region had been forced to convert to the Muslim faith during the Turkish reign, between the fourteenth and nineteenth centuries. When the Turks left the Bosnian Muslims hadn't bothered to pick up another religion. Why should they? Religion didn't even really define them or their way of life. The Austrians took over the land, and they blended in and did it again in the post–World War I Kingdom of Serbs, Croats, and Slovenes. In other words, Bosnian Muslims were just Slavs until Milosevic and Karadzic turned them into the enemy in 1991, and began calling them Muslims.

Bosnian Muslims weren't preparing a religious state. They wanted their own secular state, separate from Yugoslavia and the February vote had deemed it official. On March 5, 1992, Bosnia went ahead and announced its decision to leave. Although most Western diplomats supported the move, Milosevic, of course, disagreed. In fact, his plans had apparently already been set into motion. At that moment, he was organizing to "exterminate the Muslim people." According to Vladimir Srebrov, a former Serbian Democratic Party leader, Milosevic "envisaged a division of Bosnia into two spheres of interest leading to the creation of a Greater Serbia. The Muslims were to be subjected to a final solution: more than 50 percent of them were to be killed, a smaller part was to be converted to Orthodoxy, while an even smaller . . . part—people with money, of course—were to be allowed to buy their lives and leave, probably through Serbia, for Turkey. The aim was to cleanse Bosnia-Herzegovina completely of the Muslim nation. . . . The very name of Bosnia was to disappear."

Outsiders would call the bloodshed in Bosnia, like that in Croatia, a consequence of a chaotic post–Cold War world, though that didn't entirely capture the reality. There were other countries in similarly frayed situations that dealt much more effectively with civil unrest. Take Nelson Mandela. He averted civil war in South Africa following apartheid. Then there was Mikhail Gorbachev. When the beast of the Soviet Union rusted and finally broke apart, Gorbachev allowed the Baltic nations to secede instead of taking the route of nationalism and a greater Russia. Milosevic, however, wasn't these men.

Several weeks after Bosnia's announcement, the Serb president sent Arkan and the Tigers on their first mission. The men traveled to the Bosnian city of Bijeljina. In case Arkan was unclear about his task, Stanisic at the Serbian Interior Ministry allegedly sent him instructions. Stamped "State Secret" with a top-secret code, 675-11-428-V-8/4-92, the document read: "The leadership of the SDA, Muslim members of MUP and the organizers of the Muslim paramilitary formations should be arrested and transferred to Erdut." The SDA was the Muslim nationalist party of Democratic Action, led by Izetbegovic. MUP was an acronym for the Bosnia State Security agency. "In order to frighten the Muslim population, a small number should be executed."

By the time the war ended, that small number would end up rising to more than a hundred thousand.

3

When Trax arrived at the sweetshop on his designated morning, he found the commander seated at a big desk in the back. Arkan was dressed in camo and surrounded by a suite of thugs, bulging with concealed weapons.

"I heard about you," said Arkan, dismissing an introduction with a flick of his wrist.

Trax gazed at him, nodded.

"You were in the war," he said. "I heard you were good. And we need good men."

Trax's gut was doing somersaults. His head felt light, like he was up in space or stuck inside one of those GraviTron rides at the amusement park. He tried to keep focused on Arkan, whose eyes searched him. Trax couldn't speak.

"You want to go see Mama or do you want to go to the front?" asked Arkan. He rose up from his chair. He was taller than Trax had imagined. His head was large. Standing there, he was gigantic, especially with all those military clothes on and the pistol dangling off his belt.

Trax asked, "The front?"

"The front lines," said Arkan. "You go with my guys to the war."

"Now?" He wasn't even packed. He didn't have anything ready.

Arkan pointed at the door. "There's a truck leaving now," he said.

Trax hesitated. "I have a mother," he said, trying to find a weak spot. "I'm her only son." Which was true. He wasn't lying.

"No, no, don't worry about that," said Arkan, dismissing the notion with a wave. "The jeep's leaving."

"I'd like to say good-bye to her."

Arkan didn't seem to hear. He fiddled with papers on his desk. Machine guns and grenades were piled up on the floor, like toys.

"You go outside," he said, with an agitated tone that suggested he wouldn't say it again. "You go now. OK?"

He didn't even get a chance to make a phone call home. People would worry, especially his mother and father. No one would hear from him. Weeks would pass—and then months. His parents would wonder what had happened. He was here one day, gone the next. At one point they'd ask, Is Trax dead?

4

April 1, 1992, is the date people remember. On the Serbian side of the Drina River, just outside of Bijeljina, Arkan had set up a forward operating base. The Drina meanders south from the Sava River, slicing a border between Bosnia and Serbia, before it finally empties out into the Mediterranean. The base was comprised of tents and manned by about 150 men, Trax told me. Some were core Tigers. Others were Serb refugees from the Bosnian side. The men had been training for about two weeks, and the moment had finally come to suit up and head across the river to Bijeljina.

Spring approached. It was the Muslim feast of Bairam. Hours after midnight the air was crisp and clear as two jeeps left the base. Arkan was in the lead jeep. He had twelve other men with him, including Trax. They wore black wool masks with slits and bulletproof vests under their black jumpsuits.

Each man carried grenades, two rocket launchers, a submachine gun, a pistol, a bowie knife, and a compass, just in case they got separated somewhere along the way.

All week, Bijeljina had been expecting Arkan. They knew he was stationed on the riverbank with his men. They'd heard about what he'd done in Croatia, heard the stories on the radio and seen images on television. Over the last few weeks the city had begun to divide, like a chasm in the earth suddenly opening up. Serbs slipped away in the middle of the day, or in the night, and headed to the other side of the bridge. Some Muslims fled to more Muslim-dominated cities in Bosnia. Others battened down and armed themselves, preparing for the worst. Most—Serbs and Muslims— were scared.

Pandjic Mehmedpalija, a fifty-three-year-old music teacher, hardly slept at all the week before the battle. He and his wife were Muslim and had lived in Bijeljina for most of their lives. They lived in a two-story house at the edge of downtown. "We sat inside and watched through the curtains for Arkan to come," he told me one fall afternoon. "We saw people leaving. There were days we didn't even go out on the terrace."

Pandjic wondered, where is the rest of the world? Are they going to sit and watch us be killed?

When word trickled into the city that the Tigers were finally coming, many civilians took to their basements. A Serb woman who called herself Sophia told me that she hid in a basement for days with her Muslim neighbors. Fearful of what was outside, they ate whatever they had left in the refrigerator.

Nights seemed to go on forever. "What is he going to do to us?" the Muslim neighbors kept asking Sophia. "What is he going to do?" Sophia just shook her head. These were her friends. She had known them for decades. "We grew up together," she said. "We had our kids together, took them to school together. We were good friends, like that."

Religion wasn't something that they had talked about much. Even now, Sophia wished that she could give them comfort, as they had comforted her in the past, but for the life of her she didn't know what was going to happen. No one did.

The jeeps now traveled west across the bridge into Bosnia. A picture of a tiger was emblazoned on the jeep doors. Most traffic was stopped at the border—but not Arkan. Everyone knew the warlord. It helped that he had special license plates issued by the Serbian Interior Ministry, which acted as a free pass anywhere in the region. Even later, when the UN arrived, these plates would allow him through checkpoints with just a wave. Similar to what he did this night. He waved and the two jeeps were on their way.

On the other side, the jeeps slowed down at the curve of the river. They parked and climbed out. As the river gurgled below, Arkan spoke to the men in a low, serious voice. "I don't want anyone shooting until we get into town," he instructed. Then there was nothing more to say. He had already warned them about the heavily armed mujahideen, and the men knew what was expected of them. The men were picked because they were considered the most lethal.

Bijeljina was a municipality of 100,000, with 59 percent Serbs and 34 percent Muslims. It was a city built on agriculture and some industry. Streets were cobblestone, dirt, or asphalt. There were street markets almost every day, where Muslims in filigreed caps lined up wobbly tables next to Serbs and Croats and sold everything from Panasonic batteries to freshly picked red peppers.

It was a critical battle. Situated in the northeastern part of the country, Bijeljina was a strategic gateway into Bosnia. From there the warring Serbs would move south along the river, carving out a spacious corridor in the eastern part of the country, which would eventually include Sarajevo. Later they would take out a northern part of the country, which would link them to the Serb-held stretch of Croatia. A joke at the outset of the Bosnian war was that the Serbian Tourism Ministry had adopted a new slogan: "Visit Serbia before it visits you."

Arkan slipped on his night goggles, the only pair, according to Trax, and waved for the men to follow him single file into the pitch-dark woods. The men disappeared one by one, as if diving into an ocean cave. Without goggles it was difficult to see, except in places where moonlight slivered through the trees. Winding their way through the woods, branches lashed their faces and their military boots sank into streambeds and caught on invisible undergrowth.

The walk was about an hour, though Trax didn't remember exactly. Insects called out, chickens squawked, while cows mulled the earth. At one point a cat leaped off a wall, sending Trax into the air with a yelp. Arkan turned back, looking for the culprit. In moments like this you never knew what was going through his head, Trax told me. He could snap and shoot you dead. He locked on Trax. "What are you thinking, you pussy?" he whispered in a harsh tone. "You're going to get us killed." Nevertheless, he let him go—this time.

The Tigers skirted narrow alleyways at the backs of two- and three-story buildings. By 3:00 A.M. they were standing in the town square in front of the Istanbul Café. It was here where the Muslim militia, controlled by Izetbegovic's Party for Democratic Action, had set up camp for its roughly hundred soldiers.

The battle began. Rocket-propelled grenades were launched into the café and at surrounding storefronts. A firefight ensued. Soon afterward two buses carrying more Tigers rolled into town. As the fall of Bijeljina would demonstrate, the Muslims didn't have much of a chance. A Western-imposed arms embargo, which was meant to deter the war, only made the Serbs stronger and turned the lamely armed Muslims into target practice.

The crack, crack, crack of machine-gun fire woke the sleepy city, sending up screams of men, women, and children. In the basement, where Sophia and her muslim neighbors hid, an amazing stillness settled in, as if all had stopped breathing. What will he do to us? There was hardly a resistance force, but that didn't mean people weren't going to die. Bodies fell, bloodying the streets. A Muslim man was executed in the square. Arkan announced over a megaphone, "I am Zeljko Raznatovic, Arkan. It is time for you to surrender. If you have weapons, surrender them now."

Like an evening gloom, the Tigers fanned out over the city. Mosques were vandalized and soldiers took pictures inside flashing the three-fingered salute. The biggest mosque downtown was burned; the four other mosques would fall in the months to come. Guided by a list drawn up by local Serbs, the militia soldiers searched out prominent Muslim politicians, businessmen, and intellectuals. Young men suspected of being fighters were murdered. If Muslims didn't give up their friends' and relatives' whereabouts, they were strung up on door frames and beaten black and blue with pipes or gun butts. "They were animals," said Jesla Antonio, a Muslim who was there. "They were just cutting down people in the streets. I saw them shoot down a man on a bike who was screaming." Sophia watched Arkan himself storm into a butcher shop and gun down an entire family. "I don't remember how many people were there," she told me. "Seven or seventeen, but it was a lot. He said they wouldn't give up their guns and he killed them all."

Meanwhile, businesses and houses were ransacked. Mattresses were flipped, safes blown open. One man witnessed a soldier search a woman's vagina for a diamond ring she'd secreted away. Forty luxury cars were stolen from a rich Muslim and shipped out of town. One afternoon Trax rode off on a Yamaha 1000cc motorcycle he found in a garage. Jewelry, gold, cash, whiskey, and factory equipment were loaded into trucks and shipped back to Erdut, where all would be distributed for sale.

Ron Haviv, a New York–based photographer, wandered into the city that first morning. Arkan had given him "permission" to photograph the city under siege. He saw men in masks roaming the streets with guns, people fleeing, mosques being defaced, and a lot of dead bodies. At one point he watched several Tigers march a Muslim man into an apartment building and then throw him out of a fourth-floor window. The man was a terrorist, the Tigers explained to him.

Not long after, Haviv heard shots ring out, and then saw two fresh bodies slumped on the street in front of him. An older woman stood over one of the fallen men, her husband, and he watched as she placed her hand over a bullet hole in his chest. Partly hidden by a vehicle, Haviv snapped photos of one of Akran's Tigers as he walked up to the woman and kicked her in the head. The Soldier was dressed in green camouflage, had a brush cut, sunglasses perched on top of his head, a Kalashnikov in his right hand, a burning cigarette in the other, and a rocket launcher strapped to his broad back. The women fell as he struck her again and again with his black boot. Soon she was motionless. Was she dead? It was hard to tell.

The pictures Haviv got that day captured the utter insanity of the battle, the casualness with which someone could kill or maim a stranger without thinking twice about it. To one looking now at the picture of the fallen woman, the soldier could have just as easily have been kicking a soccer ball.

Haviv almost didn't get out of Bijeljina with his pictures. As he was preparing to leave, the Tigers he'd been traveling with announced that he wasn't going anywhere. "You must wait until Arkan sees you," they said.

When Arkan came the Tigers whispered something into the commander's ear. The warlord stepped up to Haviv. "I'll take your film," he said. He wasn't angry. He spoke evenly, politely. "I'll process the pictures and send them to you."

Haviv resisted. He said that they wouldn't be able to process the pictures in Belgrade the way he wanted them done. It's better if I take them with me, he said.

They went back and forth like this, as Arkan's men stood around looking at Haviv, guns ready to go on command. "Look," said Arkan, definitive now. He wasn't playing around anymore and Haviv knew this. "Give me your film," he said, opening his hand.

Haviv surrendered the roll from his camera and Arkan thanked him. Surprisingly, the warlord didn't ask for the film in his pocket, but Haviv decided not to offer it. After Arkan sent him on his way, he took a car straight to the Belgrade airport. By week's end the photograph of the Tiger kicking the fallen woman had been splashed all over the world—*Time* did a photo essay and singles ran in *Paris Match* and Germany's *Stern*. Throughout the war, that photograph would be published dozens of times more. Arkan, of course, was enraged. He sent a message to Haviv, "One day I look forward to drinking your blood."

Who was the soldier in that famous photo? Some believe it was Trax, and that theory was supported by rumors in Tigers' circles, though Trax would never own up to it. It would be hard to prove, anyway. In the photo you can't see the solider's face. His back is to the camera. Still, the man does share features with Trax—the wide back, the height, the short blond hair, the slightly pointed ear, and he's a smoker.

Either way, a question arises at this point: How could someone like Trax, who had led a pretty average teenage life before the war, turn around during the war and start committing such gruesome acts, others like it if not this? I didn't understand. How does one decide to cut a cross into the forehead of a next-door neighbor or kill the father of his best friend? When I asked Trax, he had a two-part answer. First he said, "Arkan was

Bijeljina, April 1992. Here, Ron Haviv, a New York–based photographer, captured the notorious brutality of the Tigers. People still wonder about the identity of the Tiger kicking the Muslim woman.

fucking nuts and you didn't say no to him." Second, and most revealing, he explained, "It was war. And during war everyone was doing bad things. Bad was normal."

In other words, after months of sustained fighting, war and death had become people's reality, a fact that changed the entire moral dimension of a land and its people. In some, the human spirit was completely transformed: What would have once been considered atrocious was now considered commonplace. To warriors like Trax, the world of peace, the world of easy relationships, the world of simple, civil living was not real any longer. War was Trax's coming of age, a tragic time when growing up and adulthood was easily mixed up with dying.

I wanted to make sense of this, because it confused me. Listening to Trax talk about the war was a lot like standing out in a strange lawn in the dark staring into the window of a stranger's house. I wanted to get a glimpse of what went on inside that house, how it shaped the lives of the people in it, but all I felt was separate and far away. I told Trax this and he shook his head sadly. "It won't make sense to you," he told me. "Ever. Because you weren't there. All I can say is that it was all very bad. Like a bad dream." In some ways, Trax is probably right. Though I was trying, I probably wouldn't ever completely understand.

5

If anyone slept those first nights in Bijeljina, their personal nightmares would certainly have been better than the reality of what was happening in the streets. Martial law was enforced. Curfews were established for non-Serbs, and any Muslim caught outside between 4:00 P.M. and 6:00 A.M. was beaten or executed. Those who hadn't fled yet were still in their basements or locked up in bomb shelters or secreted away in some other hiding place. Several phoned Sarajevo radio to get out word about Arkan and his men. They needed help. Rightly they were scared. Rightly so, they thought they were going to die. Ahmed Salihbegovic, who lived in Bijeljina, told CNN, "Arkan came in with his cannon, and he was shooting at anyone and everyone he could. I was in the square when the firemen were washing the blood off the street with their hoses. That whole day, that whole night, we just waited to see if someone was going to come by or knock on our door, and we would be finished as well. That was just terrible to survive that day."

When Pandjic Mehmedpalija peeked out of his lightless window, all he saw were men in black with guns "looking to kill." Later he would hear that his cousin was picked up on the street and executed after digging trenches. Nevertheless, he still couldn't bring himself to leave. War or not, it was hard for many in Bijeljina to leave. Serb or Muslim, this was their shared home. Their families had lived in the region for generations. They'd walked these lands, farmed these fields, made a life out of the place, a good life. They had private swimming holes and fishing spots in the river. They were as familiar with the stars that nightly stretched out above them as they were aware of all the minute and trivial contours of their own bodies.

Soon news came out that Arkan had located a local Muslim leader named Seval Begic. As Begic later recalled to CNN, Arkan told him to go on the radio and explain that the local Serb population was in "danger of Islamic extremists." When Begic refused, he claimed he was beaten for two and a half hours and then ordered to make the address at gunpoint. He was also instructed to organize a detail to clean the city. After days of fighting, corpses littered the streets and sidewalks and a sweet stench had begun to creep into the spring air. The Muslim cleanup crews were dispatched in pickups and dump trucks. A fire engine helped.

Eventually, the "men in black" got to Pandjic. They didn't kill him. They took his TV and telephone, and then on their way out ordered him to report for clean up or "death duty." They told him to wear a suit, and laughed when he did. When international news crews began arriving in the city, Arkan was unapologetic. "Those extreme Muslims are wild as dogs," he told cameras. "This is war—us against the wild dogs which only want to kill the people around here. That's what I want to say for your television."

Days passed and the cleansing continued. An elderly woman was found on the street with her eyes gouged out. I heard about several women in one basement shot dead in front of a plate of cheese pastries. Some Muslims were given fifteen minutes to pack and move out of the city. Before leaving, many were forced to sign documents deeding their house to local Serbs. Hundreds left every few days. After they signed away their hard-fought lives, I heard that some were dropped off at a nearby minefield separating a Serb town from a Muslim town and ordered to walk to the other side. Good-bye.

There was also a technique called the rationalization of living space, a more psychological form of cleansing that involved moving Serbs into the homes of Muslims and Croats who refused to leave. "Rationalization of living space" was an ancient law that dictated how much space a person is entitled to occupy. No one paid any attention to these laws until the war came.

When the war started, Muslims and Croats occupying more than the allotted amount of space in Bosnia were forced to open their doors to incoming Serbs. According to most, the situation often went something like this: A Muslim family is living in a two-bedroom house in a Serb-dominated town and a Serb family decides that, wait a second, they'd like that house. Maybe it's bigger than theirs, or maybe it's a little nicer, or maybe they've just moved there from a Muslim-dominated town. So what do they do? They crash open the door and take over the living room, which forces the Muslim family to move into the bedrooms. Of course, cohabitation is unbearable. The Serb intruders make noises through the night, kick the walls, bang furniture, shout, then start issuing subtle threats—boy, it'd be a pity to lose your lovely daughter, wouldn't it? What can the Muslims do about it? They certainly can't go to the police, because the Serbs are now the police. So after a week or so—or a couple months for the stronger ones—the Muslim family packs up and leaves and it is now a Serb house.

The Tigers stayed for a week or two weeks, depending on whom I asked. By the middle of the first week the JNA tanks and armored trucks had lumbered into the city, though the army didn't do anything to impede the Tigers. The Tigers did what they wanted, and the final results were nothing less than shocking. Within fourteen days over twenty thousand people had been expelled, transferred to concentration camps, or killed. In Bijeljina, it was estimated that Arkan and his men were responsible for dozens of those deaths. Even after Arkan's men left, the terror continued. The May 4, 1992, issue of *Maclean's* described a war-dazed city, with bloodstained walls, families clustered into damp basements, diminishing food supplies, and the omnipresent sounds of mortar fire like a never-ending rain on a metal roof.

6

There was one big surprise for Arkan during that first year of the Bosnian conflict; his Swedish son, Michael, came looking for him in Belgrade. It had been a long time, almost thirteen years since Arkan had seen his first child. No longer the baby Arkan had left behind, Michael was now a young man. Like his father, he had grown up to be tall and broad, but unlike Arkan he had a striking mane of blond hair, which stood out as he strutted into the grim Balkan city. "I came to see who my father was," he told me. "I wanted to know him."

Arkan wasn't difficult to locate. At the Belgrade airport Michael report-edly stepped up to the curb, flagged down a taxi, and said that he was the son of Arkan, but he didn't know where to go. As a person close to the family ex-plained to me, "The taxi driver just starts the car and drives him straight to his father's house, which at the time was headquarters of his army."

The two reunited, and soon Michael joined the Tigers. Although he was athletic and brave, after playing hockey for years in Sweden, he didn't have any military training. That turned out to be a minor point. He traveled to Erdut and then to Bosnia with the Tigers, and fought on the front lines.

People told me that Michael was too "nice" for the war. His tempera-ment was more California surfer than bloody mercenary. Perhaps that's why I didn't hear much about his exploits in Bosnia.

Although he stayed with his father through the war, his most notable event with the Tigers seemed to be the time he disappeared during a battle near the mountainous area of Treskavica. When fighting died out one day, no one knew where he'd gone. Soldiers told me that Arkan appeared un-bothered by his son's absence, even though seven hours passed before he reappeared. The story was that Michael had gotten lost in the Bosnian wilderness.

7

There were more Bosnian towns and cities for the Tigers to conquer, and in-creasingly, Bosnian refugees noted the packs of armed men in black masks roaming the countryside. It was like "the plague moving through our land," said one man who witnessed the Tigers' arrival in Zvornik. "They came, and if they didn't kill you, they got inside your head because of what they did, and that was just as bad as death." The man, along with his mother and sis-ter, fled into the woods.

Before Arkan, Zvornik was just another mountainous Bosnian city in the Drina Valley, south of Bijeljina, on Serbia's western border. In many ways it resembled a postcard you'd send your mother on a backpacking trip through the Balkans—a deep blue river that wandered through verdant forests and rows of four-story homes with alpine roofs that slouched along a rugged escarpment known as "neck-breaking hill." Of the eighty-two thousand who called the city home, about 60 percent of them were Bosnian Muslims, while the rest were mostly Bosnian Serbs.

Local Bosnian Serbs wanted that percentage changed, and they specifically requested Arkan's men for the task. As an incentive, they paid him a $250,000 "cleansing fee," a practice that would become more frequent in the later stages of the war. Other Bosnian Serbs would reportedly pay him up to $2 million to cleanse a city; the feeling was that he would do a better job than the army or other irregular Serb forces. As a Serbian government spokesman explained after the cleansing of Prijedor, a Muslim town in western Bosnia, "He [Arkan] is very expensive, but also very efficient."

According to news reports, the Tigers entered Zvornik from Serbia on April 9, 1992, three days after the international community recognized Bosnia as a sovereign country and offered it a seat at the table of the United Nations. Though there was a moment where the army stalled to negotiate with the Muslim governors, Arkan said he wasn't waiting.

While the JNA launched shells from the hilltops and the river, the Tigers and several other paramilitaries stormed the city. As refugees fled, they told stories of Arkan's men placing children on the road and running them over with tanks. One Serb woman told of mutilation: "Ears, noses, and genitals" were sliced off. Two hundred houses were burned. Thousands were transported to Keraterm and Omarska, two new Serbian-sponsored concentration camps. Arkan's men took over the courthouse, the police station, and the Drina hotel, where people were tortured in hopes of extracting information on opposing forces. By the end of the siege several thousand had been reported missing or dead and more than half the city—about 40,000 people—was gone.

Weeks passed, and then months. It was hard to keep track of all the conquered towns. There were so many that they all seemed to blur together. Kamenica. Grbavic. Rogatica. Kozarac. Foca. Veljina. Bodies fell. Summer passed. In Bratunac, twenty-five miles southeast of Zvornik, the Tigers allegedly escorted two thousand men, women, and children to both the Vuk Karadzic primary school sports center and the FC Bratsvo soccer stadium. Iron rods were employed for beating, jammed into anal cavities and down throats. Crosses were cut into foreheads and chests. Body parts were chopped off. Of these prisoners, forty or fifty prominent businessmen, politicians, and religious figures were killed.

In another village, not far from Brko, witnesses told UN investigators that the Tigers, with supporting troops, collected five thousand people and escorted them to a torture camp housed in an old brick factory and pig farm. Orthodox crosses were again carved into foreheads and some Muslims were even forced to convert to Orthodox Christianity. According to witness accounts made to UN investigators, between two thousand and three thousand were executed, their dead bodies dumped into the river, packed into a mass grave, or destroyed in a rendering plant that once boiled swine into lard. As one report stated, "They have photographs of trucks going into Brko with bodies standing upright, and pictures of trucks coming out of Brko carrying bodies lying horizontally, stacked like cordwood."

I heard a lot of stories like this from firsthand witnesses as I traveled through Bosnia, following Arkan's murderous trail. The stories made me sad and depressed and angry. At times it was hard getting through interviews. Other times I found it difficult to believe people; the stories exceeded my imagination. One Bosnian man told me about a grown Serb raping a twelve-year-old in front of her mother and father, who were both tied up. A Muslim woman told me of a soldier cutting out the tongue of a crying baby. "Like the Nazis," she said. I traveled up and down Bosnia. I heard stories from numerous people, mostly older, about how they just didn't want to get out of bed during the war. Gunshots would explode outside their windows. Knocks would come at their doors. But they just wanted to sleep, as if they could sleep away the war.

"Why didn't you come help us?" a man named Juka asked me. It's a question that I got a lot. He meant the United States. Why didn't America intervene? I met Juka in a small town south of Sarajevo. A Bosnian Muslim, he was in his sixties, and his face was tanned and hardened from a life spent working in the fields. His eyes were tiny black rocks. "You are strongest power and you did nothing," he said. I started to say, I know, but didn't finish. I didn't have an answer for him, but he wasn't expecting one. He told me Serbs drove him out of his house and that he lost a brother, sister, cousin, and "many friends." I asked how they had died, and expected to hear more of the same nightmarish stories that I had read about, but he just shook his head. "Why should I explain that to you?" he asked, his eyes dropping to his work boots. "It is too late now."

Arkan and the rest of the Serb military forces, of course, weren't the only team of bad guys perpetrating mass killings, rape, and torture. I asked Milivoje Ivanisevic about this. As director of the Center for Research of Crimes Against Serbian People, he worked out of an attic floor of a run-down concrete building in Belgrade. On the walls were portraits of two Serbian men who would become the world's most wanted war criminals: Radovan Karadzic and General Ratko Mladic. Through the Bosnian war, Ivanisevic and almost fifty others in his group tracked atrocities committed against Serbs. Of the thirty-four thousand Serb deaths that he'd recorded so far, he said, he knew the causes of almost twenty-four thousand of them. Many were the result of Muslim aggression. "Have you heard of the mujahideen?" he asked me.

Investigators from the Hague recorded fourteen Muslim paramilitary groups operating with the Bosnian Army, including the Black Swans and the mujahideen. As Ivanisevic suggested, the mujahideen did stand out as particularly brutal. Muslim fighters from the Middle East, they began arriving in Bosnia in June 1992 in the name of jihad, or holy war. Jihad was a call to arms that few in the country had heard of before. Most mujahideen were veterans of the Afghan war in the 1980s. After fighting the Soviets, the mujahideen warriors had come looking for a new religious front. In Muslim-dominated towns—mainly in central and western Bosnia—the Muslim fighters robbed, tortured, expelled, and murdered Serbs. There were also reports of circumcision with dull knives and beheadings. In a town called Brandina, on the outskirts of Sarajevo, the holy warriors allegedly executed scores of Serbs, after forcing them to kneel and recite a Muslim prayer. "They killed many, many Serbs," said Ivanisevic. Even officers in President Izetbegovic's Bosnian army, guys who were fighting the Serbs, didn't fully disagree with this assessment. "It was a mistake to let them [the mujahideen] come here," Colonel Stejpan Siber, deputy commander of the Bosnian army admitted to the Sunday *Times* in June 1993. "They committed most of the atrocities and work against the interests of the Muslim people. They have been killing, looting, and stealing."

Did all of that excuse Arkan's murderous work? Ivanisevic smiled. He didn't say yes or no. (In 2007, Ivanisevic would publish an article in the Belgrade newspaper *Glas Javnosti*, claiming that only around four hundred people had been killed in the Bosnian Serb siege of Srebrenica, when in fact over seven thousand had died.) He called Arkan a hero and, though he acknowledged that the Tigers could have committed some crimes, he asserted that stories about the war were replete with much embellishment. "The foreign media made Arkan so big," he said. "There were a lot of Serb groups that went to Bosnia and said they were Arkan's boys and did all of these things and they weren't even associated with Arkan."

This was true. It was also true that everyone had his or her own version of what happened in the war. The Serbs had their ideas; the Croats and Bosnians had theirs; and the media and human rights organizations had theirs.

When the media accused Arkan of murder and profiteering, he flicked away the allegations like a fly on his shoulder. It was a mad world, he admitted, but not mad because of him or because of his men, and in some ways, he was sort of right. It was a mad world. It was a world where God, whatever his religion, had forsaken his believers and left them to duke things out to the bitter end. It was mad because of Muslim thugs and it was mad because of Bosnian Serb thugs, but it was also mad because of Arkan's thugs and the other paramilitaries.

Still Arkan would always cultivate the image of a gentleman in this god-forsaken world. At one press conference, surrounded by sharp-jawed men in dark uniforms, guns dangling off their thick shoulders, he explained that they had him all wrong. "The Serbian people was [*sic*] in a very bad situation here from the part of the Muslim population, and we, Serbian Volunteer Guard, we came here to help these people," he said. "About the stories that we are looting and bad-treating people here, that's simply not true, because we are Serbian Guards, Serbian gentlemen officers."

By fall Arkan's gentlemen had helped Serbia gain control of between 60 and 70 percent of Bosnia, a figure that would not change much in the three years to come. By winter, tens of thousands would be butchered or go missing, and although no one would know for sure how many had been killed by Arkan and his Tigers, the group was universally considered the most brutal of all right-wing nationalist paramilitary outfits. Witnesses, fleeing on foot through woods, in rafts on rivers, or loaded onto tractors, told Western observers that Arkan was gutting the Muslim population.

Arkan was not just a physical force. He was also a psychological one. Over time, his terror contaminated the soil and infected the air, and the resulting condition was mass fear. It didn't matter if he hadn't personally come to a town. He didn't have to, because others did and used his name, as Ivanisevic said. Before long, Arkan was everywhere, even if he actually wasn't: He had become a trope for the ugly war that would not end.

Back in Bijeljina, Pandjic Mehmedpalija, the music teacher, was still trying to figure out how to recover his life post-Arkan, if it was possible at all. It wasn't only Pandjic. It was almost every Muslim who had made it out of the spring siege alive.

Although Pandjic was still conscious and seeing the world around him, he couldn't shake the feeling that he'd been killed. He told me that he felt like a dead man walking, and I'm sure that this emotion was not uncommon for others who had lived through Arkan's hell. "My wife and I sat inside for months, looking out the windows of our house. We didn't go anywhere. We didn't do much of anything," he said. "We worried that he [Arkan] was still here. It was like we didn't exist."

8

More and more the war fucked with Trax's head. It fucked with every soldier's head. He was twenty-one years old but felt ten times that. He
couldn't sleep. His legs hurt, and he had headaches, probably caused by the
constant pop of gunfire, mines exploding, rockets blasting in his ear-
drums like death metal music cranked to eleven. Finally, Trax resolved to
leave the war.

The decision came after Zvornik. He told Arkan that his mama was sick.
He used that word. Mama. "My mama needs me," he told the warlord one
day. "I need to go home. To help her."

It was a lie, but what else was he supposed to say? He couldn't take it. He
felt like he was going to blow up. He didn't want to die.

Arkan told Trax he could go, but he needed to come back. "Take a week,"
he said.

Trax left, but wasn't going back. He climbed on a motorcycle—a Suzuki
750 that had been stolen from the front lines—and headed for Belgrade. It
was great—for a stretch. He went home, reunited with his parents, who were
happy to see him. He got drunk, went to old haunts, found a girlfriend, and
worked on getting his life back together. Although he still had some cash
stashed away, he needed to figure out how he was going to support himself
now that he didn't have the war money coming in.

He worried some, having firsthand knowledge of what Arkan was capable of doing to a traitor. He knew about Arkan's death squads, Tigers who
did his dirty work for him around town, but he wasn't a traitor—was he? He
had done his time at the front. He had trained soldiers and fought the war
he was told to fight. Still, he made an effort to lay low, kept an eye out for
Arkan's blacked-out SUVs. You knew which ones were his because they
had special plates, low numbers or VUKOVAR.

One week passed and then another. Summer came and the sun felt
good, especially after the bitter spring in Bosnia. Soon his mind even started
to fool him into thinking that he was home forever. His nightmare was over.
Arkan had forgotten about him.

However, reality had a funny way of snapping back just when you
thought you were in the clear. He was on his motorcycle one sunny afternoon, girlfriend hugging him from behind, when one of Arkan's SUVs
pulled up next to him at a red light. At first, he didn't even notice. Then a
door opened, a guy climbed out, and a pistol was aimed at his girlfriend's
temple. She was told to get off the bike, don't even think about running.

"You know who's looking for you," the man said to Trax. Traffic just moved around the scene. Everyone knew Arkan's men.

Trax looked into the SUV and saw other men packed in the back. How many he couldn't tell. He figured he was dead. "My mother is sick," he tried to explain. "I need to take care of her. That's why I left."

As he watched his girlfriend get shoved into the truck, Trax's life raced through his head. He thought of the others who had tried to leave the Tigers, the story of the man beaten with a bat at Erdut. He didn't want to die. How did this happen?

"Let's go," said the man.

Trax left his bike and stepped into the truck, where there were three other men. He recognized one of them. Vule. In Bijeljina, Vule was a maniac. Walking down the center of a street in the middle of a firefight he kept screaming, "Come out Muslims, get the fuck out of your houses." He blasted off dozens of machine-gun rounds, challenging anyone who wanted to try him. Vule thought he was invincible until a sniper got him. Luckily Trax was there. He saved Vule's life, carrying his bleeding body to a medic, though that fact didn't matter now. If you left Arkan, you were a traitor to everyone. Deserters died.

"Who the fuck do you think you are?" shouted Vule, as the truck pulled away from the curb and headed to Arkan's place. His face was right in Trax's face. The men had their guns out, waiting for a chance to shoot. As they drove, Trax tried to get them to free his girlfriend. Why do you need her? he asked, but they just turned up the music.

When they arrived at Arkan's mansion, they led Trax out of the truck but left his girlfriend behind. Inside, Arkan smiled. "What a big surprise," he said to Trax. "It's like a birthday present seeing you."

Trax felt blood rushing to his head. He felt warm. Although Arkan in-structed his men to let his girlfriend go, Trax couldn't get it out of his head that she would be hurt.

Vule wouldn't let up. He screamed and bobbed his head like a strychnine-pumped fighter cock. "I'm going to kill you, motherfucker," he shouted, as Arkan looked on. "Do you understand that?" He got in Trax's face, veins popping from his neck.

Arkan laughed. "Don't talk that way to him," he said, serenely. A psy-chological game now. He patted Trax on the shoulder. Vule backed away, suspiciously.

"He was fucked up," Arkan said to his soldiers in the room. "But he's not fucked up now. Are you?"

Arkan looked Trax right in the eyes. When Arkan looked at you, it always seemed like he could enter your skull.

Trax shook his head, eliciting a smile from the warlord. He didn't try to explain anything. Silence was what saved him.

"We have some more work for you," Arkan told Trax. "OK?"

Trax didn't argue. He was lucky to be alive. He knew that. He would always remember one thing about that sunny afternoon: Arkan allowed him to live and his girlfriend, too. That day he was happy to go home unscathed, even though he never saw the motorcycle again, and even though he was being shipped back to war. "You get in with Arkan," Trax told me later, "and you never get out. That was rule number one."

Still, that didn't mean Trax wouldn't try again. There were always other escape hatches. Right? Maybe he just had to go farther away from Belgrade. Like to another continent—but even then, you never knew.

22

I DON'T GIVE A DAMN

1

As the body count clicked upward in Bosnia, stories about Arkan and other Serb irregulars began arriving in Washington, D.C. from on-the-ground sources. Jon Western, a human rights analyst in the State Department's Bureau of Intelligence, was one of a few who paged through thousands of reports detailing raided villages, acts of mutilation and rape, and assembly line–like killings. "Many of these atrocities looked an awful lot like what we had heard and read about during World War II," he told PBS's investigative show *Frontline*.

Western saw photographs of victims that "looked like they had been through meat grinders." There was one report that described how a nine-year-old Muslim girl had been raped by Serb paramilitaries and then left to die in her own blood while her parents looked on from behind a fence. Although Arkan continued to defend his actions vociferously, Western could see the truth on his computer monitor. "We could see the attacks by watching our computer terminal screens, by scanning the satellite imagery, or often just by watching television," he recalled. "We knew exactly what the Bosnian Serbs were going to do next, and there was nothing we could do. Imagine you could say, 'In two days this village is going to die,' and there was nothing you could do about it. You just sat there, waited for it to happen, and dutifully reported it up the chain."

Every day new atrocities streamed in from newspapers, international human rights groups, local press translations, classified cables from the field, satellite intelligence, refugee testimony, and telephone and radio intercepts. Western's job was to collect the intelligence and then generate a realistic picture of what was happening. "Milosevic was not going to call up his henchman and say, 'Go commit genocide,'" said Western. "We had to develop the case." Daily reports were delivered to Secretary of State James Baker. Though the Bush administration eventually saw everything Western saw, and read everything he read, no one moved to do anything. George H. W. Bush seemed determined to stand on the sidelines, as he had in Croatia. Repeatedly Secretary of State Baker claimed that the United States "doesn't have a dog in this fight."

In fact, talk of the war and the brutal conquests of warlords like Arkan seemed to irritate the administration. Months into the carnage, Defense Secretary Dick Cheney explained to CNN that the war was "tragic, but the Balkans have been a hotbed of conflict . . . for centuries." That summer Bush would echo the sentiment, describing the war as a "complex, convoluted conflict that grows out of age-old animosities." Later that fall, Deputy Secretary of State Lawrence S. Eagleburger, who personally advised the president on Yugoslavian affairs, would say that what Arkan and other Serb militias were doing was simply just "not rational," as if there was nothing they could do about it. In general, the administration hoped that the war would just "burn itself out." The last thing they wanted was to get bogged down in another Vietnam, especially after just coming off the first Gulf War two years earlier, when the United States had to drive Iraqi forces from Kuwait.

There were, however, some attempts made to talk sense into the Serbian president, as if Milosevic could be persuaded to reconsider his actions. In April, not long after the siege of Bijeljina, Warren Zimmerman, U.S. ambassador to Serbia, confronted him specifically about Bosnia, and even brought up Arkan. Milosevic hedged. He said that Serbia didn't have anything do with the Serb aggression in Bosnia. "But why do you come to me, Mr. Zimmerman?" he asked. "There isn't a single Serb from Serbia involved in the fighting in Bosnia."

This was patently absurd and Zimmerman knew it. "But I saw Arkan on your own Belgrade television boasting about his capture of Bosnian villages," Zimmerman responded. Arkan had been seen parading across the ashes of

Muslim towns. There were even pictures of him and Bosnian Serb president Radovan Karadzic standing over Muslim corpses.

"Our television is free to broadcast whatever it wants," Milosevic answered serenely. "You shouldn't take it so seriously."

Besides, Milosevic added, as he'd done before, Arkan was "no more than a simple sweetshop owner."

Of course, Milosevic was just trying to escape responsibility for any war crimes perpetrated while he pursued Greater Serbia. His name couldn't be attached to the battlefield. To help with the smoke screen, the JNA troops operating in Bosnia had recently switched the patches on their uniforms, so that they were no longer officially associated with Serbia. Instead, they were now the Bosnian Serb army.

Zimmerman, however, wasn't easily fooled. As he deadpanned in his memoir, *Origins of a Catastrophe: Yugoslavia and Its Destroyers,* "Arkan, who did own an ice cream parlor in Belgrade, was a sweetshop owner in the same sense that Dian [Dion] O'Banion, the Chicago gangster and Al Capone's rival, was a florist."

Zimmerman pressed his superiors on Bosnia, but his superiors didn't seem to want to hear about it. Then on May 16, a month after he met with Milosevic, his job as ambassador to Yugoslavia was finished and Washington recalled him. The White House no longer needed his services.

Still, he didn't leave quietly. As one of his last acts he submitted a confidential cable to Secretary Baker entitled "Who Killed Yugoslavia?" The cable, which was divided into five sections, echoing a verse from "Who Killed Cock Robin?" predicted that the worst of the war hadn't yet come. Milosevic, Arkan, and all the other sadistic nationalists were, in fact, just getting started. Western leaders, he wrote, were about to become "witnesses at Yugoslavia's funeral."

2

Zimmerman was right. As night crept across downtown Sarajevo on May 27, 1992, a mortar shell slammed into a breadline, blowing a crater-sized hole in the sidewalk and sending white-hot shards of knife-sharp metal slicing through the crowd. Even by the war's bloody record, this was an absolute horror show. Men, women, and children, most of them Muslim, had been waiting for a loaf of bread, which had become scarce during the conflict. The air stank of cordite. Orphaned shoes and purses were scattered about, and there were body parts—arms, legs, some fingers, and a torso. A preliminary count indicated that there were twenty-two dead and over one hundred badly injured.

That night, images of the massacre were broadcast on CNN, the BBC, and almost every other international news network. Although most experts would conclude that it was the Bosnian Serbs who had shelled the breadline, the Serbs blamed the Muslims, claiming they had done it to force the West to act.

The West did act, though not militarily. Three days after the massacre the United Nations, backed by President Bush, imposed strict economic sanctions on Serbia. The UN-imposed sanctions made it illegal to supply almost anything to Serbia—from oil to food. The sanctions, Western diplomats hoped, would put an end to the madness. They didn't.

President Milosevic played the victim card. Serbia didn't do anything wrong, he claimed, distancing himself from the shelling. Be strong, he told his people. We are being unfairly punished. As usual. We are a heavenly people. We will get through this. As the sanctions took effect, the Serbian State

Buildings in Sarajevo shelled by the Bosnian Serb Army, which had been dug into the surrounding hills.

Security and other high-level government officials organized intricate smuggling channels, enabling products to be brought into Serbia. Milosevic knew that if he wanted to stay in power, he had to continue providing food, gas, and heating fuel to his people.

So everything that had once arrived through official distribution networks now moved underground and a gray market emerged. yet, it didn't exactly improve the state of things for regular folks. The country, which had been struggling for years, continued trending downward. Two thirds of the country was unemployed, and those who still had jobs made pocket change. The average monthly wage, once at $500, slumped below $100. Inflation climbed to 200 percent. The unemployed and bankrupt were forced to break international law to survive—they set up rickety stands on the streets and in their front yards, where they sold contraband food, cigarettes, and gas. Some at that point decided to form or join paramilitary crews and traveled to the front lines to loot. You did what you had to do to turn a dollar for your family.

It was a grim moment for ordinary Serbs, and Uros Komlenovic, a Belgrade crime journalist, guessed that it was only going to get worse. "Ideal conditions," he warned his readers, "now exist for a rapid increase in crime: pervasive poverty, a corrupt government, a police force from which citizens cannot expect protection, and the concentration of experienced heavily armed criminals."

Of course, for Arkan and a handful of other government-connected criminals, the sanctions were a beautiful development. Although the state-created smuggling operations had the superficial appearance of serving the state by bringing essentials to the country's people and allowing Milosevic to play up the victims' narrative, the sanctions quickly became a massive money-making opportunity for a new criminal elite, with hundreds of millions of dollars in profits. At the top of those criminals was Arkan. The money in play was about to make him one of the richest gangsters in the world.

3

There is a well-worn maxim: The best gangsters operate like the best businessmen. They don't have to come up with all the ideas. They don't have to be constantly inspired to try new angles. What they do is recognize the weightiness of an idea when that idea presents itself. When that idea appears, in this case in the form of strict, all-encompassing sanctions, they recognize its greatness, seize it, and work hard to squeeze every single dime out of it. Arkan aimed to become a gangster CEO.

Sure, looting and trading the loot was profitable, but that sort of enterprise had limits, especially in a world without strict sanctions. There was only so much territory to loot, and the prices you got for what you looted were average or below market. Sanction busting was a different creature altogether. Under heavy economic sanctions—Serbia now had a naval blockade, border checks, and international police trolling the Danube—there was always going to be a scarcity of products within the country's borders and, because of that, there would always be a massive demand for the stuff that got in. As every first-year economics major knows, immense scarcity coupled with immense demand drives up prices—not just by little steps, but by quantum leaps. So if under the sanctions you could get the products that people needed into the country, the essentials, you would make millions. There was also a situation that was even more desirable: If you could not only transport the products into the country but kill off most of your competition as well, you would make hundreds of millions. That was the best idea.

So while the West sat back and hoped for Serbia to shrivel under its new stranglehold restrictions, Arkan got to work at building his brand-new sanctions empire. Soldiers were trained and put in place, and official government allies, especially within state security, were greased. Most say that there were three central smuggling arteries into the country. The first traveled across Lake Skadar, the largest lake in the region. Controlled by the Montenegrin mafia that had links to Italian crime families, products were loaded up on cigarette boats on shores in northern Albania and driven two to fifteen miles to Montenegro and then moved by automobile into Serbia. A second channel entered from Bulgaria and Romania; sometimes shipments came on boats across the Danube, other times by truck, train, and even tractor. The third channel, considered one of Serbia's most prolific, ran through Russia. Most deals involved grain from Serbian land, which was shipped to Russian territories, where it was bartered for oil, which was shipped back through the Black Sea and then up the Danube.

According to Arkan's personal secretary, known as protected witness B129 at the International Criminal Tribunal for the Former Yugoslavia at The Hague, the commander relied heavily on Mihalj Kertes, Milosevic's handpicked chief of Customs, to sort out various smuggling details. Arkan's secretary worked for the warlord briefly in 1993 at his Belgrade home and headquarters, and then again there from 1994 to 1995. When she testified at The Hague in 2003, she explained that Kertes and his deputies provided Arkan with, among other things, fake licenses and friendly eyes at the borders. "Mihalj Kertes," she claimed, "was always called when there was a truck coming in from Bulgaria or Macedonia and when it had problems at the border crossing."

When Arkan's secretary was asked how she could possibly know about these highly secretive details, she said it wasn't all that hard to figure out what was going on. Injured Tigers who worked alongside her at the Belgrade headquarters, including a man known as Sicko, told her stories, and she'd also "seen through the documents, because there were always facts and information at the headquarters written down in documents that related to the operations they were engaged in."

In no time, Arkan's illegal shipments were flowing into Serbia: cigarettes, food, wood, whiskey, and oil. According to international observers, drugs, too, were moving in and out of the war zone. Amid the chaos, Arkan was rumored to have been expanding his heroin-trafficking empire through Western Europe, a network that he'd started in the eighties. Whatever he shipped, it slipped through the border untouched. "Our vehicles," Arkan's secretary testified, "had the mark of the Serbian Volunteer Guard and the tiger on the front part of the vehicle so that the regular police—and I am thinking of the regular police force—did not dare to stop those vehicles."

Selected deliveries traveled to Belgrade, where Arkan's secretary told the tribunal that things were "sold to people who would come to our headquarters and who knew that we had the goods, that the goods were available." Other shipments went to Erdut, where trucks arrived around the clock: tankers, vans, jeeps, and school buses. In the background, new Tiger recruits speed marched, fired rifles, and sang fight songs while other Tigers set off for war. One hundred yards down the road the UN peacekeepers had their own headquarters, but could do nothing about Arkan except watch.

Erdut quickly became the warlord's own private state, not unlike Monaco, with its own rules and politics. Following Serbia's domination of large swaths of territory in Croatia and Bosnia, the complex had swelled into the region's most expansive distribution point for black market goods. In the days of sanctions, it grew even larger. In addition to his training camp, he constructed a gas and contraband depot. Soon, people back in Belgrade began to refer to the place as Arkansas.

Profits were considerably high. As expected, whatever Arkan had charged for his products in the past, international sanctions allowed him to charge triple, quadruple, and, in some cases, twenty times as much, according to people familiar with his activities. For example, during the sanction years, one liter of whiskey, which once sold for about $20, now demanded as much as $100. A pack of Marlboros got $30 in some places, while a pound of coffee ran upward of $40.

Oil, however, owned the biggest dollar signs—there were millions of dollars of gasoline cash at stake. No official numbers exist, but former Serbian police officials told me that Arkan bought a liter of gas for the change in your pocket and turned around and sold that same liter for about $4. UN investigators estimated that every tanker that left Erdut in defiance of international sanctions made Arkan roughly $30,000, and that during the darkest, scarcest slogs of the sanction years, UN documents suggest that it was possible for an oil-smuggling kingpin like Arkan to profit as much as $1 million a day.

Arkan, however, didn't own all of the region's oil smuggling. It is believed that he split territory with Milosevic's son, Marko, as well as with several other high-level government officials. Sometimes the territory sharing became a source of tension. Who liked to share profits? On several occasions Arkan complained to his secretary that Serbia's state security chief, Jovica Stanisic, was greedy. "Badza," he told her, "wants to keep everything to himself and for himself." Still, there's persuasive evidence that Arkan quickly exceeded his competitors' earnings. Not only did he have strong smuggling connections, but thanks to his Tigers' quick and definitive work in Croatia, he controlled every major oil plant in eastern Slavonia. "He was definitely the biggest in the business," one former government official told me on the condition of anonymity. "There was no one like him, but they were all dirty."

Dirty indeed. In time, the sanction-busting world in the Balkans would resemble something the West had always been fighting off—the infiltration of the mob where there was no legal economy. In America, the mob had taken over prostitution, gambling, and drugs. In Serbia, in the absence of any legitimate economy, the mob took over everything. The mob was not just a few people, or one family. The mob became the whole damn state.

That this world-gone-mad situation could even happen is instructive in a way that sheds light on what began to happen in Serbia under Milosevic's watch, a disturbing reality that Zimmerman had hinted at in his confidential missive to the U.S. president: The country was in the throes of a dramatic moral crisis, with massively lethal consequences. Sanctions alone weren't going to deter the madman dictator and his country. Morality had been tossed to the wind a long time ago, and it was clear that within this new gaping void crime paid millions, if not hundreds of millions, more than any legitimate or honest way of life.

When Arkan's secretary testified, she recalled how she began to see a man increasingly obsessed by war profit, even as he continued to declare publicly that his soldiers were fighting solely for his broken and bankrupt people. She described his troop's frequent hijackings of Red Cross supplies, and millions of dollars going from the government to his troops and into his private coffers. At one point, in her crossexamination at The Hague, President Milosevic questioned how she could possibly remember all the details of her tenure at Arkan's after nearly a decade. Her response was haunting: "If you had worked over there [at Arkan's headquarters]," she told the court, "you would have remembered things your entire life." Specifically, she mentioned that she'd attended the funerals of twelve young Tigers. "To bury twelve young men who were fighting for the Serbian people was very difficult," she said. "That is why I wanted to speak out, because it appears that the war boiled down to smuggling and that those young men died for no reason whatsoever."

4

Things were good until the bad news started rolling in. In October 1992, a judge in Osijek, Croatia, ordered Arkan's arrest. The court had heard testimony about his reign of terror and wanted him put away for life—or executed. Soon after, Interpol issued a warrant—his seventh. The warrant indicated that Arkan was wanted for "genocide" and that he "is considered to be violent and armed." Leoluca Bagarella, an Italian mafia boss known as the "brother-in-law," was also on that Interpol list. Believed to be one of the most homicidal mob bosses in history, Bagarella was said to have murdered over three hundred people, including his wife.

In December, the United States began to consider arresting him and other alleged war criminals. Eagleburger, who was now George H. W. Bush's secretary of state, had traveled to Geneva to speak at a conference on the fighting in the Balkans. Before a packed room of international delegates, he detailed war crimes—the annihilation of Vukovar by Serb forces, the attack on Sarajevo, and the slaughter of three thousand non-Serbs near Brko, a mass murder thought to have been perpetrated by Arkan and his men. "We know crimes against humanity have occurred and we know when and where they occurred," Eagleburger said. "We know, moreover, which forces committed those crimes, and under whose command they operated. And we know, finally, who the political leaders are and to whom those military commanders were—and still are—responsible."

Eagleburger presented a list of ten criminals, a major move in bringing diplomatic clarity to who was doing what in the war. Until then the United States had been mostly silent about those it thought were guilty of crimes against humanity. Although the list included a couple of Croats, most of the men were Serbs—Slobodan Milosevic, Radovan Karadzic (president of the self-declared Serbian Bosnian republic), General Ratko Mladic (commander of the Bosnian Serb army), and Zeljko Raznatovic, Arkan.

"Naming names" sent ripples through the world, especially in Serbia, but many skeptics wondered why Bush had waited so long to do what seemed so obvious. Why now? The most apparent reason was that he'd lost the election that fall to Bill Clinton and wanted to save face. It was about the history books. Tens of thousands were dead, millions were homeless, and the Serbs had continued carving away at Bosnia. The war wasn't just going to burn itself out. Because he was leaving office, Bush needed to be remembered for doing something, even if it was saying what everyone knew, that there were men like Milosevic and Arkan committing gross and inexcusable crimes and that they needed to be stopped.

In addition to a cease-fire, a no-fly zone, and the lifting of the arms embargo against Bosnian Muslims, Eagleburger called for the creation of a war crimes tribunal. The tribunal, he said, would resemble the trial of major Nazi figures after World War II. In front of the audience that day, he insisted that Arkan and the others be tried for their "crimes against humanity." "Over the long run," he warned, "they may be able to run but they can't hide. . . . We're going to pursue them."

Specifically, the job of putting together a case for a tribunal fell to the United Nations. That year the UN organized an investigative arm, the UN Commission of Experts, with a mandate to determine what atrocities had been committed, who committed them, and if there was enough evidence to build a tribunal.

Cherif Bassiouni, a compact man with large squarish glasses and bushy white hair, was elected chief of the new commission. A professor of international law at DePaul University in Chicago, Bassiouni, an Egyptian-born

American, had devoted his life to being a crusader for human rights. At one point he was nominated for the Nobel Peace Prize.

To help him, Bassiouni hired young lawyers and law professors to travel around the war zone in Croatia and Bosnia and catalog witness accounts of everything, from mass rape to summary executions. His crew of about thirty would talk to hundreds of people and learn about atrocities committed by all sides, from the height of the war in 1992 to its less intense years in 1993 and 1994. When he wasn't traveling, Bassiouni worked out of a book and document-jammed office at DePaul University, sleeping little. He compared the work of investigating this complicated wilderness of war to the intense, detail-oriented work of the "FBI or a U.S. attorney."

Although the Tigers were hardly his only target, Arkan's group was high on his list of paramilitary groups to be examined. In fact, Bassiouni was one of the first Western investigators to get extensive on-the-ground information about the Tigers. Jon Western had been stuck in an office, but Bassiouni was out in the field, where he learned about the looting, the payments for ethnic cleansing, the ransoming, and the brutal killings, which included throat slitting and gang rapes."

In Vukovar, Bassiouni dug up mass graves, and one night he slipped into coveralls and sneaked into Arkan's compound in Erdut, where he witnessed the Tigers speed marching and training. He also saw the oil trucks and all the other sanction-busting hardware, which amazed him.

Out of all of the volunteer Serb gangs, the commission learned that Arkan's Tigers were the worst. "Arkan's gang worked in more operations than any other gang," Bassioni told me over the phone one day from his office in Chicago. "So, statistically speaking, they probably committed more war crimes than any other gang." That didn't mean that Bassiouni wasn't investigating Croats. The commission did, but the Serb groups stuck out as the most prolific.

"They were absolutely unscrupulous," he added, speaking of the Tigers. "They would kill anything in sight. The only limitation is that they would not kill Serbs, but beyond that, they would kill anything."

Bassiouni's investigation went on for about two years. Then in the spring of 1993, Bassiouni and his team began stitching together what they had learned. At the end, the UN commission had collected sixty-seven thousand pages of documents and thirty-five pages of incident summaries. In July 1994, nineteen months after Bill Clinton had replaced George H. W. Bush as U.S. president, Bassiouni presented the materials to the UN Security Council.

"They told us, wow, you have enough evidence to prosecute." Shortly after, the UN court was established, and Clinton began to think about military intervention.

5

Around this time, Arkan probably should have started considering an exit strategy, but he didn't run. Hiding most likely didn't even cross his mind. "I don't give a damn," he said about Eagleburger, the UN, and the rest of the Western world that wanted his head. "That's how I feel about that. I'll say it in English for you: I don't give a damn."

The thing was: Much of Belgrade didn't seem to give a damn either. Instead of dismissing Arkan as an amoral, psychopathic killer, countless Serbs embraced him. As one thirteen-year-old Serb told *The New York Times* at the time, "I love Arkan because he's a hero. He looks like a real man."

Many followed Arkan's war the way Americans had followed the crime trails of Al Capone. Though Milosevic could have filtered the information that Serbs got about him, he didn't. It was easy to learn about Arkan's nasty history. If anything, the international scrutiny seemed to elevate him around town. In the years before few had dared speak about the crimes of mobsters, but now the media was abuzz with Arkan's stories. Tabloids covered every inch of his personal life, even when his marriage to Natalia was finally fading. He seemed to crave the attention. His ego was inflamed. More than once he talked about making a movie about his life. Old friends told me that he planned to call it *I, Arkan*.

Though he never made that movie, he did produce a love letter of a documentary, *Arkan's Tigers*, about his soldiers, which featured him training his men, leading them into battle through smoky and bombed-out Croatian towns, and presiding over funerals. During the war the videos were sold on street corners. Years later they ended up in other parts of the world, passed around the Internet on YouTube and peddled on eBay, where their prices beat most Hollywood movies. In one of the last scenes of the documentary, Arkan is shown in a church, where he asks a little boy to sing the "Tigers" fight song, which the boy did. When he finished the song, Arkan hoisted the boy up into his arms. "Do you know who I am?" the warlord asked him. Of course he did. "Arkan," the boy responded on cue. Arkan looked pleased. "Bravo," he said, kissing the boy on the cheek.

Naturally, he soon began appearing on television news and talk shows, mainly on Radio TV Belgrade and its famous program *Minimaks,* Serbia's *Tonight* show. The cameras suited him. In the electric yellow stage sheen, he spoke of his patriotism, as though the war were his life duty and he could think of nothing else but defending his people. He was charismatic and good-looking, and had a beguiling wide, white smile that made him look less like a mass murderer and more like another famous person peddling a new brand of toothpaste. To his fans he aspired to be a protective father figure, not unlike God or Jesus. "I am a patriot," he said over and over again. "I am here to protect you from your enemies."

It was the time of the gangster. With the war heading into its second year, gangster life had consumed the city at every level. It wasn't that the entire population was evil. It was just that evil had gotten so deep into the core of the city that there was nothing to do but to be evil yourself or stand by and watch the evil go on, because doing anything about it was unhealthy.

In many ways, Belgrade became an extension of Arkan's mobbed-up life. On the weekends people lined up for stadium-sized outdoor fairs trafficking in black market food, cigarettes, guns, foreign currency, gasoline, and cars. Nightclubs and hotel bars swarmed with cellophane molls in napkin-sized minis and ice-pick heels. In 1990, there were eleven escort services, and by 1992 that number had climbed to ninety-three. Strip clubs popped up downtown on every block. Ponzi schemes and fake banks flourished like bathtub mold, and there were droves of international "businessmen" showing up at the Hyatt with suitcases full of cash.

The police? They had little control, and many, bankrupt as most of the population, engaged in side dealing with gangsters for quick cash—mostly for help with protection and smuggling rackets. To make matters worse, the justice system, like just about every other system in the country, was on the verge of crashing, as judges threatened to leave their posts over salaries that averaged thirty dollars a month.

Matters weren't helped by the abundance of guns. They flooded the streets. In 1990, there were ten places that sold weapons. By 1992, seventy-two gun shops had sprouted up. That same year the local Yugo car manufacturing facility stopped producing cars and started making .38 and .40 caliber pistols. Guns became so ubiquitous in town, such an integral part of the new criminal culture, that apartment blocks hired armed guards, and restaurants and cafés posted signs requesting that patrons "Please check in your weapons."

On the streets gangs battled furiously for city blocks, fighting over heroin-

and hash-trafficking routes, stolen cars, and protection rackets. Regularly, there were shootouts, car bombings, and exploding houses and businesses. Gunshot victims no longer showed up at the city's emergency center with a couple of bullet wounds to a leg or an arm. The rules had changed, and entire magazines were emptied into heads and hearts. Once a city of a handful of annual murders, Belgrade in 1992 counted seventy-two killings. Most of those cases went unsolved. In 1993, the murder figure doubled. "It's as though an invisible hand of death is sweeping through the city," lamented Belgrade's *Politika* daily newspaper.

Having left his post as police chief in 1992, Marko Nicovic just shook his head. There was nothing he could do anymore. He'd tried. Arkan and all the other crime stars, facilitated by Milosevic, had won. He'd seen this coming. "Since Yugoslavia was excluded from Interpol and other cooperative law bodies, it [Belgrade] became a big black zone, where crime flourished," he said. "Criminals came here from Italy, Albania, Russia, and Turkey. Many of these people had been thrown out of their own countries."

Marko Lopusina, the Belgrade journalist, was equally disturbed. Wartime Belgrade, he said, "epitomized Chicago in the twenties and thirties, the economic crisis of Berlin in the thirties, the intelligence intrigues of Casablanca in the forties, and the cataclysmic hedonism of Vietnam in the sixties."

When Arkan wasn't doing television or on the front lines, he cruised the city streets in a Pajero jeep, the war truck of choice. The white suits were back. He favored big lapels and colorful ties and aviator glasses that were black enough so you couldn't tell what his eyes were doing. He spent time luxuriating at the Hyatt, considered the gangster hangout. The hotel had the city's top restaurants, a high-end spa, and a swimming pool, and the lobby always seemed to be filled with guys wearing too much gold accompanied by slinky, barely dressed blondes on their pumped-up arms. Sometimes he traveled with female bodyguards who looked like centerfolds for right-wing gun magazines—dressed in shrink-wrap black dresses and stiletto heels with heavy guns slung over their hammer-hard shoulders.

At one point it seemed like every young gangster wanted to be Arkan. Everyone knew about his bank robberies, his covert executions, and the great escapes. They knew about his life on the front lines, a place where few of them went, and looked up to him for it. They could recite his stories like passages from the Old Testament, just like they did years later to me. Do you know that story about Arkan in San Remo with the casino and the speedboat? What about the story with the rose? Or the Stockholm court-room breakout? No one cared if they were true. Details didn't matter. "Arkan is who I look up to," said a twenty-year-old criminal named Bane Grebenarevic in a documentary called *See You in the Obituaries,* about the city's scary coming of age in crime. "He is the most organized, and that is especially hard in Serbia."

Produced by B92, the independent Belgrade television and radio station, the film featured numerous local gangsters talking candidly about their brutal escapades, and about how the work was getting more violent—three of the men would die before the crew finished filming.

Arkan only sat for the filmmakers for a minute, announcing to the camera, in reference to war crimes allegations, "I don't give a damn." One of the most interesting interviews in the film, though, was Goran Vukovic, a Serbian mobster known for murdering another crime boss, Ljuba Zemunac. Many murder attempts had been made on his life. Once an anti-tank missile had been fired at his car. In the film, Vukovic, who was an old friend of Arkan's, criticized the police for being overly violent, shooting when they didn't have to, and warned them to watch their backs. "They hit our families, we'll hit theirs," he said. But in 1994, Vukovic was dead, taken out with twenty-five bullets as he stumbled away from a dinner date.

It was easy to die in Belgrade, but none of the young criminals seemed to give death much thought. "Every single young kid wants to be a criminal, if only for five minutes," declared Bane, who had the neck of a football player and fists that could drive you into the sidewalk. "He would like to ride a fancy car, with a fancy girl, and [have] some gold around his neck." Oddly, to some extent, this was just like Arkan when he was a kid in Belgrade trying to find a way out of his own lost youth.

A poll taken in 1992, near the height of the Balkan War, reported that Arkan was the most desired man in Serbia. His life was *Scarface.* As a Belgrade magazine commented at the time: "In Arkan, we have a real character, one that is artistically rounded off, and worked out to the minutest detail. There is no work here for a writer: anything added or invented would not be able to compete with the documentary conviction of Raznatovic's biography."

Pop culture reflected the decadent times. Local turbo-folk music videos featured rap star–quality bling: gold jewelry, luxury cars, and megamansions. Young women wore knockoff Versace and lived it up in Belgrade's mirrored clubs and casinos, several owned by Arkan. Young men had military haircuts and tucked their two-hundred-dollar track jackets into their jeans. There were also the men known as "Dizelasi," because they wore Diesel brand shirts and jeans, all purchased with dollars from smuggled fuel.

Despite his popularity, Arkan still had to watch his back. Weekly, if not daily, there were strategic considerations: how must he beat back challenges from rivals while somehow ignoring them, so as not to give them power and legitimacy. There were rules. Everyone occupied a place in the gangland's economic hierarchy and owed fealty, as well as cash, to the person above him—in most cases Arkan—who in turned provided help or protection. Arkan, I was told, owned most of the protection rackets in town, including ones over major drug traffickers. The situation was like paying extra rent, with some monthly rents exceeding $1,000 ($100,000 to $250,000 supposedly for international drug dealers), a hard price to pay in wartime when money was short and inflation sky-high. The rules of the system were simple, even for an idiot: Pay or you suffer. For business owners that meant your shop was burned or robbed. For low-rung gangsters, it meant you ended up in a shallow grave in New Belgrade, under a bridge or in an overgrown lot.

At the time, rivalries and grievances among the city's gangs were, as in local politics or WWF wrestling, hard to keep up with. One gangster said that the city had so many criminals vying for power and riches that it made him think of "a small pond with too many crocodiles." Crocodiles, of course, killed.

There was one story that everyone mentioned when they talked about the crocodile pond. The story involved a twenty-one-year-old up-and-comer who apparently got in Arkan's way. Alexander "Knele" Knezevic had iron balls and wanted to take over the underworld, and everyone knew it.

In 1992, Knele presided over a burgeoning enterprise of drugs and stolen cars. Magazines featured him shirtless, his buff chest covered in gold, like a rap star. He drove a Porsche, wore Air Jordans, and caroused with a long line of ladies in miniskirts and fake breasts. For a young kid, he had ambitions, but he started stepping on big toes. Not only on Arkan's but on those of other crime kings, too. Knele became an example for those who didn't understand Belgrade's rules of respecting the guy above you on the crime ladder. In the fall of 1992, hotel employees at the Hyatt walked into his suite and found a corpse. Knele had taken two bullets to the skull and three to the body. Who killed him, no one knew for sure, but chatter on the street suggested Arkan.

The longer the war went on, the longer the people suffered, and the deadlier the gang wars became. Bane, by the end of the documentary, began to understand this fact. "Everybody sees only the bright side of it," he said. "Nobody sees the ugly side. When a young guy is driven to an early grave or goes to prison or becomes crippled—they never see that. It is pressure that gets you. When you have to watch your back around-the-clock, and mind where you sleep, who you eat out with, whether you parked your car in the right place—the pressure is huge."

No one would begin to understand this more acutely than Arkan.

23

MAN OF THE PEOPLE

1

Civilization seemed to pause for a moment in the drafty auditorium in Obilic, a grimy industrial town in the southern Serbian province of Kosovo, where smokestacks were about the only thing that poked through the depressing winter ceiling. Schoolteachers, businessmen, children, unemployed—they all took a break from their days and watched as a man in a neat, black, double-breasted suit and a dozen or so armed men swept through the entrance and approached the front.

Then the chanting began, "Arkan. Arkan. Arkan." These were the voices of several thousand people. It was mid-December in 1992 and freezing cold, even inside the auditorium. Stopping in front of the crowd, Arkan absorbed the whole scene. A gold, diamond-encrusted Rolex peeked out from under his shirt cuff and caught the lights. Around him stood men in black with angular jaws, automatic weapons dangling off shoulders, their hands lethal. The men scanned the gray crowd, some of them dirtied from mining, some of them muted and scarred from war, most hungry and exhausted and desperate from the sanctions and the very punched-up and dazed world around them. The bodyguards especially kept their eyes fixed on the doors, watching for anything suspicious.

When the chants diminished, Arkan leaned toward the crowd, as if he were going to take them all up in his arms, a minister and his flock. In the past a scene like this was just a prelude to men being snatched away from women and children, followed by gunshots or bats t-balling skulls. Not today. Kids were tossed up on fathers' shoulders, elevated into the swirling mass to catch sight of the man and hear his words.

The man. The mobster. The warlord. His voice was level but slightly high-pitched, which must have been a surprise to anyone expecting to hear the roar of a tiger. He spoke about the war, Orthodox Christianity, Serb togetherness, and the future. He didn't waste any time getting to his point. "I cannot promise you new telephone lines," he said to them. "I cannot promise you new highways, but I pledge to defend you with the same fanaticism that I've used so far in defending the Serbian people."

December 1992 was a month to remember. Arkan was running for parliament in Kosovo in the direct Serbian elections. It seemed so far-fetched. Even saying it was more than a little odd. Arkan, the political candidate. Many times it made me wonder: What was he thinking? Why would he want to run for office? Wasn't it antithetical to everything that he'd done before then? Being in office would force him to work through ideas with other people and to try to arrive at a compromise. What did he know about compromise, and what point did that have in his life? Then again, something else occurred to me. Maybe there really was something to this decision, Parliament as the ultimate form of power. Whether or not he actually participated in legislating, he would be immune to prosecution by any international body. So as a parliamentary man, he would be allowed to go on doing whatever he pleased and say fuck you to the world, try to get me now.

His entry into politics got a lot of people scratching their heads both inside and outside of Serbia. As a Belgrade weekly commented not long after his decision to run, it was a scary development that clearly echoed the bizarreness of life at that time in the Balkans: "If someday someone decides to write the social history of Serbia, today's events and customs will be best described through the personality and career of Zeljko Raznatovic."

"None should be surprised if he is entrusted with the task of drawing up a new constitution one day," the article's author went on to say. "No one will be able to take care of our cause and protect it better than he will."

It was a joke—but still.

2

Kosovo was a dreary place that God seemed to have deserted long ago, though it was still home to many of Serbia's most sacred monasteries. Poverty was as prevalent as the decrepit streets and buildings. Some houses didn't have windows. Many didn't have regular heat. International sanctions meant that people barely ate a meal a day. Standing in front of the three thousand or so Serbs in Obilic that day in 1992, with his fresh suit, perfectly combed hair, and shiny black shoes—he was visibly different. Given that he wasn't even from the region, it was reasonable to think they'd ask what this interloper thought he could do for them, but they didn't. Not because they weren't interested, but because they already knew who he was and what he had to offer.

It wasn't that Arkan was a convincing politician. He didn't offer any discernible vision for change, or even pretend to have the answers, but he was a practical politician. Instead of balancing budgets or health care or tax cuts, he offered protection to the local Serbs, who lived in a tense land dominated by a population that was 90 percent ethnic Albanian. I am here to save you from them, he said. Traveling in a convoy of a half-dozen Mitsubishi Pajero jeeps, he dispensed the same message all over Kosovo, standing up in front of thousands in sports stadiums and school auditoriums. No one will help you but me, he told them.

It wasn't a good time in Kosovo. In June, the province had attempted to declare their own state, and since then things had grown noticeably combustible between the Serbs and Albanians. Local Serbs knew about Arkan's war adventures. They called him patriot and savior. When he spoke, they listened. "We will create a super-Serbian police force to defend the rights of the Serbian people," Arkan told them. "We will create a state ruled by law where the Serbs will rule."

The words were vaguely familiar. Serbs will rule, and no one else. This is our land. We are the cops. It sounded just like Croatia. It sounded like Bosnia. Which was exactly what the local Serbs hoped for, and why the Albanians worried. For the Albanians, seeing Arkan's convoy of armored jeeps coming into town and tearing across a landscape of agriculture and industry, must have been a lot like watching the approach of Mr. Death—and not being able to do a damn thing about it.

The Albanians held meetings. Some armed themselves, a precursor to the Kosovo Liberation Army. They saw the Serbian warlord's nationalistic posters. Heard his threats on the radio and in the newspapers, about how

Kosovo was the "cradle of the [Serb] nation," and a "holy land," their Jerusalem. They heard him when he promised Serbs that "Albanians who do not obey the Serbian law, who have their reserve homeland in Albania, can leave and never return." They wondered, what does that mean? Never return? Was war around the corner?

Arkan said he wasn't planning anything violent. He was just a politician. Why wouldn't they believe that? "I am a Serb who cares about his country," he told his minions. Milosevic, waving the Socialist Party banner, was also running for reelection as president of Serbia. Although there was competition for his job, including the antinationalist challenger Milan Panic, a Serbian-American businessman, Milosevic couldn't be bothered. As far as he was concerned, competition was no more than a fly on the shoulder, just flick it off, smash it with your fist, or don't even pay attention to it, because eventually it will fly away.

It was a totally warped election. Arkan couldn't win, could he? The odds were against him. How could he triumph in a region where 90 percent of the population hated his guts? Others, however, knew different, knew of Arkan's magical ways. "Ah, Arkan," said Pavle Ivic, a prominent nationalist Serb academic. "He's a flower of the bad weather. A criminal, but an extremely skillful man. And very powerful. He has all these other skillful people with weapons. We have terrible inflation, unheard-of poverty, and so many weapons. It's a bit chaotic."

When polls opened on December 20, 1992, the Albanians decided to boycott the election; they didn't even show up, no doubt figuring that the polls would be rigged by Milosevic's state security apparatus anyway. Though some 90 percent of the two million people living in Kosovo stayed home, 17,352 of the region's Serbs cast their ballots for Arkan. That was all it took. Arkan won, as did Milosevic. It was one of history's saddest victories. That night the former bank robber and now war crimes suspect was handed a place in Serbia's 250-seat Parliament, and life there suddenly became a bit more unpredictable.

3

The Parliament building looms over downtown Belgrade. An old, stately edifice, it gives the impression of a headquarters for superheroes, featuring several prominent domes, dozens of tall, arched windows, and two giant leaping black horses that guard the sweeping entrance steps. History, in fact, has proven it to be a solid building, having survived the Luftwaffe saturation bombing of Belgrade during World War II, which killed more than seventeen thousand people and leveled several thousand buildings, including the national library.

When Arkan climbed the steps for the first time after his election, he actually seemed a little unsure of himself. Bratislav Grubacic, editor of Belgrade's VIP news services, remembered his inaugural press conference. The first question sailed in from a woman who wanted to know about the embattled economy. Inflation had grown to 10,000 percent, and more than half of the Serbian population was unemployed, with the desperate queued up daily in the freezing streets waiting for rations of flour and sugar that wouldn't adequately feed their families. What was he doing about it? Did he have any plans?

Vaguely baffled, or maybe just perturbed—what right did this journalist have to ask him questions anyway?—he stared back at the woman. After a moment of silent consideration, he stepped away from the podium and without saying a word exited the room. End of press conference. "Later his people claimed he had a last-minute appointment," said Grubacic. "But we knew he was terrified of being up there. That's probably why he didn't drink. He had complicated nerves. If he drank, he'd probably kill you after a couple."

As a politician, Arkan became known for being unpredictable. Sometimes he walked out in the middle of official Assembly speeches. Politeness did not seem to interest him. I heard a story from Nesa Pavolovic, one of Arkan's personal attorneys, about how one day Arkan stood up and interrupted a colleague's address to Parliament, after deciding that the man had been talking too long about a government program. "What's with this old guy?" Arkan asked, shaking his head. "He doesn't even talk in the same language. He's so boring." After the session, Pavolovic told me, a couple of the politicians tried to take him aside and explain that what he'd done was inappropriate. "But he didn't care," said Pavolovic. "He laughed at them."

During his time in Parliament, Arkan's only discernible agenda seemed to be the subjugation of non-Serbs and the perpetuation of Milosevic's Greater Serbia project. In his own speeches to Parliament and in public, he spewed ethnic hatred and made threatening remarks about Croatia and Bosnia. He called himself a mouthpiece of the divine ("When I tell you, it is as if God told you") and promised other ethnic groups that they would not sleep as long as he was in power ("To Croats, I'll fuck their Ustashi mothers"). To those who asked what kind of politician spoke this way, he offered, "I have not finished college. I'm a caterer. My college is the city's tar."

In January 1993, the war was back on Arkan's agenda. He slipped out of his designer suit and back into his combat boots and led his Tigers to fight in Ravni Kotari, on Croatia's Adriatic coast—a direct violation of the peace accords. The land was important. It would extend Greater Serbia to the ocean, and it was also important to his black market empire. Other Serb volunteers joined the battle; it was a short one. After a couple of weeks, the Serbs won, and by February Arkan was back in Belgrade.

Yet the war and his investment in it were never completely out of his mind. There was still fighting in Bosnia, though it mostly came in fits and starts now, with the Serbs in control of 70 percent of the territory. When his Tigers weren't fighting, he employed them in his businesses in Belgrade and Erdut. In addition to his black market dealings, he at that time owned several casinos, money exchanges, a detective agency, and a protection service. Like Arkan, his soldiers were untouchable around Belgrade. All they had to do to get out of trouble was flash their Serbian Volunteer Guard badges. Most of the soldiers told me that it was better than a diplomat's ID; it even kept police from inspecting their cars. "We were celebrities," said the Tiger who called himself Mr. X.

Even as a leader of Parliament, bodies continued to fall around him. That winter there was a shootout at his sweetshop involving the Tigers. Apparently, one Tiger soldier shot another, who nearly died. No conviction, of course. Soon after, one of Arkan's adversaries—a man named Isa Les, aka Dzamba, or Jumbo Jet—went missing. As the story goes, Jumbo Jet arrived one night at Arkan's casino in a downtown high-rise, wanting to talk about money owed to him, but Arkan wasn't there. Threats were made, then the Tiger named Vule—the soldier who had bullied Trax— stepped up and escorted Jumbo Jet out of the building. Days passed before Jumbo's car was discovered in a desolate street in New Belgrade. Jumbo, however, was never seen again, though rumors hinted that his body was buried in Erdut.

Months passed like this, where Arkan traveled from the halls of Parliament to the underworld to the war zone and back as if it were the most natural thing in the world. The way he so deftly straddled such divergent worlds seemed to be a sick trope for how very screwed up and broken the country had become. Sometimes Arkan even joked about the crazy situation himself. One night, as *The New York Times* reported, he appeared on a television talk show and presented the hostess with a tennis racket. "I heard you have lots of rackets," said the hostess, referring to the fact that most businesses in Belgrade paid him a protection fee. "I see you have one to spare." One of her funniest jokes, however, involved Mujo and Haso, two recurring characters in a Muslim joke at the time. In front of Arkan and the television audience, the comedian told Arkan the "final" story of Mujo and Haso. "Mujo and Haso go into the woods and they meet Arkan," she said. "End of joke."

4

Dr. Vojislav Šešelj was a pudgy, middle-aged man with a violent streak. He wore thick-framed glasses often seen in 1970s pornography and unfashionable suits. If he had resided in Florida, he might have been mistaken for a traveling vacuum-cleaner salesman. In Serbia, however, Šešelj, who had a doctorate in political science and a soft spot for automatic weapons, was the chairman of the ultranationalist Serbian Radical Party and leader of the White Eagles and Chetniks, two Serb paramilitary gangs that sometimes operated with the Tigers.

In 1991, Arkan and Šešelj were in Vukovar, where their troops did battle and probably executed and tortured hundreds of civilians. In 1992, Šešelj's men were killing in Bosnia, and, like Arkan, the United States secretary of state had named Šešelj a war criminal. That same year Milosevic backed Šešelj's political ambitions and helped get him elected to Parliament, but in 1993, Šešelj wanted the top spot. The only way to do that was to knock out Milosevic and Arkan.

When rumors began circulating in the fall that Milosevic was inching toward a peace agreement with Bosnia, Šešelj, whose ultranationalist party held the second-largest bloc of voters in the Serbian Parliament, made his move and called for a vote of no confidence. Seeing betrayal, Milosevic ordered the arrest of some of the White Eagles and Chetniks on charges of rape and murder. Milosevic then hit the political restart button—he dissolved Parliament and called for snap elections in December. That's when it got messy for Arkan. Suddenly, he had lost his seat and had to go back on the campaign trail. This time Šešelj wasn't going to make it easy.

When the news of his lost seat spread, Arkan must have thought back to a Red Star game a couple of years earlier, when he almost killed Šešelj. The war hadn't happened yet. Šešelj was just a burgeoning politician, and he wanted to enter the stadium like all the other fans, but Arkan denied him access. When Šešelj approached him after the game, Arkan reportedly laughed and asked, "Do you know how many people I've killed for the state?" It should have been over then, but Šešelj was a fighter. "No, I don't," he replied to Arkan. "I haven't killed anyone, but I'll start with you. I'll strangle you with my bare hands."

That's exactly what Šešelj was about to do.

5

Arkan, however, wasn't going to take anything lying down. In the fall of 1993 the warlord flung two thunderbolts that rocked Serbia: He launched Serbian Unity, his own ultranationalist political party, and then announced that it was running candidates for all 250 seats in Parliament. Not 5. Not 100. All of them. The decision left Serbs a little confused, until a theory emerged, which was that Arkan aimed to prove to the country that he was the Man. On November 23, he and his armed motorcade of fifteen cars and trucks kicked off the campaign in downtown Pancevo, a gritty industrial suburb not far from Belgrade. Arkan, dressed in a double-breasted black suit, strolled into a basketball stadium and, with visible emotion, told several thousand supporters, "We have a Serbian Dream."

He invested millions of dollars into his campaign dream—millions more than any other candidate. The jeeps were back, blazing the countryside, honking their horns, and showing up at schools and sports complexes. The campaign was designed to be grandiose, like campaigns in America. To his motorcade he added a press bus and two political headquarters— one in Belgrade and one in Pristina at the Grand Hotel, where he owned a casino. Posters of his smiling mug popped up all over the place, in store windows, on street lamps, on city buses. A slew of television commercials were launched, like a nuclear attack. In one he rhapsodized, "We want one beautiful, peaceful land called the United States of Serbia."

His campaign became a spectacle, something to be seen. It wasn't just him and the armed men anymore. He traveled with television personalities, movie stars, and professional athletes. He invited turbo folk singers along and turned his rallies into concerts. The concerts were huge, attracting thousands, many of them young people. Everyone was crazy about turbo folk. The music had replaced rock and roll during the war. A cheesy blend of Middle Eastern music and trumped-up techno rhythms, turbo stars—mainly young, curvy women in skimpy outfits—belted out lyrics about storybook love affairs and struggling country people. One of the biggest stars at his rallies was a slinky twenty-year-old named Ceca—the soon-to-be Madonna of the Balkans and Arkan's future wife.

Questions about Arkan's motives loomed over his spectacular charge. What was the point, really? Was he doing all of this to help Milosevic drain votes from Šešelj? Did Milosevic put him up to this? The questions irritated him. He was no one's puppet. He did what he liked. And what he liked was Serbian unity. "I respect the president," he told people. "Just as I will respect the next one." Milosevic, he added, merely "awoke" him to the job.

At one point there was speculation that Arkan would actually pick up at least thirty seats, and some journalists and political insiders even wondered if they were seeing the preview of a presidential bid.

Then the mudslinging began. It had to come, and it came in force. The accusations were worse than any witnessed in American politics. Šešelj described Milosevic as a war criminal, and called Arkan "the main criminal." In newspaper and television interviews, the pudgy professor linked Arkan publicly to state security operations in Croatia and Bosnia, and implicated him in civilian killings, as well as in the theft of truckloads of property. Šešelj called Arkan a thief, not a patriot. Same with Milosevic. "They have taken an enormous amount of money to Cyprus and to other foreign banks," Šešelj told a local television station. "Several billion dollars were taken from the country." Another time, he said to Arkan, "I bet you've put a black sock on your face more often than your foot."

Arkan fought back. He called the professor a liar. He said that Šešelj was the war criminal. Not him. "You will hear a thousand stories about me," Arkan advised reporters at one of his rallies, minutes before the pop stars danced across the stage in their cleavage-baring tops. "It's up to you whether you believe them or not."

Of course, they were all liars and they were all guilty. That didn't matter. This was Serbia. The sick thing was—the fight could have been even dirtier. What about the pig farms? The crosses carved into foreheads? The sexual assault chambers? Šešelj, who had once said (jokingly, he later claimed) that he would gouge out Croatian eyes with rusty forks and spoons, told the press he would "gladly" appear in front of any war crimes tribunal because he had done nothing wrong, unlike the others. (He would later be sent to The Hague.) Arkan was no less defiant. "I don't know if there is a warrant for me," he told the men and women on his press bus one day. "I know they are hounding me for war crimes." He explained to them that, unlike other people he knew, he was a defender of Serbian unity, and paused for a moment before adding, "I should ask them to go to Nagasaki, Hiroshima, Vietnam, and Angola. These were places where war crimes were committed. I committed no war crimes. We were defending our homes and families."

Arkan, however, did make some glaring oversights in his political battle, something he never did when bullets were flying. For instance, one newspaper couldn't understand why a man being accused of looting was still talking about his money and wearing expensive clothes and jewelry. "The people who conducted Arkan's campaign forgot to advise him to take off his gold Rolex," the magazine *Vreme* wrote. It looked especially bad when he went on TV and bragged to the sanction-starved nation about the two floors he planned to build atop his already large mansion. To add insult to injury, Šešelj asked him if it's true that he was the richest man in Serbia, and Arkan laughed. "I hope so," he replied. Of course, the response was supposed to make him sound more important than Šešelj, more accomplished, but it just seemed arrogant.

Arkan plastered new posters on the streets. "Our program is one in which mothers will have everything," one read. "We will give everything to officers and soldiers; we will have everything: milk, bread—cake, even." The rallies continued, and crowds of young people who wanted to be Arkan continued to mob them. "What do I love about Arkan?" one nine-year-old told an Associated Press reporter. "He is beautiful."

Beauty didn't matter in the end. When election day arrived on December 19, 1993, Arkan was definitively shut out. His Serbian Unity Party received less than forty-one thousand of the several million votes cast, picking up no seats. Arkan lost not only his seat in Parliament but also the parliamentary immunity that went with it. Meanwhile, Milosevic kept his power and Šešelj, though he didn't make any gains over Milosevic, didn't lose a whole lot. In the end, it was hard not to wonder if both men had played Arkan. Was it all just theater created by the president to give Šešelj a chance to appear as though his party was something other than a creation of state security, while at the same time reminding Šešelj who was in charge?

Of course, there was a great deal of talk of cheating, of forged ballots, of miscounting, of police intervention—and all were probably factors. As a newspaper in Belgrade noted at the time, that year the political process suffered "a general falling apart of the system, camouflage, special actions, police infiltration, the interference of the army, propaganda smoke screens, warmongering, slander, the instigating of crime, changing convictions, mass hypnosis, and the loss of common sense as a guiding light."

In all of this there was undeniable truth. Arkan had been beaten. No amount of public relations, bullying, or free turbo folk concerts had been able to save him. "The people came to your rallies to hear the music, not you," his wife, Natalia, was heard saying. The very same people Arkan thought he was defending had shunned him. Even the Serbs in Kosovo had not voted for him—what had he done for them so far? The Albanians were still around. Not only did he invite the Albanians into his new casino in Pristina, but word on the street was that he'd used his Parliament position to extend his black market operations into the region.

Arkan blamed Šešelj for his underwhelming poll numbers, and there was, indeed, some truth to this. The professor's ultranationalist party had siphoned votes from his campaign, but that's not what most irked Arkan. He felt Šešelj's personal attacks—all lies!—had done him the greatest damage, had given the voters a false image, and had turned them against him.

If he weren't such a visible figure, Arkan probably would have found a way for the professor to disappear. Dig a hole for him in Erdut. Right next to Jumbo Jet. Or boot his feet in concrete and sink him in the Danube.

Instead, Arkan sued him. It seemed like a joke. Maybe he was trying to look legitimate. Like he'd really suffered personal injury. He was an emotional man. The decision would garner headlines. His political party, however, would go on, even after he died. Later, Arkan would even consider a run for president. With the election over and his seat gone, there were other things to get back to: like that pop star Ceca. She was a real looker.

24

POP STAR

1

Svetlana "Ceca" Velickovic always knew she wanted to be famous. Born in 1973, she grew up poor in the small Serbian southern town of Zi-toradje, not far from the Romanian border, where streets are dirt and farmers still plow fields with horses. Her father was a grocer and her mother taught at the local elementary school. She started singing at five, and by ten she was touring all over the Balkans. There was no *Star Search* or Mouse-keeters, so Ceca performed at weddings, hotels, and *kafanas,* the family-styled restaurants at the center of every town. At home she practiced in front of a mirror alongside her younger sister, Lidija. "I couldn't get away from the mirror," Ceca told me. "I loved to look at myself."

At fourteen, she recorded her first album, *The Nagging Flower*. It sold over a hundred thousand copies in the Balkans and established her as one of the rising stars of turbo folk. Mainly, her lyrics told the love stories of struggling rural people. "If I was American, I would definitely be singing country music," she said. "It's the same as Serbian folk—it speaks to the people."

As Ceca matured into her late teens, she made the delicate transition from teen idol to sex symbol. She traded in her mall hair and tacky outfits for tight tops and miniskirts. Onstage she mixed belly dancing with pole dancing and played sold-out concerts to expatriate communities in Germany and Austria. Newspapers chronicled her love life, and she enjoyed the attention. Her first boyfriend was a Red Star soccer player, but he was too soft and she dropped him. "I'm a girl who likes someone to fight with me," she told the press.

When she was twenty she bolted for Switzerland with a Muslim businessman, a decision that got headlines in her mostly Orthodox Christian world. Her mother was dumbfounded; she woke up every night crying for her lost daughter. Speculation emerged that Ceca had left to escape her domineering father, who had pushed her career and was now after her money—not unlike messed-up Hollywood families. Her father, however, disputed the accusations. "It's a lie that I took all of her money," he complained to a local newspaper. "The fact [that] there's a lot of money to be made in this business isn't our fault."

A year later she was dating gangsters in Belgrade, a city unraveling fast. One mobster boyfriend, Dejan Marjanovic, was murdered, some say by Arkan's men. The incident only made Ceca bigger. "She became a major icon fast," said Eric Gordy, a sociology professor at Clark University and author of *The Culture of Power in Serbia*. "For many, especially rural people, she was the symbol of a girl living out a dream—an innocent girl from the country making it big."

Ceca's career continued to expand in the 1990s, as Milosevic's war swallowed the country and gangsters became kings. Her records sold in the hundreds of thousands. Turbo folk replaced the countercultural rock and roll of the 1970s and 1980s and became the kitschy soundtrack of nationalism and the underworld, with its stars appearing on Milosevic-backed Pink TV and Palma TV and at swish nightclubs like Folkoteka. The music reveled in Serbia's new elite criminals. Videos narrated the gangsters' outsize life—buxom women in fancy clothes, fast cars, gold, and sprawling mansions. Brand names were sacred bywords—Versace, Rolex, Diesel, Adidas, and Mercedes. Lyrics celebrated hedonism and exhibited a cavalier, who-gives-a-fuck attitude about Serbia's international isolation. There was one song titled "200 Miles per Hour" about driving fast cars, and another about a couple making love work at all costs. Lyrics in the songs at the time went like this, "Coca-Cola, Marlboro, Suzuki/Discotheques, guitars, and bouzouki," one of the more famous songs went, "Nobody has it better than us."

Of all the turbo-folk stars, Ceca emerged as queen. She was tall and curvy with long brown hair. She sold the most records (nineteen million albums during the 1990s), earned the most money, and had the slickest,

most expensive MTV-styled videos. During the war she sang, "It was probably time for Arkan to start running. If you were wounded, I'd give you my
blood." Serbs saw her on billboards, posing in catsuits in front of expensive
cars and in commercials for perfume. There was always talk around town
about how Madonna was thinking about producing a movie about her life,
a rumor that never went anywhere.

Ceca met Arkan for the first time on October 11, 1993, in Erdut. Arkan
had asked her to help him celebrate the Tigers' three-year anniversary—a
three-year spree of killing, looting, and torture. Getting a chance to see
Ceca up close, prancing around in her tight skirt and razor heels, was probably a lot like Jessica Simpson performing for the American troops in Iraq—
the Tigers freaked out.

At the end of the show, Arkan turned up. "He looked right into my eyes,"
Ceca recalled. "That was how it happened." She fell for him right then. "I
could tell he was a very strong man, and I liked strong men." Later, he took
her to a quiet place and they talked. The world seemed to melt away. "We had
a serious conversation," said Ceca. "He even studied my hands, pulled up my
sleeves to make sure there were no needle marks."

Of course, the leggy pop star was far from the first woman to be seduced
by his power; at that point, Arkan was on his way out of his second marriage,
with a handful of rumored mistresses. Still, Ceca was unworried. "He wasn't
aware that we were together from the moment we met," she said. "I knew I
needed to have him, at whatever cost."

2

The relationship moved lightning fast. Despite his marriage, the couple began turning up in public together and appeared on national talk shows, including *Minimaks*. After his campaign for Parliament flopped, she performed
events for his Serbian Unity Party. In front of fans, she encouraged others to
come along for the ride. "You can be as happy as me," she cooed. "Just join
the Serbian Unity Party!"

As the couple grew closer, people warned her. They mentioned his past
life, the bank robbing, allegations of war crimes, and rumors of him beating
up his women. At one point her father reportedly tried to step in. She pursued him anyway, playing naive mob girlfriend. "We didn't talk about business," she'd tell me later.

Arkan (in the light jacket) and Ceca right before Ceca's concert at Hala Pionir sports arena/concert hall in downtown Belgrade. It's October 28, 1995, the war is over, Arkan is just back from Bosnia, and it's time for him to start thinking about his next move.

What about Europe, did you talk about that? "Like everyone else, I read things in the paper, but nothing more."

Some suspected that Ceca had the potential to be just as dangerous as her new man; she just needed someone to unleash that side of her. "She is sweet and charming in public," said Ivana Kronja, a Belgrade media critic. "She has the skin of a lamb, but you don't know what's underneath."

Meanwhile, Arkan and his wife, Natalia, continued to drift apart. The war had strained things, and the death of her brother still loomed over her. "Natalia was the love of his life," Dinic, the publisher of *Svedok*, told me. "He was crazy about her. But then Ceca came along. He fell in love with her, too, and he told me he couldn't love two women. So he took Ceca. It made his career."

Arkan and Natalia finally divorced in 1994, and shortly afterward Natalia fled for Greece with the kids. Arkan reportedly bought her a house in Athens and shipped all of her belongings south.

The first night Arkan and Ceca spent in the warlord's mansion was the beginning of a new life. "The house was totally empty," Arkan recalled in Marko Lopusina's book *Commander Arkan*. "Ceca and I sat on the floor."

3

Not long after Natalia's departure, Arkan and Ceca appeared on state-controlled television and announced that they were in love and would marry. They would go to the station again when their first child was born. It was a huge deal. As one commentator put it, "The relationship between Arkan and Ceca is more than just an ordinary love affair between two mortals." Tabloids universally predicted "the wedding of the century."

They married on February 19, 1995, a year and a half after their first encounter. She was twenty-two and he was forty-three. Spanning an entire day, costing around a quarter of a million 1995 U.S. dollars and featuring automatic weapons, shiny SUVs, dozens of luxury cars, numerous costume changes, and bags of cash and gold, the affair resembled a twisted Hollywood take on an antique ritual—Quentin Tarantino doing *Romeo and Juliet*.

It began on a gray dawn, a Sunday, when Arkan climbed into his black armored Panjero jeep and led a fifty-car convoy south to Ceca's hometown of Zitoradje. Two hours later the vehicles entered the small village, and Arkan's men stuck their guns out the window and announced their arrival by blasting hundreds of rounds into the air as crowds pushed into the roads to get a look.

Arkan emerged from his jeep, gripping a pistol in one hand and a Heckler & Koch machine gun in the other. He wore a traditional Montenegrin costume, which included dark baggy balloon pants, a black cape embroidered with gold, a pillbox cap, and a thick gold cross the size of Flavor Flav's clock.

He fired the pistol and then emptied his Heckler and Koch. Finally, he was directed to an apple dangling off a fishing rod–like pole on the roof of Ceca's family's three-story house. As a surging crowd stood by, some snapping pictures, others firing guns, he took a rifle and, after six missed shots, blasted it into the sky. He was now in.

Ceca's mother and father greeted Arkan on the street, and the warlord handed over a suitcase of cash, a couple of gold watches (one directly from the wrist of Arkan's friend), some rings, and a bag of gold. In Arkan's world, you still paid for your wife—or maybe he was just doing the whole thing for the video cameras. Two hours later the group was off again. They climbed into their vehicles, firing guns and shouting, Ceca now in tow, and headed back to Belgrade for a ceremony at the Holy Archangel Gabriel Church. In their wake they left over one thousand spent cartridges. Although no one had been injured or killed by the gunfire, one stray bullet had sliced through the main power line, leaving the village without electricity for a day.

At the Holy Archangel Gabriel church Arkan quickly changed into a World War I general's uniform and Ceca slipped into a silk wedding dress, described by one local newspaper as "cocaine white," and inspired by *Gone with the Wind*. Beforehand there was some dispute about who would conduct the ceremony. Two bishops were scheduled, but Serbian Orthodox Church patriarch Pavle reportedly forbade them at the last second. Pavle objected to the twenty-one-year age discrepancy between the bride and groom, and the fact that Arkan had already been wedded twice. In their place a local priest stepped in. He placed crowns on the heads of Arkan and Ceca while they held tall white candles, and went through the vows.

Milosevic embraced the marriage, as he'd tacitly embraced the rise of Arkan. The day was videotaped and broadcast on state television, just like the lavish nuptials of Prince Charles and Princess Diana, and the day was pronounced good. Tens of thousands either tuned in at home or showed up on the streets and, for a moment, some Serbs glimpsed a future that was not dreary or miserable. Desperate to forget about the twisted war that was gouging out the country's soul and emptying bank accounts, the fairy-tale romance of Arkan and Ceca was a welcome diversion; it was a lot like everyone receiving a free pass to Disneyland for the day or, better, an intravenous hookup to a morphine tube.

The reception was held at the ritzy Intercontinental Hotel, which was encircled by two hundred of Arkan's well-armed private army. Seven hundred guests arrived, including some of Serbia's state security officials and news crews from the BBC, Reuters, and Associated Press (CNN allegedly was banned). There were toasts. Lots of them. Arkan sported a black tuxedo and sipped sparkling apple juice. Ceca, in a glittering white gown with the shoulders cut out, sang a few numbers. Later, a video of the affair was made, and over one hundred thousand copies were sold—today you can find it on eBay.

The partying lasted past midnight. By the end, Serbia had witnessed the equivalent of a coronation. An unofficial royal family had now emerged. It was very good news for Milosevic. Having a celebrity couple would help distract the population from his apocalyptic vision and even made some wonder: Had the Serb president secretly masterminded this whole affair, from Arkan's rise to his marriage? The new couple benefited most, of course. While Arkan gained celebrity and glamour in the deal, Ceca got guns and money. Overnight they became one of the richest and most dangerous couples in the nation. Some newspapers began referring to them as Beauty and the Beast. When *The Sopranos* debuted on HBO, they became the Sopranos of Serbia.

25

WAR'S OVER

1

The newlyweds talked about a honeymoon somewhere warm and far away: maybe Brazil or maybe Mexico. Several weeks after the wedding, however, Croatia opened a counteroffensive against Serbia and began retaking territory. Sitting in his Belgrade mansion with his wife, he watched in disbelief as news clips showed the Croatian army storming land that he and his Tigers had torched, raped, and pillaged four years earlier. What the hell? It looked like they had new weapons and bigger troop numbers. What was going on? Was he dreaming? He made a face, shook his head, then exploded. "I won't let them do this to my people," he shouted at Ceca. "I must go back to war."

Ceca tried to dissuade him. "You're married to me now," she said. They had talked about having kids right away. He promised her nine. "We're building a family," she said. "Remember?"

He did remember—but he didn't stay. His mind was already racing ahead, imagining, plotting battlefield moves, and what to do next. Ceca could tell, which worried her. Before she could argue he disappeared upstairs to the bedroom.

After fifteen minutes or so she went to find him, and he was in full camouflage and a red beret. They wouldn't be going on a honeymoon—not now. He made a phone call and, less than an hour later, a gaggle of armed men in fatigues were assembled across the street at the Red Star stadium. The Tigers were back.

2

The war would not end quietly or without a bloodbath. In January, former U.S. president Jimmy Carter had negotiated a peace deal between Bosnian Serbs and Muslims, but several months later the deal was shot. In the void, the Croatian army, which had been armed and trained by U.S. forces over the previous year or so, began an effective and violent retaking of their homeland in western Slavonia. In addition, the Croats joined up with the Bosnian Army, which had lately been armed by several Middle Eastern countries, and launched a second strong offensive against the Serbs in Bosnia. The feeling seemed to be that the Serbs now had to pay for their war.

Although the joint Croat and Bosnian forces came on strong, the Serbs hit back hard and the blood flowed. The Serbs began their counterstrike in Srebrenica, an old silver-mining town in eastern Bosnia. The city had a population of about forty thousand, but it was not just any other Bosnian city to be conquered. In 1993, the UN had designated Srebrenica a "safe area," along with five other Bosnian cities. Soldiers were forbidden to enter, and tens of thousands of Bosnian refugees, forced out of their homes with little else but the clothes on their backs, had flooded into the safe cities to wait out the carnage. Guarded by UN peacekeeping troops and protected by international law, the safe areas were meant to be exactly what they sounded like: safe. Safe from the war. Safe from the warlords. Safe from dying.

Nevertheless, on July 2, 1995, Srebrenica was flooded with Serb troops and the "safe area" was no longer safe. Arkan and his troops had arrived at the heels of General Ratko Mladic and his Bosnian Serb soldiers. Mladic, who had the neck of a horse and a permanent sneer, easily muscled his way through the UN's blue-helmet forces. At first, he promised the refugees safety. "Please be patient," he told them as the UN troops looked on. "Those who want to leave can leave. There is no need to be frightened." His men actually handed out chocolates to children, but when the empty buses started arriving, things got ominous.

It was just like before, a nightmare relived again and again. Men, women, and children were split up. Women and children were shipped north, the men were kept behind. Meanwhile, the Tigers began hunting for a Muslim warlord named Naser Oric and other Muslim "terrorists." Oric, the Serbs claimed, had been using the city as a base to attack and plunder nearby Serb-held towns, and he had to go. I wasn't long before a couple thousand men identified as terrorists and Oric fighters, were lined up, like a soccer team about to run suicide drills. All of this was in direct defiance of the international community, but that seemed to be the point. The Serbs were going to send a message to all their enemies, including those funding their enemies: No one can protect you, no one.

The killing began. More trucks and buses came: now for the Muslims. In side the vehicles, the "terrorists" were driven to *vukojebina,* those desolate places where the wolves fuck, and erased—tortured, executed, and then covered with fresh earth. The purging went on for about ten days. By the end, seven thousand men, women, and children from Srebenica were killed, making it one of the biggest massacres in modern history. Later the world court would rule it genocide.

News of the horror radiated across the world. Bill Clinton told his staff, "This can't continue. We have to seize control of this." He demanded that Milosevic end things, and sent in Richard Holbrooke, the United States special envoy for Yugoslavia, to sort it out. Holbrooke is a solidly built man with a bulldog demeanor. He insisted that the war end, but Milosevic, as before, said he had no control over Bosnian Serbs, including General Mladic and Bosnian Serb president Radovan Karadzic. The soldiers were acting independently of him. They were rogues, he claimed. What about Arkan? Holbrooke asked. His images were all over the newspapers and television.

Arkan? That crazy Serb? He was powerless over him, responded Milosevic. In fact, Arkan was so wild that he would probably kill him, the president, if he had the chance. "He's my sworn enemy," asserted Milosevic.

It was a laughable claim, all of it, and Holbrooke didn't believe him for a second. "I continually told Milosevic that Arkan was a major problem, and that his close associations with Milosevic were a direct challenge to Milosevic's international credibility," Holbrooke recalled to CNN after the war. "My arguments with Milosevic over Arkan were continuous. It agitated him. He didn't want to discuss it."

Still, what incentive did Milosevic really have to come out honestly and make peace in his world? Since Clinton had entered office the United States had issued the suicide man a bunch of hollow threats. The same went for the rest of the international powers—Britain, France, Germany, and Russia. It was a joke. When the international powers did intervene, their actions were pathetically ineffective. As in the spring of 1994, when Bosnian Serbs shelled another marketplace in Sarajevo, and sixty-eight civilians died. Pictures of the massacre turned up all over the media. Instead of bombing the Bosnian Serbs out of their tanks, Clinton simply instructed the army to move its heavy artillery twelve miles away from Sarajevo. Sure, the tanks rolled out, but instead of backing down, the Bosnian Serb soldiers rumbled into Gorazde, a Muslim "safe area," and began shelling there. When news of this trickery got out, Clinton backed a terrifically weak NATO bombing; jets exploded a Bosnian Serb tank and some tents but killed no one.

However, that was then. Little did Milosevic know those times of non-aggression were gone. After Srebenica, sentiment at the White House had shifted. In August the United States green-lighted a massive Croat-Muslim offensive in Serb-held Krajina. Dubbed Operation Storm, the joint army of 100,000 Croatian and Bosnian men, supported by 350 tanks, hundreds of heavy artillery pieces, 18 MiG "Fishbed" fighter jets, and 12 attack helicopters, hurled across the Serb-won territory recapturing stolen land. In several days of fighting, the Croatian and Muslim armies also decided to do some of their own ethnic cleansing. Two hundred thousand Serbs abandoned their homes, and tens of thousands were killed or went missing.

The offensive was a disaster for Milosevic, and sent Arkan and the rest of the Bosnian Serbs reeling backward. The war began to shift fast, and suddenly signs of internal cracking appeared among the Serb ranks. Newspapers chronicled soldier fatigue rippling through the trenches. There were rumors of a cease-fire. At one point Arkan clashed with General Mladic about strategy, and complained publicly that the Serbs were losing land because the army was just an unskilled bunch of drunks. "They are too stupid to stop an attack by Boy Scouts," he flared. If the Serbs were going to win this war, he seemed to suggest, he would have to go it on his own.

Although outwardly brash, Arkan himself seemed to suffer from some of his own late-war distractions. Once he confessed to a few men after a strategy meeting that he had Ceca on his mind. "I got a twenty-two-year-old wife at home waiting for me," he said. It was cause for concern. Some of his own soldiers couldn't help but wonder if they were with a different man. Was he thinking of the abandoned honeymoon? Was he considering a break away from this warrior life? As one Tiger said later, "I think Ceca made him soft. He didn't yell as much. He seemed to be in a haze." I heard the same complaint from Curly at Red Star's stadium. Ceca was getting in his way.

Yet, if there was ever a haze, it most surely lifted off him and other Serb fighters on August 30, 1995. After another Serb shell killed 38 people in downtown Sarajevo, NATO, supported by Clinton, struck back at the Bosnian Serb army with a gigantic bombing campaign. Stretching over two weeks, NATO unleashed a series of fierce air attacks—3,515 sorties against 338 targets. The bombing was so surprising and intense that it finally persuaded Milosevic and Karadzic to intiate talks about a way to end the war. Not Arkan. Incensed, he packed up a couple hundred troops (1,000 were mobilized in Erdut, according to his personal secretary), and pushed hard westward to stop the oncoming enemy.

By now there were thousands, if not tens of thousands, of Bosnian and Croatian soldiers on the battlefront, but he plowed on, as if a fire were burning inside. In quick succession, his men fought in Bosanki Novi, Prijedor, and Banja Luka. Behind Serb lines he mopped up remaining non-Serbs and made sure that local Serbs stayed put. By mid-September, he was heading full speed into Sanski Most, a death march some said. That city would become notable for two reasons: It would be one of the war's last battles, and Arkan would finally meet his ultimate nemesis.

3

Hamdu Abdic, the Muslim warlord, couldn't believe his luck. When the news came crackling over the radio waves that Arkan was in Sanski Most, he shook his big shaggy head and laughed. Hamdu's brigade had been part of the Croat and Bosnian armies' recent three-month surge across Bosnia. Now, helped out by Croat tanks and rockets, he and his hundred or so men were stomping over a northwestern swath of Bosnia, deep in the ragged mountains, where the fierce chill of autumn had long taken hold. He and his men were restless.

The intelligence about Arkan's arrival was an inspiration. Ever since the thirty-two-year-old Hamdu had climbed into camouflage, stuffed a hunting knife in his boot, and picked up an M72 machine gun three long years earlier, when this godawful war had shuddered to life, he'd become obsessed with killing the Serbian warlord and doing to him what Arkan had now done to thousands of his Muslim people. Although he and his soldiers were known as the Bosnian Army's 502 Brigade, Hamdu had dubbed them the Tigers. He also

owned a pet tiger, like Arkan, and people called him "Commander." The simil-
iarities all seemed like one big sick joke—naming your gang after the gang you
aimed to kill, and even getting yourself the same mascot—but this was Bosnia.

Hamdu the Tiger was tall and cadaverous, with a long, bronzed face,
deep dimples, and revolver-black hair. He bore an unusual likeness to a
young Herman Munster and, with a two-pack-a-day cigarette habit—not to
mention a soft spot for whiskey—his voice was gravely and his teeth were
stained yellow. Though he set out to kill Arkan, his Tigers spent most of the
conflict slugging it out in northwestern Bosnia, protecting Muslims and
evicting Croats and Serbs. Hamdu's Tigers were accused of torture, rape,
and murder. Though Hamdu would never admit to any of the allegations,
and would never be indicted by the International Criminal Tribunal ("We
were angels compared to the others," he said to me, with a Cheshire smile),
still, the rumors didn't seem too improbable, considering his history.

Before the war Hamdu seemed to be a sort of aspiring gangster in the

*Hamdu Abdic called his Bosnian Muslim group the Tigers. During the war, one of Hamdu's
goals, aside from beating the Serbs back, was to hunt down and kill Arkan. His men finally
clashed with the Serb Tigers in Sanski Most on October 11, 1995, but Arkan had already
fled.*

northern Bosnian village of Bihac. A small-time version of Arkan, he lorded over the tiny city. A black belt in karate, he carried a pistol, drove fast cars, and ran a "number of businesses." He had some influence over local politics and worked black market deals. "It was a frontier kind of world," he told me. "You had to fight to succeed."

His urge for riches and the fast life didn't subside during the war. War was a business opportunity, just as it was for a lot of other strong men with Donald Trump–sized visions. Hamdu allegedly profited handsomely from smuggled cigarettes, coffee, and gas. His name started getting around. "I know a lot of the Tiger," a Bosnian intelligence officer told me. "All I'll say is that he was a good soldier in the middle of the war, but at the end and after the war he became a criminal who committed a lot of criminal activities and got rich."

Much of the war money was apparently transferred into personal bank accounts, but some of it was funneled back into Hamdu's army. His men, like most of the Bosnian troops, were apocalyptic looking, ragged, and mismatched, like they'd stepped out of a garage sale or a dump. At first, crippled by the international arms embargo, his men fought with kitchen knives, bats, and hunting rifles—whatever they could get their hands on. Most of the time they wore no specific uniform and piloted windowless cars, rusting tanks, tractors, and even horses. When the Bosnian Muslims bought guns, they actually bought them from the Serb-controlled JNA, which didn't exactly make sense—buying guns from your enemy—but not much did. Hamdu had been shot three times. Showerless for weeks now, his body stank of sweat and cordite, his feet ached, and his side was in pain from a recent bullet wound. Despite his suffering, he told his men to get ready for the battle of their lives.

Soon Hamdu's Tigers were hunkered down about fifteen miles from Sanski Most, in tents and abandoned houses, locked in a shroud of mist. Additional men were called in for the job, and scouts were dispatched to get a look at what Arkan was doing in the city. The scouts slipped through the woods, along the River Sana, around roadblocks, sticking to the shadows. When they returned to Commander Hamdu, the news was as expected. There was torture going on; the city smelled like a charnel house; dead bodies littered the streets; there were men in masks all over the place, probably two hundred, maybe more. It was ugly, but Arkan was definitely there.

Hamdu prepared his men to strike out. By now there were almost one thousand other soldiers on the line waiting to attack, as well as Croat artillery. Hamdu would make his intial entry with only two hundred men. He wanted to move fast, and he wanted it to be his operation.

Shaking off a mean hangover from a night of drinking and hardly any sleep, he knew one thing for sure. This was the last time Arkan would get away with his crimes. He would be hunted down, like a wild boar, and killed. He had to be stopped.

It was October 10, the eve of the peace accords, when Hamdu headed in for his famous kill. The sun hadn't come up yet, the River Sana's fog lingered in the naked treetops, and the air was dead cold. A glittering frost clung to the ground and cracked under the tank treads and forward-stomping combat boots. After three years of missing each other, the two Tigers were about to do battle. Hamdu knew this.

4

When Arkan arrived in Sanski Most, he and his men commandeered the three-star Hotel Sanus, a white blocky building downtown, at a curve in the River Sana. He took the suite for himself and set up a jail and torture chamber in the building's dingy basement and a command post in the manager's office, where he organized the purge. Tanks were parked in the grass, along with mortar shells and armored personnel carriers. Machine guns were stacked in the lobby.

Sanski Most is a river city. In English, Sanski Most means bridge over the Sana River. Before the war sixty thousand people called the tranquil place of water and hills home, with an almost equal split between Serbs and Muslims. By mid-1992, most of those Muslims had been run out, but as the Croatian-Muslim army sprang back to life, some were returning, Serbs were starting to leave, and the city was rapidly showing signs of unrest.

Right upon Arkan's arrival, checkpoints rose up on major roads and at city entry points, and local Serbs were gathered up and forced into the Tigers gang. Working from lists, the Serbs entered Muslim houses. "They knew my name and that my husband was working in Germany," Razia Beharemovic recalled later to *The New York Times*. "They broke down my door, blindfolded me, grabbed my hair, and began to beat me with their fists. They asked for money and jewelry. They held my twenty-six-year-old niece and said they would kill her if I did not give them everything." Beharemovic gave them everything before she fled to the woods. "I took all my money and jewelry, which I had strapped around my waist, and handed it to them. One of the men with Arkan's troops was a Serbian neighbor."

Arkan's Tigers worked fast, expecting the Muslim army to show up at any minute. Dozens of Muslim men were transported back to Hotel Sanus, where they were interrogated and beaten and prepared for execution. One Muslim man, identified later at the war crimes tribunal as protected witness B-1047, remembered being captured and taken straight to Arkan. "Who are you?" the warlord asked him. Arkan was dressed in clean green fatigues and wore grenades on his chest. The man told him his name. "We have work for you," he said. "Go stand over by that wall and wait." What B-1047 didn't know was that he was waiting to be murdered.

As he stood against the wall, B-1047 saw other captives tied to trees (some were Serbs found drinking) while others were directed to unload weapons from arriving vans and buses, which B-1047 noted had Vukovar license plates. That night, B-1047 and thirty others—twenty-nine men and one woman—were jammed into a basement boiler room measuring roughly five square meters, with inadequate ventilation. It was lightless and hot, and there was not enough room to sit. Sometimes soldiers in black appeared and issued beatings.

After three days of standing in the room, two died, and then twelve of the prisoners, including B-1047, were tied up and loaded onto a bus. The bus transported them approximately two and half miles on roads alternating between asphalt and dirt and gravel until they reached an unfinished cinder-block building along the river. By that time, it was night. The pitch-black woods around the river were loud with unseen things. Two by two, the prisoners were led out of the bus, and minutes later shots rang out. When Arkan's men reached for B-1047, he begged for his life. "People," he pleaded, "can you *not* kill us somehow?"

B-1047 couldn't tell how many of the Tigers had come for the execution. He couldn't see if Arkan was there. It was too dark to see much, and it was hard to focus with the gunshots going off.

"You're lucky," one soldier finally replied. "You're lucky to be in Arkan's hands. Give us five thousand deutschmark each, get into the truck, and we'll drive you to your home." B-1047 didn't have the money, but even if he did, there was little chance that they'd let him live. With nothing left to say, the men led him into the concrete building. A bullet entered his left shoulder, another entered his left leg, and, as he fell to the ground, one sliced through his chin.

He was sure he was going to die, though somehow he remained conscious as the last executions were carried out. "I heard them order them to kneel," he testified at The Hague tribunal about the final murders. "One of them was begging, 'Don't, please,' and the other one started swearing at him and said, 'Kneel, Bre.' Then I heard a knife being taken out of the scabbard and then this soldier said, 'Zeljo, you can do the honors. You can do the best part of the job.' This young soldier of Arkan's (he was fifteen or sixteen) slit the throats of these two men. Then we could hear other people gurgling in that pile of human bodies."

Eventually, B-1047 heard the Tigers lumber out of the room, then the bus rumbling away. "I asked whether anybody was still alive. I put this question several times; however, nobody answered," B-1047 recalled. "Since my left arm was numb, I put my left hand on my belt, the belt on my trousers, and I somehow managed to get up. I got out of that room and set out toward the road. I thought I could not take this for very long. I thought I'd die very soon, so I wanted to be somewhere by the road so that someone could find me. From time to time, I couldn't see anything, and then I could see again. And at one point I felt very thirsty. So I started walking along the road, trying to find some water." B-1047 walked for miles through deep forest and mountains. Though he eventually escaped his killers, he would never forget them. Not only because of what they did to his mind, but because he now lives as an invalid.

B-1047 wasn't the last casualty. More prisoners, including the remaining ones in the boiler room, were loaded onto a bus and trucked away. The story was much the same, except this time the soldiers took them on a half-hour drive through the night to the foot of a hill below a church. The *Toronto Star* interviewed one survivor, a forty-five-year-old mechanic identified as H. On the bus, H. remembered, one woman was gang-raped as a radio played and the killers sang a Serb fight song, which went "Who's saying, who's lying (that) Serbia is small." The woman "did not make a great deal of noise, but the Serbs were screaming," said H. "None of us made a sound." H. recalled how the prisoners were later beaten with hammers or shot. H. was shot in the right leg but managed to scamper away. As he lay in a soggy ditch, it began to rain, and he heard the sounds of dying. "I could hear the weird noises from the bodies that were still dying." After a day of lying in the ditch, he escaped. Less than a year later, sixty-five bodies were exhumed from the church site. By the end of the Tigers' stay in Sanski Most, between two hundred and three hundred were slaughtered, ranging in age from fifteen to seventy-four.

The killing and looting stopped only when word trickled in by radio that the Croat-Muslim army was closing in on the city. There were rumors of opposing forces triple and quadruple the size of his Tigers. It would have been smart for Arkan to call in backup troops, but there was no one else to call. The war was ending. It was in the gun-blasted air. He would fight this battle on his own. He told his men to be ready.

5

The two Tiger clans clashed on October 11, 1995. The battle was vicious and intense, first in the woods surrounding the city, and then in the city streets. In addition to Hamdu's men, several hundred other Muslims ended up joining the fight against Arkan. The Serbs had haunted them for three years now, and they weren't going to take any chances, though it was still Hamdu's operation. Marching into the city, the Muslims took heavy rocket fire, and tank blasts glowed in the murky fall light. Before they reached the city they found dozens of corpses in a house along the river. The fulsome stench of decaying bodies filled Hamdu's nostrils. "It made my stomach turn," he said.

By the second day, a Bosnian peace agreement had been accepted, but the fighting dragged on. It had to. Both sides knew this; at this point they were isolated from the rest of the world, the battle seeming almost separate. Inside Sanski Most, Hamdu cornered twelve of Arkan's men in a post office. He called for them to surrender and told them to give up their leader. Machine-gun fire was exchanged, killing four of Hamdu's men instantly. Hamdu burned the post office and killed them all.

The fighting carried on, both sides suffering casualties. As daylight slipped away, the Muslim Tigers finally entered Hotel Sanus, but no one was there. The building was empty and the buses were gone. According to a witness, the Serbian Tigers had left ten minutes earlier. Arkan was with them, along with about three hundred Muslim prisoners.

Hamdu was dumbfounded. He had almost a thousand men storming the city now from all directions, covering all major roads. How could this happen? In the manager's office, he found Arkan's maps plastered on the walls and communications papers scattered on tables. There was blood on the floor of the boiler room, traces of what had happened.

Eventually, Hamdu stumbled into Arkan's suite. On a side table there was a lukewarm cup of coffee. He sat down on the bed, ran his hand through his dirt-and-sweat-matted hair. It seemed like he had been fighting forever. He had two thoughts: Arkan had gotten away and the war was over.

"I wanted to kill him," Hamdu told me later. "There would have been great satisfaction in killing Arkan. But I guess I will be remembered as the guy who stopped him, and that was a good thing." That night, after celebrating with bottles of Serb whiskey, Hamdu the Tiger passed out in Arkan's unmade bed and slept late the next day.

6

Arkan retreated east to Belgrade, but kept a watchful eye on his back. Soon he holed up in his mansion, rejoined his young pop-star wife, Ceca, and waited for news to come. With the peace on, one of the first things he did when he stepped through the front door, Ceca recalled, was sleep. "He didn't say anything about what happened," she said, referring to the war, "and I didn't ask him."

By late October, as the Bosnian cease-fire held steady, Milosevic climbed aboard a private jet and flew to Wright-Patterson Air Force Base near Dayton, Ohio, to hash out a final peace agreement with leaders from Croatia and Bosnia. Richard Holbrooke, the U.S. special envoy to the former Yugoslavia, was there to broker the deal. Every major newspaper and television station in the world covered the negotiations, which dragged on for twenty-one days and twenty-one nights, before Bill Clinton finally stepped in and concluded the deal, which was to be formally initialed in Paris on December 14, 1995.

At the end, the Serbs walked away with 49 percent of Bosnia, giving up the now bullet- and bomb-riddled Sarajevo, while the Croatians got 25 percent (as well as most of the recaptured Slavonia in Croatia), with the skimpy balance going to the Bosniacs. A toothless central Bosnian government would govern the divided-up land, with three revolving presidents. In addition, sanctions on Serbia would be lifted and twenty thousand American troops would ship out to enforce the peace in Bosnia.

Still, as the signing parties packed their bags and flew home to their broken world, there were other more complicated issues to be hammered out. After the deaths of some two hundred thousand, the displacement of millions, and the loss of billions of dollars in property, who were the criminals to blame? How and when were those criminals going to be brought to justice?

It was now a time of reckoning. People had to pay for the blood and profit. Justice had to be meted out. Heads had and would roll. The fat cats had to pay. Thus began a deadly board game, as the great and aspirant powers—politicians, warlords, mercenaries, and madmen—jockeyed to outmaneuver one another. The losers of this game would go to jail or take a bullet to the forehead.

The move for justice came sooner than later. That month, the UN war crimes tribunal announced thirty indictments. Mladic and Karadzic were charged with genocide. Although everyone expected to see Arkan on the list, he wasn't. What the heck had happened? It was heartbreaking, especially for Holbrooke, who had emerged as one of the main advocates for Arkan's capture. In his memoir, *To End a War,* a blow-by-blow account of the conflict and how it ended, Holbrooke had come to see Arkan as one of the nastiest of all the war criminals; he described him as a "freelance murderer" and a "racist fanatic run amok." Hoolbrooke had read the same intelligence reports that Jon Western had read, seen the same gruesome pictures. He knew about the mass graves, the stolen lives, and the war profits still being stashed away in offshore bank accounts. "It makes me angry," he said later. "I do not understand why, but Arkan has not been indicted."

It was a surreal moment. Human rights organizations had richly documented evidence excavated from wrecked villages and towns. So had Croatia and Bosnia. Officials in Bosnia indicated they possessed files tying Arkan to Milosevic. Even Cherif Bassiouni, the war crimes tribunal's chief investigator, was a little flummoxed by the tribunal's oversight. "He should be indicted, and he should have been indicted," he said. "There is ample evidence."

Meanwhile, at home, Arkan was greeted as a romantic hero, a patriot who had fought hard and willed his body to the Serbian cause. As a kid he'd admired John Wayne's cowboy characters. However, after the bank heists, assassinations, and prison escapes; after the pink Cadillac, Red Star, Vukovar, and Bijeljina; after the mob/royal wedding, and after Sanski Most, he'd outgrown them all. He was bigger than John Wayne and bigger than Al Capone. He was monstrous, epic, with millions of dollars apparently packed away from his war adventures. By some estimates the four-year conflict had netted him about $50 million. Add all of this up, Marko Nicovic, the former Belgrade police chief, told me, and Arkan was now untouchable. "He was suddenly the most powerful man in the country. More powerful even than the president."

Yet . . . he wasn't bulletproof. When Milosevic flew back from Dayton, rumors arose that the president had started to quietly plot Arkan's death.

With the tribunal talking about indictments, Arkan knew way too much about Milosevic's involvement in the war. Not only that. Milosevic couldn't have someone around the city who controlled so many professional killers. It wasn't only Milosevic, there were countless other jealousies coalescing in Belgrade's underworld. These men saw Arkan's oil money, they saw his leggy wife, his gleaming jeeps, and his BMWs, and they wanted a bigger piece of the action. As far as they were concerned, every man had his day. Even a Serbian hero. They had allowed him his time in the spotlight. It was time for someone else to rule.

As Arkan lay down in his own bed that first night, thoughts of his expanded fame and power, and all of the forces threatening to swallow him up, no doubt ran through his head like a dark melody. Although no explicit threats had been leveled against him yet, it would soon become clear that the war had made Arkan too big—and too big was not to be tolerated. Truth was, at this point there was already a bullet out there with his name on it. The question now was: When his enemies came to kill him, when they stepped out of the shadows with all their hate and envy and firepower, would he be quick enough to kill them first?

7

Arkan officially disbanded the Tigers in 1996. Erdut, capital of "Arkansas," was shuttered and, after five hard years of war, all operations finally ground to a halt. The Tigers were brought up to believe in the war, and now what they believed in was over. In those four years they had operated in more battles than any other Serb force. This was well known. Although there are no exact figures, the U.S. State Department estimated that the Tigers killed about two thousand people, innocents and soldiers combined. Of its core members, the paramilitary force lost between fifty and eighty men, though they'd lost hundreds of the weekend warriors, or Vikendashi, and Serb refugees who had been forcibly drafted from captured towns. That spring, as the snows melted away, Arkan gathered his men together and told them it was done—for now. "He told us to stand by," recalled the Tiger who called himself Mr. X. "He said, 'You never know how this is going to work out. If necessary, we have to be able to be armed in twenty minutes.'"

Hundreds of the Tigers, like Mr. X and Sloba, joined Arkan's criminal family in Belgrade—some as foot soldiers, others as members of his security firm, and still others in his casinos. Some put the number of former Tigers working for Arkan at almost one thousand, which seemed reasonable, because war or no war, as one Tiger put it, "we were always Tigers and always for our commander."

Others joined Serbian state security. The most talented were recruited into the SBD's Unit for Special Operations, or JSO, an "antiterrorist" unit widely perceived to be Milosevic's praetorian guard.

There were also reports of Tigers who decided it was time to disappear for a stretch. The concern was that the International Criminal Tribunal would come for them. Dozens left; one source told me as many as fifty. Some traveled as far as Australia, or the United States. One former Tiger, who had allegedly videotaped every one of the group's operations, packed up his tapes and fled with them to Canada.

There were other ones who lost their minds. This wasn't unusual for a soldier. Without the constant thought of battle, they finally got a chance to think about the ugly things that they'd done, and they began to crack. I was told one Tiger, addicted to heroin, shot a man dead in a dispute at a house party, went to jail, was freed by Arkan, and then died shortly after of an overdose. I was never able to confirm the story. There was another who, like a character out of a David Lynch film, killed someone with a chain saw.

Trax was different. When he returned to Belgrade, he didn't stick around for long. He grabbed his girlfriend and hopped on a jet to India. He'd never been there, but he'd heard about the sunny beaches in Goa, the blue moon parties, and the hard techno scene. The idea was to go somewhere that was the opposite of Serbia. "I needed to get away," he told me. "I was desperate."

In Goa, Trax fell deep in love, and kept hoping that the hot sun and pounding music would melt away the bad memories of war living inside him. "We didn't sleep," he said. "Just music, all the time."

Three months later he returned to Belgrade. All the unspeakably horrible stuff roared back. His girlfriend's twin sister overdosed and died, and then several months later his girlfriend, the girl he planned to marry, died of the same thing. Was he next? It was hard moving on, but he had no choice. Suicide was out of the question. Trax was too big for that. At night he went out to clubs, drank, popped pills, and lost himself in the heavy beats. He slept all day. Music was better than the drugs. With some leftover money, he decided to buy mixing tables and speakers and began making his own beats. It felt good. He moved out of his parent's place and into a basement apartment downtown, where he DJ'd for friends. Sometimes he just turned all the lights off and let the music play. It was the only way to keep out the ghosts.

All the while he tried to stay away from the Tigers still connected to Arkan, but they were always around. He saw them at cafés. He saw them at the pool hall. When he DJ'ed at clubs, they were there. They urged him to visit the commander, but Trax stayed away. He didn't give a shit anymore. Though it probably wasn't the healthiest decision, the Tigers eventually stopped coming around, and then it began to look like Arkan was going to let him go. Trax was still skeptical—always would be. "No one gets out of that world," he said later. "You get pulled into Arkan's world and you stay. Or else. I was probably one in a million."

When I heard these stories about life after the war, I couldn't help but wonder how in the world these former Tigers were even allowed to go on with their lives as if Croatia and Bosnia had never happened. What about justice? That raised an interesting question. Were all the Tigers war criminals? The answer is no. According to international law, only the ones who killed civilians were criminals, though proving which of them did what would be a hugely difficult, if not an impossible, task. Investigations into their specific roles, however, would go on, but they weren't easy. For instance, when word leaked out that Natasa Kandic, director of Belgrade's Humanitarian Law Center, was considering prosecution of local war criminals, she began to receive death threats. "Some of the Tigers told me that they would prevent me from doing that," she said.

Ron Haviv's photograph of a Tiger kicking an older woman (probably dead) would forever haunt human rights organizations. Who was the soldier in the picture? The consensus was that a case could be made that he was a war criminal. Although Trax would never cop to it, people in his circle always told me not to talk about the photo with him. Most thought he was the guy. I wasn't sure. The first time I asked about it, he either didn't hear or pretended not to hear. The second time I asked, he looked surprised, but just shook his head sadly. "I don't know," he said. Like the other Tigers, he also didn't know if he killed any civilians. "It was war," he said. "Lots of people died."

Soon Trax was making cash DJing at small clubs. He was the first to play techno in Belgrade, and a grain began to sprout alive in his head that there might be some real money in it. Next he was thinking about putting together a production company.

No matter what he did, he would never forget the Tigers. Aside from the nightmares, he had shrapnel in his right leg from a grenade explosion, and it hurt whenever he stood on it for too long, or when it got cold. "Those were fucked-up times," Trax told me. "I can't even tell you."

Other Tigers disagreed. They longed for the old days—always would. "I still have all my equipment from the war," said Mr. X. "It's in my house, like a shrine."

Actually, it was good that Mr. X kept his equipment, because little did he know, another battle was coming.

PART III

THE ASSASSINATION

26

THIS IS SERBIA, YOU WOULDN'T UNDERSTAND

1

It was a bitter cold autumn night in Belgrade in 2004 when my battered Volvo sedan arrived at Arkan's heavily guarded fortress. Since Milan was out of town, I'd hired another Serb named Alex to go with me to visit Ceca, the warlord's wife. After much negotiation, Ceca agreed to grant a rare interview—with precautions. As I exited the car, I was surrounded by burly men who looked steroidal and just out of Sing Sing, guys dressed in leather and clean white athletic shoes, carrying Heckler & Koch submachine guns. Expressionless, they frisked me and Alex, then escorted us up a dark, treeless road of unsettling quiet, through a steel gate and toward a set of marble steps leading to the gargantuan seven-story house. That's when a pair of huge dogs—Japanese Tasas—lunged out of the gloom, scaring me and sending me stumbling backward.

Then I heard laughing. It was Ceca, standing at the top of the stairs.

"Don't be afraid," she called down to me. "Come into my house."

Arkan's compound, with the glass elevator. Today, it is home to his pop star wife, Ceca, and their two children.

2

At thirty-one years old, Ceca looked like a weathered swimsuit model. She wore tight, bleached blue jeans and an orange sweater that complemented her fake tan and accentuated her (most likely) fake breasts, which were bigger than everyone had described—and everyone who talked about Ceca talked about her breasts, sort of the way people in America talk about Pamela Anderson. Her brown hair fell in a curtain down her back, and her features were sharp, like something cut from wood. She wore diamonds everywhere—her wrists, neck, ears, and fingers.

"It's been a long day," she said wearily, in Serbian, as she knocked out a cigarette from a pack of Cartiers and fired it up with a gold lighter. Smoking was the only thing that calmed her nerves. "If I were to tell someone outside this place about my life," she said, "they wouldn't believe me."

Before the interview, Alex had warned me to be careful about pushing her too hard about Arkan. I was curious about what she knew about his war crimes. Most believe that while she did not participate in the Bosnian rampage, she was far from an innocent naïf. "She's not guilty of war crimes," said Ivan Kronja, a Belgrade media critic. "But she profited from the war in every way, from getting love and adulation and popularity. She was a public promoter of the ideology and the spirit of nationalism and chauvinism. She was in very deep."

We settled down in leather couches in her living room. An older woman served us Heinekens and brandy. "I love Heineken," she volunteered, holding it up. "Yes," I said. "It's good."

Six video screens on a far wall watched the street and the dark edges of the house. Her cell phone rang, distracting her for a moment. It would ring constantly through the night. A mystery person would call repeatedly, and every time her response was something like, "You can't come now. Not now. The American is here."

The mansion is a stunning place, and more than a little strange. When I asked about the number of rooms, Ceca shrugged. "I have no idea. It's a big house." Arkan spent around a decade building the enormous home, finally completing it after the war. There are two fake waterfalls, a solarium filled with botanically unidentifiable plastic greenery, marble pillars, crystal chandeliers, and a mosaic swimming pool in the basement. Its walls are covered with oil portraits of Arkan as well as a dozen or more World War I paintings, most of them of beleaguered soldiers and assassination scenes. When I inquired about the meaning of the paintings, Ceca shrugged again. "They're Zeljko's," she explained. "I don't know anything about them."

When the discussion finally turned to the war, her eyes flickered and then dropped to the floor, and she placed her hand on her forehead, as if to staunch the memories from flowing back. What did she think about her husband being involved in the conflict? I ventured. She didn't answer right away. When she did, she said, "He was a Serbian patriot. He was very brave. That's what I loved about him. He was a very strong man."

She suggested that many of the accusations against him were flat-out wrong, a belief shared with thousands of other Serbs. When I asked her about his war crimes, she called them "nonsense," sounding just like the wife of a mobster, as we know from TV and the movies—all loyalty and denial.

"I don't know everything that Zeljko did," she told me, fussing with her sweater sleeve. Unlike almost everyone else in Belgrade, she never referred to him as Arkan. It was always Zeljko. "When he came through the door of our house, all of his business was left outside. We were just ordinary people. I called him Zeljko, and I was Fatso."

This time she looked over at a photograph of him on the wall. In it, he had donned a World War I uniform, like the one he wore at their wedding. It looked like she was going to cry. She ran her right hand over her face, and then pushed her long hair behind her ears. "It is hard for me to talk about him," she said, looking up. She was only a couple of years older than me, and yet she had probably lived seven more lives. She said that it was especially hard for her to explain what had happened with Zeljko. "Serbia is not the same as other places," she told me. "You try to tell people about the things that happened here and they won't understand. This is Serbia. It's a different world."

That evening, she would begin, a little reluctantly, and with considerable conflict, to explore the last years of the man she called Zeljko.

27

GOING LEGIT

1

In 1997, a young Belgrade journalist named Milomir Marić wrote a story entitled "Legend of Arkan." In it he attempted to puzzle out Arkan's criminal history, from his childhood through his days as a bank robber and hit man, and on to his life during and after the war. After the story was published, Marić received a disturbing phone call. "This is Arkan," a man's voice declared. "You have six months to live. And when you die, I will speak at your funeral." Then the phone went dead.

Die? The slightly high-pitched voice replayed in his head. It was Arkan's voice. He knew that for sure. For a second, he didn't move, the voice playing itself over and over. Die? He wondered: Is he fucking serious?

Three years earlier, there was another journalist who wrote about the warlord and turned up dead. Her name was Dada Vujasinovic, and most in Belgrade knew something about her tragic story. After she had written a similar exposé, her boyfriend found her body sprawled out on the living room floor of her two-bedroom apartment in New Belgrade, a bullet wound to her head and an antique Russian rifle next to her.

It was April 1994. City police labeled it a suicide, though Dada's family and many journalists were unconvinced and called it an underworld hit. What most persuaded them of this was not that Dada was a happy girl, but that all of her investigative files concerning Arkan and the Belgrade underworld were stolen on the night of her death. Nothing else was misplaced: not her money or jewelry. The missing files had been locked up in a bedroom safe. The family pressed the police on the question of the files, complained of a hasty crime scene investigation, pointed out that the perpetrator must have known her because there were no signs of a break-in, and lobbied them to continue investigating. The case languished, and the search for resolution continues even today.

After spending time in Germany, her father and mother now live in Dada's old two-bedroom apartment. When I visited them the father reproduced, in eerie detail, the scene of his daughter's death as it had appeared in the living room. From a closet he produced a dark fabric armchair, stained with his daughter's long-dried blood. He leaned the antique rifle against the chair and, on a coffee table, displayed the photographs the police had taken that bloody night over a decade before. "This is what my daughter got for telling the truth," he said sadly, as he looked over at his wife. "We can never forget this."

Marić knew the story, too. He couldn't get it out of his head. At the end of the month, his phone rang again. "You have five months to live," the man told him. The same high-pitched voice. Arkan. He began to taunt him now, a rusty knife twisting in an open wound. The call came again at the four-month mark, then at three. It didn't stop after that. Time was running out. The knife digging in.

There was no one to go to. What were the police going to do? Or the government? Arkan had influential people everywhere. When Marić confided in friends about the situation, some urged him to leave the city, maybe even the country. Dada was not the only dead journalist. Between 1991 and 1995, forty-nine others had died in Serbia, though most of them in the war. With one word, Arkan could easily add Marić to that list. His friends tried to persuade him to lay low for a while, wait until things cooled down. Come back in five years. But Marić stayed, and so he was punished.

As he strolled out of a downtown hotel one night, with two months left to live, one of Arkan's hired killers confronted him. According to Belgrade lore, the man, known for his terrifically lurid hits, had cut up one of his victims with a chain saw. Marić had no reason to believe that he'd be spared—but he was. Instead of a bullet to the temple, the chain-saw man pounded him with his fists and left him bloodied on the ground. Just a preview of the pain to come. The knife twisting deeper.

The phone calls came two more times, and then it was days before his appointment with death. A moment before his scheduled assassination, however, there was a development. "I got very lucky," Marić told me, which was a huge understatment. Somehow, a family connection was established between Marić and Arkan. It turned out that the two men had long-lost cousins in common, and word of the relationship got back to Arkan. Only in Serbia. Having a soft spot for family, the warlord called off the hit, but that didn't change the meaning. Although Marić was spared, Arkan's threat was abundantly clear to everyone else: Negative talk of his past would have consequences, a message that was more important now than ever. Arkan was about to reinvent himself, and no one was going to get in his way.

2

It was time to become a legitmate businessman. Arkan aimed to be reborn. It wasn't exactly a novel concept. Over time many mobsters had washed their hands of a grim past and reinvested ill-gotten wealth in a life of legitimacy. The problem always was: The mobsters can change, but can the world forget?

Ceca's career was the start. Arkan was determined to keep her on top of the music world, maybe even bring her to the West. He invested hundreds of thousands of dollars into the production of her videos, put her in transparent gowns with thongs, and apparently paid for her superduper-sized breasts and a nose job. "He dressed me up," Ceca said. "He was into that." Sometimes he arrived at her concerts carrying her ice-pick heels. After shows, he sold her special dresses and gowns in a new boutique. Just like Marilyn Monroe.

Most agree that he was a tough husband, and an even tougher manager. Just as in his days as the commander, he demanded perfection, and the only way to get that was through rigid discipline. Stepping out of line carried consequences, and so there were always rumors around town that Arkan hit Ceca—from light slaps to full-on punches. Though I was never able to confirm it, the most brutal story I heard involved Arkan walking in on Ceca sniffing a line of cocaine—drugs were one thing that Arkan would not tolerate. He supposedly beat her so badly that she ended up at Narodnog Fronta hospital. To keep the incident from the public, a part of the maternity ward was closed off until she recovered. Two people said she was in for a week. A third person said two weeks. In 1996, Ceca produced an album that seemed to sum up her new life with the warlord: *Emotivna Luda,* or *Emotionally Crazy.* Whatever the reality at home, however, tens of thousands of records sold.

In addition to his work with Ceca, there were other businesses. He opened a chain of bakeries; invested in casinos and property development; bought a construction company, which planned to build the city's largest business center; and launched Third Child, a philanthropy that gave financial aid to Serb families that had three or more children. The business grew fast. At one point he had over four hundred employees. "He became like a Fortune 500 company," said Marko Nicovic, Belgrade's former police chief.

Meanwhile, he dreamed of owning a championship soccer team. He imagined it would bring him global clout and admiration, maybe even clear his name. He didn't want just any team. He wanted an elite squad on the level of Chelsea and Manchester. A team that people all over the world would know and talk about—and envy.

Red Star was his first choice, but the owner rebuffed his offer. So he bought Pristina Football Club in Kosovo. According to local lore, his first management decision was to fire all of the Albanian players. When the team floundered, he dropped it. In 1996, he purchased Belgrade's Obilic Football Club, and that was the start of his soccer stardom.

Obilic, however, wasn't exactly a glory-destined team. In fact, it was widely considered a middling squad, at best, that had been languishing in the minor leagues for more than a decade. The record wasn't what inspired Arkan. He derived hope and meaning in the team's name. A son of a dragon, Milos Obilic was the supernatural Serb hero who fought at the tragic Battle of Kosovo, where the Serbs fell to the Turks in 1389 and lost their country for five hundred years—the event that turned the Serbs into a "heavenly people" and eternal victims. On the night before the battle, Milos slipped through the lines of the fierce Turks, entered the tent of Ottoman Sultan Murad I, and stabbed him to death.

Arkan fancied himself a modern-day Milos Obilic, a military man who had sacrificed himself for the Serbian people, and it became increasingly apparent as he immersed the team in his personal history. He changed the team uniforms to yellow, like a tiger, and plastered pictures of his private killing force all over the stadium. On the cement walls outside there were murals of war scenes, including a list of the Tigers killed in battle and a close-up of Arkan in a beret.

Over time, millions of dollars were poured into a new glass-and-steel stadium, a testament to Arkan's power. When complete, the stadium became one of Belgrade's most modern buildings, rising above the decrepit city like a beacon. Arkan worked out of an office at one end of the stadium, with tall glass windows looking out at the pitch. There was a long wood table for meetings, a collection of antique swords, a set of armor, and a flavored-coffee machine. The stone floor was covered in Persian rugs, and his desk was as large as a compact car, with a sculpture of his own serious face prominently displayed for visitors.

3

Within a year Obilic was on the road to becoming national champions. While Arkan paced the electric green pitch, Ceca could be seen on the sidelines, dressed in leather or leopard prints, her stomach bulging with the couple's first son, Veljko. After a slew of victories, the team was promoted to the first division, which made Arkan a happy man. When people asked how he did it, the new owner sounded a lot like George Steinbrenner did when his Yankees were winning. He bragged about smart management, critical drafting decisions, and discipline—though the truth was much more sinister.

Although he did outspend most teams in his league and displayed a knife-sharp temper when things went wrong—qualities he shared with Steinbrenner—the way he steered his team to victory was unprecedented in professional sports. He treated soccer like war, and the stories of his stewardship became legion. One of the most memorable was the time when a rival center fielder was told that his kneecap would be shot off if he scored in the second half. Rival managers were told to throw games to Obilic—or else. Once, when a manager refused to trade a player to Arkan, the manager was allegedly killed and then the player jammed into a car trunk, driven to the Obilic office, and forced to sign with his new team.

Playing Obilic was unhealthy. Before games the stadium filled up with young men dressed in black, just like the Tigers. "We were tough guys," one Obilic supporter, a national wrestling champion, told me. "You didn't want to fuck around with us." At the gates, referees were greeted and offered "suggestions" about how the game should be officiated. In the stands the supporters brandished guns in players' faces and shouted threats. Some of the fans' famous chants included: "If you score, you'll never walk out of the stadium alive" and "We'll break both of your legs; you'll walk on your hands."

Some opponents needed to be reminded that they were supposed to lose, and Arkan's supporters allegedly paid half-time visits to the opposing team's changing room. They weren't gentle. There was shouting, more threats. Star players mysteriously withdrew from the game. Others were forcibly extracted—one player claimed later to reporters that Arkan's men locked him away in a garage.

When people talked to me about the days of Obilic, some of the stories reminded me of Arkan's crazy bank-robbing legends. I found them hard to believe. Specifically, there was one about a sedative gas being pumped into the visitors' locker room through the ventilation ducts. "Are you serious?" I asked the guy. He was a Red Star soccer fan. "Do you think I'd make that up?"

True or not, the stories were enough to cause some teams to take precautions. When Red Star visited Obilic, they decided to change in their bus and, instead of retreating to the locker room at halftime, stayed on the field. During Arkan's tenure as club owner, reports of hooliganism got so bad that they even inspired some players to rethink the value of soccer in their lives. Who wanted to die for soccer? After one game against Obilic, Perica Ognjenenovic, a Red Star striker, told reporters, "This is not soccer, this is war." He added that he was thinking of leaving the country for good.

It wasn't only the opponents of Obilic who suffered. Obilic players, too, had to deal with Arkan's twisted soccer vision. Drinking before games, people told me, resulted in lashes, and losing was, of course, unforgivable. One time on the journey home after a loss, the team bus suddenly pulled over to the side of the road and the doors flopped open. "Get out," said Arkan. They were twenty miles from Belgrade, but so what. The players had to walk home.

Yet, the tactics worked. After only a year in the first league, Obilic took home the national cup and qualified for the European Champions' League. They were finally winners.

4

Despite his soccer success, Arkan's past continued to nag him. At one point he and Ceca appeared on a TV Pink chat show, and a female viewer called in to compliment Ceca on her beautiful gold-and-diamond necklace. The viewer also accurately described an inscription on it. When the host of the show asked how she could possibly know what was written on Ceca's jewelry, the woman said, "Because Arkan stole it from me in Bijeljina." Ceca's mouth dropped. She looked horrified—and she probably was a little confused. Arkan shook his head and, of course, denied any wrongdoing. He told the woman he had a receipt for the necklace. In fact, he said he'd be happy to settle this whole misunderstanding if she provided him with her address. He would pay her a visit. Wisely, the woman hung up.

That summer, after he had intimidated Marić and sent a message to local media and Serbs in general that talk about him would not be tolerated, CNN aired Christiane Amanpour's documentary. Titled *Wanted,* the story painted a damning picture of Arkan's gruesome crimes in Croatia and Bosnia. Amanpour, CNN's chief international correspondent, interviewed victims of Arkan in Bijeljina and Zvornik and a number of top government officials gunning for the warlord, including U.S. special envoy Richard Holbrooke and Cherif Bassiouni, the UN war crimes investigator. By the end of the film Amanpour seemed to ask: Why is Arkan still operating freely in Belgrade and not in a jail cell?

Arkan was furious. The next day he convened a press conference. Appearing with his son Michael and his lawyer, he wore a black suit coat and dark pants. Although his hair was thinning and flecked with silver, his smooth baby face was unchanged from when he was just a twenty-year-old crisscrossing Europe with dreams. Looking directly at the army of cameras in his face, he lashed out against Amanpour and the documentary's content for almost an hour. In general, he claimed that CNN had lied about him and that he was "a good soldier." "That Cherif, whatever his name is," he went on, "isn't telling the truth." He did, however, note that there might be some war criminals on the Croatian side, because they had killed four of his Tigers, but he wasn't going to push for a trial. At the end of the press conference he threatened to sue CNN for libel. Then, as a journalist wrote at the time, he climbed into "his Chevrolet 2500 which had been parked illegally . . . and drove home."

The documentary, however, was the least of his concerns. Close friends and associates who formed a protective circle around him began to disappear. Not just disappear, but die, a trend that little by little slashed away at his power. One of the biggest losses was former Serbian interior minister Radovan Stojicic, or the Hulk. The Hulk, Arkan's chief link to Milosevic, was shot to death in a Belgrade restaurant. Weeks later there was the death of Zoran Stevanovic, the man arrested with Arkan in Croatia for gun smuggling; followed by Vule, the Tiger who had threatened Trax and knocked off Arkan's rival, Jumbo Jet; and finally Suca, a major in the Tigers.

When asked if he was concerned that Milosevic was behind the killings, Arkan reportedly responded that the president wouldn't think of it. "He has a son," Arkan pointed out as he quietly plotted revenge. Payback killings proliferated. Though Arkan was too smart to get caught with a murder weapon, most knew what was going on. As one reporter wrote at the time, "Some one hundred personalities were killed in Belgrade [in the mid and late nineties]. . . . Ministers, politicians, businessmen, and criminals. Arkan's name was tied to many of these eliminations."

Funerals appeared around the city, like fungus after a hard rain. At night, guns blazed, cars exploded, buildings burned. Locals dubbed the time "the decade of assassinations." Newspapers overflowed with obituaries, and tabloids devoted entire issues to the shady hits, which sold out as soon as they hit stands.

Not surprisingly, most cases went unsolved. Arkan, master manipulator, blamed the murderous atmosphere on the sensation-minded press. "You start writing about a criminal," he said, coyly, "and he starts thinking he's really big. And then the blood circle starts unwinding."

However, the blood circle really *was* unwinding. No matter what he said, no matter who he allegedly killed, no matter what businesses he started, there was no getting around his past. In late 1997, as the icy fall winds whipped through the rolling Belgrade streets, the war tribunal at The Hague secretly indicted Arkan for war crimes. Although no official announcement was made, everyone knew the real one was moments away, and the press collectively speculated on Arkan's next move. Would he take his money and family and escape to some remote island? Would he fake a disappearance? The great escape was one of his oldest tricks, dating back to his European adventures. The feeling was that he must have something planned—but what?

Even though he denied the existence of a secret indictment, the European Championship League didn't care; the soccer group went ahead and banned Obilic from play. League coaches said they weren't going to host a thug like Arkan. The European ban also emboldened coaches at home. After bowing to the warlord for two seasons, the Yugoslavian teams joined forces and decided that they weren't going to give in to Arkan's sadistic tactics anymore. As far as they were concerned, they'd rather die together than lose another championship to Obilic. So Obilic, like Arkan, who was now forty-six, began a descent into oblivion.

The war in Kosovo, however, would halt this inevitable fall but only for a moment.

5

The Serbian people wanted Milosevic out of office—or dead. In 1996, the dissenting voices were louder than they'd ever been. After he'd attempted to engineer the municipal elections in favor of his party that fall, tens of thousands of people mobbed the streets and forced him to back down. He tried other things—muzzling the media and sending his security apparatus out to assassinate those who challenged his vision. In 1997 he named himself president of Yugoslavia, thinking that would elevate him, but the mobs kept coming, and his rivals were proving to be surprisingly bulletproof. The pressure began to consume him, but Milosevic wasn't one to walk away, even if staying killed him.

So he did what he had to, his last line of defense: He dreamed up another conflict, this one in Kosovo, the southern province where he'd started his career almost a decade earlier, in 1987. Like the wars before, the airwaves filled up with stories of suffering Serbs, this time at the hands of local Albanians. There were rumors of church burnings, beatings, and deaths. Milosevic said that the nation needed to protect the Serbs down there—no one should beat them—and he hoped that his people would follow.

It wasn't going to be an easy or straightforward fight. Kosovo was a barbed mess. Kosovar Albanians were a significant majority in the province, and by 1998 they were sick and tired of being perceived by Milosevic as second-class citizens. For years, there had been talk of an armed resistance, but in 1995, in the province's poverty-choked industrial hellholes and farmlands, a shadowy guerrilla force finally emerged. The group, which called itself the Kosovo Liberation Army, or KLA, and soon numbered in the thousands or tens of thousands, depending on whom you believed, was funded by Albanian émigrés from as far away as Chicago and Queens and armed by the Albanian underworld. The men were hard-nosed, many of them unemployed, with nothing much to lose but the ratty clothes on their skinny, food-deprived backs. In the cover of the surrounding mountains, the KLA trained, made plans, talked of an independent province, and gradually began pressuring Serbs out of towns around the province.

In the spring of 1998, all hell broke loose. The KLA killed three Serb police officers, and Milosevic in turn sent busloads of heavily armed troops rumbling into Kosovo. To his troops Milosevic issued a simple mission: Drive out the ethnic Albanians—torture, kill, burn, whatever it takes—and claim once and for all the country's spiritual heartland.

At first Arkan made a grand show of not joining the warring Serb presence in Kosovo. It was a strategic move to deflect international attention. Instead, he spent time lounging around the swanky Hyatt hotel in New Belgrade. Almost daily, he'd arrive out front in a heavily tinted Chevy SUV and glide through the front doors in a crisp blue or black suit, trailed by a crew of bodyguards. Sometimes the bodyguards were women, dressed like

Calvin Klein models in mobster black and stiletto heels. Occasionally, he showed up with his wife, Ceca. No matter who came with him, he attracted attention. He strutted through the marble halls, and then plopped himself down in the tearoom, where he liked to conduct interviews about the conflict. On many occasions he told eager reporters, "Everyone keeps saying that I'm in Kosovo, but I'm not, as you can see." Outwardly, he didn't laugh, but there's no doubt he was cracking up inside.

While Arkan waited things out, a professional killer named Milorad "Legija" Ulemek filled his shoes as commander in Kosovo. Legija, or Legionnaire, was tall and muscular and handsome, like an NFL quarterback. After allegedly robbing banks in Europe, he'd done time with the French Foreign Legion, where he earned the name Legija, and fought in Libya, Iraq, and Chad. In March 1992, he joined the Tigers in Bosnia. Like Arkan, he also became associated with the SDB, where, after proving his skills in battle, he was eventually recruited to head the agency's "antiterrorist" unit, or JSO. The JSO operated in the shadows of official life and was immune to any legal control. After Arkan's death, the JSO, which included many former Tigers, would morph into an organized crime gang, smuggling drugs, engaging in dozens of rackets, and killing anyone who got in the way—all with the approval of the Serbian government. (Later, Legija would become closely linked with Ceca and be convicted in the killing of both Ivan Stambolic, Serbia's former president, and Zoran Djindjic, the country's first democratically elected prime minister, orders that allegedly came down from top government officials—but that was much later.)

The newfangled Tigers had several different names: Super Tigers, the Unit, and Red Berets. According to most accounts, the new Tigers blended into the Serb army, some sporting the trademark black uniforms and black masks, and others dressed in the camouflage of ordinary foot soldiers. Their methods hadn't changed from the days in Bosnia. They showed up at Kosovar houses, at businesses, at checkpoints, or on passenger trains, cleaning up the Albanian enemy. I suspect that these were most likely the same men that I had encountered on my train ride that summer. Reports of civilian deaths and pillaging followed, and hundreds of thousands of Albanians began fleeing.

Summer passed and atrocities piled up on both sides. In the fall, Richard Holbrooke, acting again on behalf of President Clinton, managed to broker a cease-fire. It brought momentary relief to the world until it fell apart in January 1999, after Serb soldiers murdered fifty-eight Kosovar Albanians in a town called Raçak. It was a massacre. Photographs surfaced of dead women and children, burned bodies, and heads chopped off with knives. Eerily, it brought to mind memories of Srebrenica and even Rwanda. This was Milosevic ratcheting up the ethnic cleansing process. Soon word was spreading that he'd called in Arkan to finish it.

Sightings of Arkan in Kosovo began to appear in local and international papers. "Arkan and his thugs are there," said Kris Janowski, UN high commissioner for refugees. "We saw these people in action in different places. There is a similar pattern [of violence against] people coming out of different areas in Kosovo, and it's very much what we saw in similar situations in Bosnia and Croatia."

Still, whenever claims of him being in Kosovo popped up, he somehow materialized at the Hyatt, slick as a panther in his expensive suit and polished shoes. Ghosts, he said. Those UN people and the reporters, they were seeing ghosts down there. Not him. No way. "They are telling the world I am in Kosovo, but I am here in Belgrade," he exclaimed to Reuters television. "I am not yet in Kosovo, but I promise the minute that NATO ground troops are in Kosovo, I will go there for sure."

6

In February, Serbia slipped into a typically frigid winter. Meanwhile, the United States and European allies organized a peace conference between Belgrade and ethnic Albanians at Rambouillet, a French château not far from Paris. In a take-it-or-leave-it offer, the Serbs were told to pull out of Kosovo, grant the province autonomy, and allow twenty-five thousand NATO troops in to police the peace. If the Serbs rejected the deal, NATO would bomb.

Milosevic didn't even show up to the talks, and the Serbs made it public that they had dismissed the offer. It was another Milosevic gamble: If the international community had taken four years to bomb them in Bosnia, why would they bomb in this war after only a year?

Nevertheless, bomb is what NATO did. On March 24, 1999, just as spring melted away the cruel winter, NATO, encouraged by Clinton, began bombing. The United States and its European allies would not tolerate another genocide.

Christiane Amanpour arrived in the capital to cover the battle for CNN. Amanpour is a tall, striking woman with dark hair cut off at the shoulders.

As CNN's chief international correspondent, she was accustomed to working at the bullet-riddled heart of the world's hot spots. Though she'd covered the Bosnian conflict in the early 1990s, it was one of the first times that she'd been back since she'd made the documentary about Arkan.

Arkan, of course, hadn't forgotten her, not even as the bombs began to fall. After she and her crew had set up at the Hyatt on that first night of NATO air strikes, she got word that Arkan was coming for her. "I got a call from Eason [CNN's chief news executive] saying Reuters in Belgrade had been 'invaded' by men in leather jackets and balaclavas [black face masks] and weapons, looking for me. Reuters told Eason they were Arkan's men."

The rumor around Belgrade was that his men had plans to cut off Amanpour's hair, and then kill her. "I hid," Amanpour told me, and waited through the night, wondering if Arkan would find her. While she waited, CNN worked furiously to find a way to sneak her out of Serbia. It was a race against time.

Much later in the night she sneaked back into her room and gathered her things. "It had been broken into and ransacked, with my papers strewn all over the room," she told me. By then, however, CNN had come through. Before sunrise, after much "diplomatic and hush-hush stuff," Amanpour was ferried out of the country. She was safe.

But Arkan was not. Days later, as bombs exploded throughout the city, The Hague announced the indictment against him and issued a warrant for his arrest. Suddenly, all bets were off, and Arkan was going down.

28

THE END

1

On the morning of March 31, 1999, the news began appearing on CNN. Louise Arbour, chief prosecutor of the International War Crimes Tribunal, had finally charged Arkan with grave breaches of the Geneva Conventions, violations of the laws and customs of war, and crimes against humanity, the worst charge, which carried a life sentence. Although not all of the charges were disclosed immediately, there were twenty-four counts, spanning the conflicts in Croatia and Bosnia, with mentions of rape, torture, and murder. Not long after the arrest warrant went out to the Serbian government, a $5 million bounty was placed on his head.

Arbour said that they would track him down. "The world is a much smaller place," she warned. She was a fifty-two-year-old Canadian judge and had been appointed to the tribunal for the former Yugoslavia in 1996. The stories were mixed on exactly why the tribunal had waited so long to indict, but there were theories. One was that the United States had worried that Milosevic would be harder to bargain with on Kosovo if they started charging people in his inner circle. Another was that Arkan would go on a killing spree if officially charged. As one tribunal official put it, "A man like him, with his capacity for violence, might eliminate witnesses."

With Milosevic unwilling to budge on Kosovo and intelligence pointing to Arkan's return to the battlefront, Arbour hoped that the indictment would serve as an "unambiguous signal" to Arkan's associates and disciples. "If the public disclosure of this arrest warrant reduces somewhat the possibility of his arrest outside Yugoslavia, it will nevertheless serve to put on notice those who might be inclined to retain his services or to obey his orders that they too will be tainted by their association with an indicted war criminal," she said. A NATO spokesman, Jamie Shea, was more candid. The indictment, he declared, was a "warning to all other . . . little Arkans."

Whatever the signal, it was an undeniably meaningful development, with broad historical implications. Serbia's soul was changing. Inflation was a deadening 200 percent, and unemployment an unfathomable 40 percent, forcing the poor to hit the streets to fight or die. Meanwhile, demonstrations were erupting more frequently in the city and all over the country, by truly oppressed people demanding political and economic change. To add to this, the Serbian Orthodox Church had just called for Milosevic to resign. Of all these things, the indictment of Arkan, one of the most prominent criminals in the country's (and probably Europe's) history—the most poignant symbol of an era of excess—seemed, at long last, to intimate the beginning of an end.

Outside Serbia other parts of the world were going through profound changes, too. Russia had clawed itself out of a grim spell of hyperinflation and was about to get a new president, Vladimir Putin. Former Chilean dictator Augusto Pinochet was on the ropes, with an English court clearing the way for his extradition to Spain to face charges on human rights violations—though he would die in Chile before being officially tried. In Eastern Europe, the Czech Republic, Hungary, and Poland had joined NATO, an event that underlined the three nations' dramatic transformation from aging Soviet allies to free market–oriented and Western-style democracies. Extending membership to these three democracies would gradually help stabilize a region that had been the staging ground for many of the century's disasters. In addition, the UN had initiated an expansion of its tribunals to prosecute not only war criminals in Yugoslavia, but also ones from Rwanda, Sierra Leone, East Timor, and Cambodia. Justice, it seemed, was becoming more important in the world.

Still, Arkan was not about to throw in the towel. Watching the news of his indictment unfold in Technicolor—it was on almost every channel, from CNN to the BBC to the local Pink TV—he shook his head. "That bitch," he shouted at the screen flickering with images of him in camouflage and the serious-looking Arbour. Days later he slipped into his trademark black suit and laundered white shirt, climbed into his SUV, and with a bevy of armed men headed for the cameras to defend himself. When he appeared on ABC's *Good Morning America with Charles Gibson* on April 15, he was defiant: "To tell you in the clear English language, I don't give a damn for that indictment . . . and Louise Arbour, the prosecutor of the court, is a bitch." In the broadcast, Charles Gibson's eyes widened, like he'd been suckerpunched in the gut.

"You understand me," Arkan continued tensely, giving off the feeling that he was about to blow. "I was killing in a fair fight. And I am ready to kill any enemy soldiers in a fair fight. I also have my soldiers being killed in a war. And I have my wounded soldiers. When you put this matter to the innocent people, innocent man, he will tell you she is a bitch."

Later, on CNN, he declared: "I will not surrender myself. I am not guilty. I will fight to the end."

He also had a message for the U.S. president, whom he felt was behind everything bad that had happened and was happening to him and his country. "This is a message for Bill Clinton," he told the world, as news cameras rolled. "Don't quarrel with Serbs. Ever."

Then he headed into war. At a torched and emptied village outside Podujevo in Kosovo, he swaggered around in designer aviator glasses. The homes had been looted and burned, and ethnic Albanians expelled or killed. As smoke rose specterlike from the ruins, he told his men and a couple of journalists, "I'm back in business."

Which might have been the case—until NATO bombed him.

2

Late on May 7, 1999, NATO fighter jets and bombers, under the command of General Wesley Clark, were roaring over Belgrade. The night sky was overcast, the air filled with thunderous sounds. When the precision-guided missiles came, they struck in a flurry. Air-raid sirens blared like a rock concert. Missiles slammed into the police headquarters, and then the Defense Ministry, turning them into a tangled mess of concrete and steel. In no time the city's electricity was out, plunging the landscape into a wilderness of darkness. "I felt like the world was ending," a woman in her thirties told me.

At around 11:05 P.M., NATO locked its telescopic, infrared-guided cross-hairs on Arkan. Three precision-guided missiles struck the Hotel Yugoslavia, where the warlord had turned one of his casinos into a war operation bunker. It was a direct hit. Though the hotel was empty, except for one man later identified as a Serbian army operative, one entire side of the bulding was reduced to a smoldering pile of rubble. Across the street, the Chinese embassy also took hits. Deemed an accident—the CIA faulted old maps—there was considerable speculation that it had been deliberately targeted af-ter word got around that Arkan was secretly using the building to transmit battlefield communications.

The bombing went on for hours, and Belgrade didn't sleep. At a NATO press conference the next morning, while the exhausted city dug itself out of the smoking wreckage, journalists got right to the point. "Was this an at-tempt to hit Arkan directly?" asked Mark Laity of the BBC. "And will you change your targeting policy after what happened last night?"

Javier Solana was the bearded NATO secretary general from Spain. He took a deep breath and nodded to the room, which was jammed full of in-ternational media, many of them bleary-eyed and burned out from weeks of dodging bombs. "It is true we have targeted the Yugoslavia Hotel," he be-gan, using his hands for emphasis. "As you know very well, these are the headquarters of Arkan and Arkan's Tigers, therefore of a publicly indicted war criminal, and without any doubt one of the persons which have been linked most closely, together with Milosevic, with the tragedy of the ex-Yugoslavia, not only the tragedy of Kosovo."

Solana paused. "Arkan is responsible for many, many, many murders, many killings, in Bosnia, in Croatia, and therefore this is a target which makes profound sense in this very moment in which we want to stop the ethnic cleansing for which he is so closely responsible personally."

Later that day in Washington, Kenneth H. Bacon, U.S. assistant secretary of defense for public affairs, echoed Solana. As if to justify the unusual tar-geting of one man, reserved later for antagonists like Osama bin Laden and Saddam Hussein, he described Arkan's dastardly résumé, including mass murder and rape hotels, where Muslim women were being forced into pros-titution. Arkan, he said, was "one of the most wanted criminals in the world." With noticeable irritation, he described the Tigers as "Arkan's Thugs" and the Hotel Yugoslavia as the "brains and nerve center" of these thugs. Before he finished, he warned Arkan that NATO was "determined to keep hitting at such targets."

Fearing that his mansion was next to be hit, Arkan rounded up his young family—which now included a three-year-old boy, Veljko, and a one-year-old girl, Anastasia—and began ferrying them to different shelters around the city. He became a ghost, like many of the other Tigers, frightened that they might be snatched up or killed. Few knew for sure where he spent his nights, but there were stories. Many told me that his family hid out in Thailand's embassy, which had been abandoned before the bombing, and then moved to the Russian embassy, before finally shuttling between friends' houses and hotels.

By late spring, Arkan surfaced at the Hyatt, where many reporters covering the war had shacked up, figuring that it was the safest place from NATO's bombs. People told me that he didn't leave the hotel often. When he emerged it was usually at nightfall, and always with five to seven heavily armed bodyguards. His four- and five-car convoys were notable because they traveled faster than most traffic, drove on sidewalks and against traffic, blew red lights. Sometimes, people spotted him at the Serbian Orthodox Church Holy Archangel Gabriel. Mostly, he used the night to be with his family or check on his various businesses, which had by now made him and Ceca one of the Balkans' richest couples, perhaps even the richest. Estimates of his wealth ranged from tens of millions to hundreds of millions.

The rest of the spring passed like this—a deadly game of cat and mouse, with bombs dropping like a storm that wouldn't quit. Summer approached. The Hague tribunal kept pushing Yugoslavian authorities to hand over its criminals, and Arbour continued to collect evidence, marshaling prodigious bunkers of intelligence gathered by Bassiouni and other investigators—photos, blood samples, battlefield reports, gunpowder samples, eyewitness accounts, and myriad statements from Western governments, journalists, and humanitarian aid groups. Lacking a police force of her own to raid the former Yugoslavia, she visited Western countries and pleaded for help. She floated the idea of Special Forces operations, and told local law enforcement to be on the lookout, just in case the criminals decided to flee. Specifically, she declared, "We require these states, including Yugoslavia, to arrest the accused if they are within their jurisdiction and deliver them to The Hague for trial."

At the start of The Hague hunt for justice, most of those apprehended were low-level thugs. One was Dusan Tadic, a former guard at the Serb's Omarska detention camp in northern Bosnia. In 1996, after being picked up in a German bar, he became the first defendant to stand trial. Although Tadic was clearly a sinister character, he was no Arkan or Mladic, the Bosnian Serb general.

Still, the lack of arrests didn't seem to faze Arbour. On May 28, 1999, she announced the indictment of Slobodan Milosevic on charges of crimes against humanity, and issued an arrest warrant. It was the first time that a head of state had been brought up on war crimes charges, and Arbour meant it as a message: It doesn't matter who you are. If you are a war criminal, you are not safe. We will take you down.

Two weeks after the president's indictment, Milosevic recalled his army and the NATO bombing ceased. After seventy-eight days of fierce air attacks, with thirty-four thousand sorties flown and thousands of Albanians dead in mass graves and hundreds of thousands now homeless, the carnage was over. The date that people remember is June 13, 1999. Most say that Milosevic had no choice but to end the war. In addition to his vulnerability as a newly indicted war criminal, with the world now calling for his arrest, Serb troops were deserting the battlefield en masse, and cronies were begging him to save their business interests, which were being disrupted or blown up.

The war in Kosovo, it turned out, left Milosevic more vulnerable than the day he dreamed up the conflict. In fact, for the first time in his years of warring, he actually lost territory. After the fighter jets departed and fires burned out, Kosovo became a protectorate of the UN, and fifty thousand peacekeepers arrived to enforce the rule of law. Suddenly, the province's future with Serbia was uncertain, and the only thing that was clear was that after almost a decade of bloodshed and power, the house of Serbia was falling.

3

Louise Arbour would never get Arkan. Nor would her successor, Carla Del Ponte, the Swiss lawyer appointed to The Hague's chief prosecutor post that August, after Arbour resigned. Instead, justice would be handled the "Balkan way," with a bullet to the skull. Although it would never be proven, it's widely believed that several days after his indictment and the war's ignominious end, Milosevic (or people close to the president) did then what he'd been planning to do for several years—ordered Arkan's execution. Arkan, it was decided, was a man who knew too much—and it was finally time for him to die.

The summer of 1999 was the summer of discontent. As Ceca explained later to me (in the understatement of the year), "You could tell he had a lot on his mind." Turf wars with local gangs had intensified for him, and the decade of assassinations continued. By now over a hundred popular figures had been killed in Belgrade, and Arkan's men were dying off as if they'd been exposed to a nuclear meltdown. Whenever he stepped out of his house, news cameras always seemed to be in his face, asking him about the indictment and what he was going to do. In spite of this, he tried to maintain a cool poise, piloting his family around town in his SUV, showing up at the Hyatt tearoom for lunch, and attending Obilic soccer games on Sundays with his kids in tow. As much as he wanted to focus on the future and his family, his old life kept pressing on him and, by late June, he began seeking an exit.

Newspapers reported that he quietly asked his lawyer and good friend Giovanni di Stefano to work out a plea deal with the tribunal. Stefano was an enigmatic international businessman and attorney, one of the many who had traveled to Belgrade during wartime for a piece of the profits to be had in the black hole. He was an honorary member of the Tigers, owned a local radio station and a casino, among other entreprises, and liked to tell people that he had a stake in the Hollywood movie studio MGM.

Few in Belgrade knew what to make of Stefano. Many called him a crook, especially after unsubstantiated rumors spread around the city that he was actually Arkan's old bank-robbing partner, Carlo Fabiani, whom Arkan had broken out of the courthouse in Stockholm. I heard about this connection all the time in Serbia, but when I asked Stefano about it, he laughed and said he was never a bank robber. "Do I sound like one?" he said. I had no idea, though most people told me not to trust him. In addition to representing Arkan, Stefano would later take on Saddam Hussein and dub himself the "devil's advocate."

Whatever Stefano's identity, he was unable to make any headway with Carla Del Ponte. The tribunal told Stefano not to bother. "There is nothing to negotiate," they said. Once indicted, there was no bargaining.

Arkan didn't give up hope. In July, he approached Belgium about asylum, where he had once escaped prison and now had a daughter. That plan also failed. "He was told there was no chance," said Jos Colpin, a spokesman for the chief Belgian prosecutor. "If Arkan was found [in Belgium], he would be arrested."

When Colpin was asked if Arkan had given a reason for wanting asylum, he guessed that he was "just testing the water. Perhaps he wants to turn himself in to avoid being shot somewhere."

Ceca couldn't stand seeing her husband frantic like this. "He was on the

run," she said about the last months of his life. "He felt the world was closing in on him." At that point, Dinic, the publisher of the local tabloid *Svedok,* began to witness a dramatic change in his old friend. Arkan, he said,
was suddenly starting to realize that he probably wasn't ever going to get
away. With 177 countries having issued warrants for his arrest, where could
he go? The realization was a scary one, probably a lot like waking up from a
nightmare and understanding for the first time that the nightmare was not
just a dream but actually your life. "I believe he was ready to pay a price not
to be Arkan anymore," Dinic told me. "He looked tired. I think that he
would have paid any amount of money to leave his old life behind and start
a new one."

What exactly Arkan was thinking as the world came crashing in on him
at gale force, we will never know, but it got me wondering. I wondered if he
regretted anything, or if he ever grasped that he'd done things in his life
that the average person would characterize as evil. I wondered what he
thought up there at the top of his Mount Everest, if he arrived at the apex
and looked back down at the kid who wanted to be a cowboy or a comic
strip character. What happened to me?

Even if he wanted to change now, changing wasn't his choice to make. It
would be like Scarface waking up one day and calling it quits, and then deciding to recede into a bland life of soccer dads, car pools, and mall trips,
and expecting everyone, including the law and his hard-core pals, to forget
the past. To a large extent, the state had invented Arkan and allowed him to
flourish—first Tito, then Milosevic. Many decades ago he had agreed to deal
with the devil, and at forty-seven years old, after reaping the riches and
earning celebrity, the devil would not let him forget.

In November, Dinic met with his friend for the last time. They had tea in
a local restaurant. Oddly Arkan had instructed his bodyguards to stay outside, and he hadn't traveled with a convoy. When Dinic commented on the
lack of security, Arkan shrugged it off with a joke. "My jeep needs protection. How embarrassing would it be if someone stole it?" he asked. Dinic
laughed, but he perceived something more ominous in his friend. "You look
more relaxed today," he observed, noting how his shoulders were loose, his
eyes bright, his jacket unbuttoned, his manner upbeat. He wasn't even
wearing his bulletproof vest. What's going on? The warlord sipped his tea,
looked at the table, then outside, before looking at Dinic and smiling. "If
they mark you," he said, "there's no way out."

Dinic described this to me as recklessness. It was as if Arkan had decided to turn himself into a target, daring people to take a shot. It was a

strange thing. Why would he do that? What damage had his life done to his soul? What had it cost his soul to push up against mankind as he had, to challenge it and its inherent evils. We know about the psychological consequences of those beaten and raped. We know about what families of the murdered feel and think about, how such a brutal act changes a life or lives, but the consequences of being a murderer are much more opaque. What the hell was Arkan thinking?

Dinic never saw his friend again. "I think Arkan had a sixth sense that it was over," he said. "That there was no way out now, and he just gave in to that. It seemed he was ready to go. He resigned himself to that."

Whatever Dinic felt or believed, less than two months later, Arkan was dead.

29

IF I HAD A MAGIC WAND

When I visited Ceca for the last time at casa Arkan, her two kids were watching the movie *The Punisher* on a supersized flat screen. Veljko Raznatovic, who was then seven and resembled his father, said he loved the film. In the movie, a special agent's family gets murdered and he takes revenge. "I like the gun scenes," he told me in perfect English.

After some loud battle scenes, Ceca finally asked him and his five-year-old sister, Anastasia, to turn the TV off and join in our conversation. Veljko raised a plastic Hercules sword over his head and swung it down playfully. "I want to be in the army," he announced, puffing his chest.

Forcing a smile, Ceca dragged on a cigarette. It's obvious that this was not one of the conversations that she'd OK'd with her kids beforehand to discuss. She had asked me not to bring up Arkan around them. "They are still very young and don't understand everything about what happened," she'd said earlier in the day. For a while after his death, she'd made excuses to them about his absence, for instance, that he was off on a trip. Even four years after his death, I'm not sure they knew exactly where he was and how he got there.

Ceca exhaled a long stream of smoke. "The army," she said, pensively.

Veljko swung the sword again.

"He always tells me that he wants to go to West Point," she said, chewing her lower lip. She fidgeted with a golf ball–sized diamond ring on her right hand. "Oh, Veljko," she murmured, as if to say "you don't have the slightest idea what the world has in store for you."

Ceca's an overly protective mother. She worries about the prevalence of ransom kidnappings. She worries about what her kids see in the tabloids and hear about her life from friends. She doesn't let her kids go anywhere without bodyguards, not even around the block or to their private English school, or to friends' homes. She wants "a good life" for her kids, a different life than hers. "I don't want anyone in my family to ever be involved in the military again," she said after a moment, shaking her head at her son. "The military is not a good life."

Veljko said something declarative in Serbian, and Ceca just smiled at him, seeming to mean "not now." Fortunately, the housekeeper, an older woman, entered the room, quickly dispelling the topic. She replaced the ashtray and took more drink orders. Ceca asked for another Heineken, her third of the night. "I love Heineken," she announced. Veljko stood up and said to me with a cute, goofy smile, "And a beer for you, too, sir?" Then he and Anastasia hurried off to help.

Ceca rose and went to a side room and returned with her 2004 album *Crazed Love*. "For you," she said, handing me a copy. It was one of the first albums that she did after Arkan's death. I asked what it's all about, but she's not one to expatiate obnoxiously on the subject of her music. Instead, she popped another copy in the stereo and said, "Let's listen."

Like her other records, the songs were thumpy dance numbers with lyrics that narrate stories of love and romance and betrayal. It's heavy on synthesized beats, and you can imagine it being played on MTV or in a sweat-soaked European dance club.

As the music played, Anastasia and Veljko returned to the room, with the beer. Anastasia, who hadn't uttered a word all night, suddenly perked up when she heard her mother's music. She started to do little hip moves, her long brown hair swaying across the back of her pink Burberry dress, and a tiny smile crept across her face, the mirror image of her mother's. Veljko, too, knew every song and sang along. It almost seemed planned, because it was such a perfect family moment. After a couple of tracks, Ceca got into it herself, the kids gravitating to her lap, and the whole gang was singing.

We didn't get back to Arkan until the kids went off to bed. A new beer in hand, Ceca began to talk about the day he died. "It was just a normal day," she said. Nothing unusual. They'd spent time with the kids. It was the holidays, and there was talk about the new year. They were going to have more kids. She couldn't remember anything out of the ordinary that day. No strange phone calls. No threats. "Nothing," she said.

The memory seemed to distress her, and tears formed in her eyes. "He was the love of my life," she said, sipping the beer. "So it's very hard for me to talk about this."

I mentioned that some people in the city claimed that she had softened Arkan. Someone had even blamed her for his death. She swatted that away. "Ridiculous," she said.

When Ceca began talking about the night of his death and the hours after, she said again how unbelievable the story was. "This is Serbia," she said sadly. "If you tell this story to people outside of here, they wouldn't understand."

This comment would always haunt me. It was constantly on my mind as I traveled through the Balkans researching this book. I remembered it when I met with victims of Arkan's Tigers and when people warned me that it was not safe to ask questions about their dead hero. I remembered it when Arkan's Tigers subtly threatened my life at the Belgrade café, and I remembered it when I got a phone call late one night from a man who said in broken English, "Trouble is for you here." I also remembered it when I changed my departure ticket that night for the next day, packed my bags, triple locked my downtown Belgrade apartment, put a dresser in front of the door, and fell asleep in an armchair with my clothes on, ready to escape out the second-floor window and down a pipe if they came for me. I remembered Ceca's words through the years as I retold these crazy stories to friends and strangers. I remembered when I recalled to people the story of my first train ride through the region, and when my friend and fixer Milan received late-night threats. I remembered when people warned us not to get too close to the "spider's web, or else," and also when someone on an Internet message board suggested I be shot for ever questioning Arkan's heroic life. "It's Serbia, it's hard to explain," I found myself saying. Which is exactly what the world had said when the war consumed the country, and what had kept anyone from doing anything about the killing and the men who killed.

When I spoke to Ceca, I didn't understand everything she told me concerning Arkan, except that it would be hugely difficult for others outside of this world to comprehend. Still, for what it's worth, Ceca made an effort with me to go through the day of his death. "I will never forget it," she said. "Not ever."

She was twenty-six years old then, with two kids, but it had seemed like she'd lived a million years already. Like most of the people in her world, death wasn't exactly a surprise anymore. After a decade of carnage, death lurked. No matter who you were, death waited to suck you up. It was an inexplicably tragic time. Ceca spoke at length about his murder at the hotel, sipping her beer, choking back tears, and chain-smoking. She talked about the men who killed him—all the blood, and the doctors racing around to save him. When she finally stopped talking it was around 2:00 A.M., and the sprawling mansion was silent.

We walked to the big marble-encased front door. She had trouble opening it, and smiled wearily when I helped. I stepped outside into the early morning chill and waved good-bye. As I climbed into my car and looked back at her now darkened house, the armed men lost in inky night, I couldn't help but think about one last thing she had said about Arkan. "If I had a magic wand, I'd wave it and bring him back," she said. "And then I'd use that wand again to move us all out of this country. We'd go to the most remote place in the world, escape everything, and be happy and alone."

Of course there was no wand. And never would be.

30

THE KILL

Arkan died on January 15, 2000. Earlier in the night, he'd climbed into his navy blue Chevrolet SUV for the last time. It was icy and cold in Belgrade, the sun long gone. With him in the heat-filled truck were Ceca, her sister Lidija, and Zvonko Mateovic, one of his many bodyguards. Navigating the city's early evening traffic, they slipped past black-spewing city buses, rusted-out Yugos, blacked-out Audis. Soon they were crossing the muddy Sava River into New Belgrade, with its jagged skyline of high-rises. The truck glided down an exit ramp, and minutes later they arrived at their destination, the Intercontinental Hotel, a sprawling eight-story complex of green-mirrored glass, which resembled an aquarium. A decade of violence and crime had caused the Intercontinental franchise to pull its corporate sponsorship years before, but that didn't stop the Belgrade elites from going to the hotel for dinner or drinks. It was a place to be seen, and Arkan and Ceca enjoyed turning heads.

Stepping out of the SUV, Ceca, always dressed for the paparazzi, wore a white mink coat, tight around her curvy figure, and her long brown hair cascaded perfectly over her narrow shoulders. It was around 5:00 P.M. While she and her sister went to check in on the upscale boutique she owned in the hotel, Arkan wandered over to the lobby's plum-colored banquettes. At forty-seven, he still had his baby face, and although he was tall and muscular, he had started to carry a couple of extra pounds around the waist, but that's what happened when you spent more time in the office and less time running around. He wore a fancy dark suit, and on his wrist, as always, a diamond-encrusted gold Rolex.

At a far table, the warlord sat down and ordered tea. Two friends joined him—Milenko Mandic, the manager of his casino in the bombed-out Hotel Yugoslavia, and Dragan Goric, a police colonel. What they talked about, no one knows exactly, but most suggested to me that the conversation involved sports bets for the following week.

Where the assassin was at this point is unclear. Official reports put him at a banquette near the piano, not far from Arkan's table. Though most would say that there was only one shooter, witnesses would remember two or three accomplices acting inside and outside the lobby. Whatever the number, the assassin and his accomplices would have been difficult to spot before they wanted to be seen. The Serbian New Year celebration had happened the day before, on January 14, and the lobby was overcrowded with visitors.

When Arkan sent his bodyguard Zvonko off to fetch sweets, the assassin made his approach. He wore a bulky overcoat. Some say he was masked. Others remembered a young face and dark, mussed hair. About two and a half feet from the banquette, the assassin stopped. Words were exchanged, and then the assassin withdrew a 9 mm automatic and started firing.

Guests screamed, and scattered for the exits. Zvonko returned and fired at the assassin, who was now in full-throttled retreat. One female guest took a stray bullet. When Ceca came running in, Zvonko took a Beretta from her purse and emptied that, hitting the assassin somewhere in the back. At the hotel's glass entrance, the man fell like a sack of sand and began crawling, still snapping off a few more rounds.

There was a second when it looked like the assassin would not make it, but then two other men materialized suddenly, dragged the bleeding man out to a waiting car, and were gone. As one waiter recalled, "I've never seen so much shooting. It was absolutely crazy." The whole event probably lasted three minutes, with twenty-eight bullets fired.

"They killed the commander," Zvonko started shouting over and over again, in disbelief. "They killed the commander." Standing over Arkan's banquette, Ceca perceived a lake of inky blood spreading over the marble floor. Mandic was splayed out on the ground a few yards off, as if he'd tried to run, while Goric, the police colonel, was slumped over in his seat, as if he were napping. Mandic was dead and Goric would be pronounced dead an hour later. Arkan, however, was still alive, though his breathing was wet and he was hemorrhaging copious amounts of blood.

There was no time to waste. Ceca and her sister carried Arkan outside and flagged down a BMW, piled in, and told the driver to go fast. In the back-seat, Ceca worked to keep her head together and scooped blood out of her husband's mouth. Five minutes later they screeched into Belgrade's emergency center, not far from the U.S. embassy. His body, now motionless, was strapped to a stretcher and hurried to the operating room.

As doctors worked to reanimate him, news of the hit spread fast. Within an hour hundreds of people crowded into the parking lot, despite the freezing weather. People climbed on top of cars for a better view of the hospital entrance and to get a peek into one of the building's lighted windows. Most noticeable on the scene was the contingent of a hundred or so gangsters and paramilitary troops, many of them dressed in black or camouflage and blocking the hospital doors, allowing no one in or out, not even the police. Locked down, the place was now under the control of the Tigers.

Meanwhile, what the surgeons saw was not promising. Arkan had been shot in the temple, the right eye, and the mouth, rendering him almost unrecognizable, even to his wife. Dragan Rvovic, the manager of Ceca's boutique at the Intercontinental, later described Arkan this way: "When I saw Zeljko Raznatovic, I was horrified. He was all bloody: His eye fell out."

Doctors worked on him for nearly sixty minutes. As Arkan's vital signs worsened, the medical staff began to fret about the mob outside. How would the Tigers respond to his death? One male staff member working that night told me that there was a discussion about who would talk to the family. "We worried that his men would come in and start killing us," he said. When Arkan's family doctor arrived, he was nominated as the spokesperson.

It was past nightfall when Ceca appeared before the crowds outside. Not long before, she had fainted on her husband's body and had to be revived with an IV infusion. Sitting now in a wheelchair, she appeared pale and fragile, according to people who were there that night. She had blood on her white fur coat, blood in her hair, blood on her face. As Arkan's men made space, the crowd jostled around her. Journalists shouted questions. What happened? Did Arkan make it?

Her face was full of sadness, but also of dread. What would she do? What would her family do—her three-year-old son and one-year-old daughter? Would the men who shot her husband now come after her? For a moment, she didn't say anything, as if trying to grasp that her husband would never come home again. He was gone forever. At forty-seven, Arkan was dead. Tears dribbled down her makeup-smeared face. She shook her head, and then, in desperation, shouted at the pitiless winter night, "God, what will I say to my son?"

EPILOGUE

1

The funeral was held on an icy Thursday afternoon, five days after his death. Thousands arrived at the city's main cemetery to say good-bye. Some even put the number beyond ten thousand. The cemetery was perched on a slight hill, and the streets around it were lined with Audis and Pajero jeeps and other shimmering luxury cars, symbols of the dead man's excessive rise and more excessive fall. There were politicians, businessmen, mobsters, celebrities, former Tigers, and many ordinary Serb folks. Near the gated entrance, vendors in heavy coats hawked white candles and white flowers. From above, the crowd was a river of black as it moved slowly into the cemetery, and the icy air was full of whispers, people wondering how in the world this could have happened to a man whom, in contrast to the rest of the planet, they perceived to be a Serb hero.

A small service was held for Arkan's family in the chapel, while the thousands waited outside, some of them weeping. When the coffin emerged, it was draped in the Tigers' red, blue, and white flag and carried by six of Arkan's men, dressed in camouflage with red berets, as if they were returning to war. A sniffling quiet descended on the people. Ceca, who wore a black overcoat with mink trim and a black fishnet veil, followed.

Arkan was assassinated on January 15, 2000. Thousands showed up at his funeral in Belgrade's central cemetery. The casket, draped with the Serbian flag, was carried by the warlord's men and followed by Ceca, his mother, Slavka, and his son, Michael.

Next to her were Michael, the oldest of Arkan's nine children, carrying a large wooden cross, and Arkan's mother, Slavka, who seemed to be staring off into another world as the coffin made its way to the open gravesite. Also there was Arkan's former wife Natalia.

Deep into winter, the cemetery was frozen and devoid of color, the trees black and skeletal without their leaves. The sun moved in and out of the clouds, but the wind was strong and wouldn't let up. At the grave, an Orthodox Church bishop in black robes led a choir and brass band in an old Serbian hymn as the Tigers fired a three-gun rifle salute in honor of their commander. The Tiger who called himself Mr. X was there. Like many of the other former paramilitary soldiers who had gone to battle with Arkan in Croatia and Bosnia, he was sad to say good-bye to a man who had made him feel alive in a broken and depressed time. "When he died," he told me later, "we knew it was all over. I went to the funeral to say bye to him. I have very beautiful memories. That's all I have now."

Other Tigers, though probably in the minority, like Trax, came to the funeral as a way to bring closure to a tragic history that they had been dragged into and still don't quite understand. "Going that day was a way to end that chapter in my life," Trax recalled to me. "I remember it was cold and snowing. My leg with the grenade shrapnel in it was hurting. I watched him go into the grave, and then I walked away. After that, it was done for me. But I will always remember what happened. I have no choice about that."

Milosevic didn't show his face. Although it didn't exactly come as a surprise, it did deepen the suspicion among the mourners that he was the man who had paid for the hit. Later, the spokesman of the president's Socialist Party, who had attended Arkan and Ceca's wedding but not the funeral, issued a statement. "Regardless of his contradictory biography," it said, "Arkan was no doubt a patriot."

Before delivering the eulogy, Borislav Pelevic, a "general" in the Tigers and later chairman of Arkan's Serbian Unity Party, waited for the crowd to draw closer to the grave. Then he stepped forward and looked directly at the flag-draped coffin. He spoke of Arkan as a war hero and patriot, reminded everyone of his life as a sportsman, and praised him as a family man and humanitarian. "You have become a legend even during your lifetime," he said, looking at the coffin and then at Ceca, who dabbed at her eyes. "You have defended the Serbs in Croatia, Bosnia. Without you, they would not exist."

He paused and contemplated the coffin some more. Wreaths and baskets of white flowers festooned the frozen earth and the black marble headstone. Later, a bust of Arkan in a World War I military uniform would adorn the grave; the grave would also be staffed with a guard. "Mr. Commander," Pelevic said at last, "let me report to you one last time. The Serbian Voluntary Guard is in good order. The Party of Serbian Unity is in good order. Mr. Commander, allow me to take my leave."

The brass band started up, as the choir sang the words "God, give us justice" over and over. When the band finished, two Tigers folded the militia's flag, and Pelevic handed it to Michael, who took it in his arms. Gradually, the crowd began to disperse, leaving the coffin to the earth. As the procession made its way out of the frozen cemetery, the wind whipped the empty trees. Several days later a blizzard would swoop down on the city and the cemetery would be encased in a deep snow.

It was over. All of it. What this meant to Serbia, to Belgrade, to Ceca, to Mr. X, to Trax, to Arkan's pursuers, to his kids, and to everyone else who had encountered him over the years was still unknown. But for a moment, as the mourners made their way toward the exit gates, some would recall that it was so quiet that it felt like the world had suddenly come to a halt.

2

It was almost a week before local police caught up with the assassin and made an arrest. The man's name was Dobrosav Gavric, a jaunty twenty-three-year-old ex-cop who had lately been moonlighting as a mobster enforcer. After being fixed up by a private surgeon in a nearby village, he had tried to vanish into the ragged countryside, where folks suspicious of authority protected him. But the police located him anyway, along with the two others who had dragged him bleeding out of the hotel that night. A trial followed. The number of accomplices would eventually rise to seven. Predictably, Gavric, who was paralyzed from the waist down from the shooting, denied any part in the assassination. He insisted that he was at the Intercontinental Hotel visiting friends. When asked why he was wearing a bulletproof vest, he replied that he always wore one. But eventually he was convicted of three counts of murder and sentenced to twenty years. As he left the courtroom, one former Tiger promised retribution. "We're going to judge you ourselves," the soldier said.

Two years later, however, the sentence was overturned and everyone was released. Gavric disappeared into the remote eastern hills of the country, where he awaited a new trial. Months passed. One judge and a number of witnesses dropped out of the case, expressing fear of retribution, not unlike people testifying in mafia- and gang-related cases in America. Behind the scenes it was clear that Arkan's people were doing battle with the people around Gavric. One witness was murdered and Gavric's brother was shot.

Despite all of this, another trial was eventually convened in 2005. Arkan's mother and sister Jasna appeared at most of the court dates. Ceca had been present through much of the first trial, but she showed her face less now. By October 2006, the trial was finished. Gavric, along with seven others, was again convicted of Arkan's murder. Gavric was handed thirty years, as were the two men in the getaway car. Five others received sentences ranging from two to five years, though the deeper mystery of the people behind the murder plot persisted.

Most in Serbia believe that Gavric and his accomplices were just bit players in a much larger killing scheme, which, according to news reports, involved a murder payment of nearly $2.5 million. As a judge indicated near the end of the trial, "It is obvious that some deal was involved, something was promised to the perpetrators, but we could not determine what or who may have ordered it."

Belgrade was a city of conspiracy theories. Hundreds of stories swirled around the streets, in newspapers, on television. Surely better than any Agatha Christie potboiler, the questions about Arkan's death consumed the country—still do. Was there one assassin or three? And who ordered it? It became a topic of conversation at dinner tables, in cafés, on street corners. Most told me that President Milosevic and his regime would benefit most from the killing, a line of thinking that Ceca and Arkan's family came to believe. Others speculated that the hit was gang-related, a bold move to claim the multimillion-dollar oil trade and black market. There was also talk of Ceca being involved, which seems unlikely, or the soccer mafia. The one truth, said Marko Nicovic, Belgrade's former police chief, is that "a hit like this doesn't happen unless it comes from the top."

Outside of Serbia, the overall mood seemed equally dispirited and baffled at Arkan's death, though for different reasons. "The surrender or apprehension of Arkan has long been sought . . . and has been a priority for the United States government," U.S. Secretary of State Madeleine Albright said at a press conference on January 15, 2000, the day of his murder. "We take no satisfaction in Arkan's murder and would have wanted him to stand trial in The Hague for his crimes." That same day, British foreign secretary Robin Cook said, "I regret his death because it prevents us from doing justice to the victims of his atrocities by seeing him in the dock at The Hague war crimes tribunal," he said. But he added, as if to imply a note of consolation, "Arkan lived violently so it is therefore no surprise that he died violently."

3

After Arkan died, Serbia began a slow march toward a new era. It started with the fall of President Milosevic. On October 5, 2000, hundreds of thousands of Serbs, angered by years of economic misery and global isolation, stormed Parliament and, in a notable act of courage, called for the president to step down. It was a surreal moment, not only because the police didn't raise their batons or pull their pistols, but because Red Star supporters, Arkan's former fan club, participated in the revolt. "We were ready to kill," boasted Curly, the Red Star fan club leader. "It was a great day. We forced him out. We wanted change, and that's what we got." By the next week Milosevic had resigned, and soon after was shipped off to The Hague to face charges of war crimes. A new government, helmed by a democratically elected president, Vojislav Kostunica, stepped into the void, promising to democratize Serbia and crack down on its underworld.

At first, Ceca defied them. After a year spent in mourning, she staged a concert in June 2001 at Red Star stadium. It was a celebration of Arkan, and more than a hundred thousand fans, most of them teenagers, packed the place. For an hour and a half the pop star danced around in a dress slit up the side and down the center, and as an encore she led the crowd in a chant of Arkan's name. Two years later, Serbia's pro-West prime minister, Zoran Djindjic, was gunned down. Immediately, Ceca came under suspicion. (Investigators believed that she was somehow involved in the assassination through her association with former Tiger general Milorad "Legija" Ulemek.) Public intrigue churned. Was Ceca sending a message to the new Serbian government?

When police searched her house, they found a secret basement bunker loaded with dozens of guns, laser guides, scopes, silencers, and hundreds of rounds of ammunition. Ceca, of course, denied she knew anything about the contraband. Whatever was there was Arkan's. As she told me later, "It's a big house. There are a lot of rooms."

Authorities, however, weren't persuaded, and Ceca was hauled off to jail and locked in solitary confinement. For weeks, she couldn't make phone calls, not even to her lawyer. She wondered if she'd ever get out. Food was handed in through a slot in the door. "I slept constantly," she remembered. "Every morning, I hesitated to open my eyes," she said. "I didn't want to wake up and see that I was actually living this nightmare." Her children were told that she was touring in the United States.

She spent four months in confinement before she was released. What had happened? Maybe the government was making its own point. You will not be tolerated. But an explanation or apology would never come. "They just told me one day that the charges had been dropped and let me go," she said. She was never tried.

The time away had hurt. Her music career, which Arkan had helped to shape, was in tatters. Gradually, radios stopped playing her songs, and she wasn't allowed to leave the country. Ceca stayed inside her home, sleeping twelve to fourteen hours a day. "I watched a lot of Latin soaps," she said.

Death threats came. She hired more bodyguards, and sometimes carried a pistol in her purse. Suddenly, Arkan's second wife, Natalia, sued for the house, claiming that it was hers. The world that she'd once dominated with Arkan seemed to be crumbling around her. In a desperate attempt to restart her superstardom, she launched a world tour, but because of her associa-

Ceca in her bed, with Arkan's portrait.

tion with Arkan, she was denied visas to America, Canada, and Australia. "All of her friends stopped calling her," said Ceca's father, Slobodan Velickovic. "It was very sad."

Then Milosevic was dead. On March 11, 2006, after five years of confinement at The Hague's prison and days away from the conclusion of his trial, the former Serb president had a heart attack. Although some believe he was actually poisoned, and others mention suicide, medical tests disagree. (The years before had also seen the deaths of Croatian president Franjo Tudjman and Bosnian president Alija Izetbegovic, as well as the capture of Croatia's biggest alleged war criminal, General Ante Gotovina.) With the death of Milosevic there was a sense that Serbia could really begin to move beyond its sordid history, to purge and at the same time heal. In some ways, that is true.

Now, turbo folk is played less and less on the radio, and rarely at clubs. Though numerous indicted war criminals are still on the run, including former Bosnian Serb president Radovan Karadzic and Bosnian Serb general Ratko Mladic, many have been picked up and are being tried, some at The Hague and others at Serbia's new court for war crimes. Croatia has finally regained full control of eastern Slavonia, which the Serbs had once taken fully, and Bosnia is a single state, though partitioned between the Muslim-Croat Federation and Bosnian Serbs, and overseen by three presidents. In 2007, after years of litigation, the World Court concluded that although genocide did in fact happen in Bosnia, Serbia, as a state, was not specifically responsible. Bosnian Muslims in general seemed to perceive the ruling as a miscarriage of justice, while Serbs called it a moral victory, and the rest of the world collectively scratched their heads: Genocide happened but no one is charged? As for Kosovo, the province, now guarded by 16,500 UN peacekeepers, continues to call for independence, though Serbian leaders won't let it go.

Meanwhile, a fresh wave of forward-looking Serbian politicians and crime fighters has emerged. These men and women are focused on Serbia's joining the European Union, just like its neighbors Bulgaria, Romania, and Croatia, which will all probably gain admittance by 2009. On the streets, in cafés, and in the newspapers there is serious talk about a society free of political and economic vice. When I spoke to a number of high-ranking officials working for President Boris Tadic, there was a common refrain of renewal and catharsis. "Serbia is changing," a foreign adviser to the president told me one morning in the now outdated Intercontinental Hotel, where Arkan was gunned down. "The old gangster days, the days of war and dictatorship, are over."

I'm not sure that's entirely true. As new buildings rise in Belgrade, as foreign business returns to the country, including companies like Citibank and Microsoft, as all the offical talk of change happens, as courts churn through more war trials and police chip away at organized crime, the spirit of Arkan remains strong in places. His portraits are painted on city walls, Red Star fans still brag about his leadership, and weekly magazines devote entire issues to him, selling out instantly in record numbers. On the Internet there are personal blogs glorifying his reign, and videos on YouTube feature him leading the Tigers; he even has his own Web page on MySpace .com, with over five hundred friends. Annually, on the anniversary of his death, crowds—family, friends, and old soldiers—still gather at his grave and say prayers, and all through the year there are piles of flowers and burning candles in the grass around his headstone, not unlike the grave of Jim Morrison in Paris. Older people seem to cling to him as a symbol of Serbia's previous brute strength and its heady gangster days of anything goes. To some younger Serbs, Arkan's legendary outlaw reputation is alluring in the same way American teens respond to stars with shady pasts, like Tupac.

All of this Arkan worshiping didn't exactly surprise me. What did surprise me was that there is still a tremendous fear of him in the world. On one of my last visits to Belgrade, I met a former Red Star soccer fan at a tiny

Arkan's gravestone draws hundreds, if not thousands, of visitors a year. Annually, on the anniversary of his death, his family gathers here for prayers.

bar. A techno version of Eminem's "The Real Slim Shady" boomed from blown-out speakers dangling from the ceiling. Like many others, he was nervous talking about Arkan and kept looking around at the dozen or so others in their thirties and forties pulled up to the bar or slumped at booths. At one point he told me he'd leave if I used the warlord's name again in conversation. "Do you know what you're saying?" he asked me, his eyes darting here and there. It was like he was expecting Arkan himself to pop out of the shadows and cut us in half with his machine gun.

So I posed a stupid question, one that had been bothering me for a long time. "Do you think he's alive?" I wondered.

The man looked me straight in the face. His eyes were bloodshot from late hours working at some nearby metal plant. He'd spent three years fighting in the Bosnian war with Arkan and still looked tired. "You never know," he said finally.

"What?" I asked. He nodded, repeated himself. "You never know."

At first I thought he was completely crazy. Sure, I had heard that Arkan's underworld network continued to thrive. I had heard that after his death, the illegal businesses were split up between several of his lieutenants, all former Tigers. Others told me that Ceca had taken over a piece of the enterprise, though that didn't ring true to me, and that his sister Jasna had also commandered a slice. But the idea that Arkan was still around doing his thing, running his empire? Absurd.

But it wasn't. There were a lot of others out there who thought he was still alive, even seven years after his assassination. How? I asked. He'd orchestrated the death himself, these people guessed. In fact, the rumor of his survival had begun as a report by a Greek TV station not long after his murder, and was echoed in several Belgrade dailies, and later even in Sweden. People thought he was hiding out, maybe in the bunker beneath his house. Or he'd fled for the islands. One man guessed that he'd gone to Greece and climbed on a cargo ship headed for southern Africa. Another man put him in Turkey, where he sat behind a computer dictating orders by e-mail and messenger.

I asked Arkan's old friend Vladan Dinc, the newspaper publisher, about the theory of immortality. "I'd say that even today, one third of our population still thinks he's alive," he told me.

"You can't be serious."

He nodded gravely. "There's a story that he had seven or eight look-alikes, and one of them was killed that day in the hotel," he said. "I don't think any of my colleagues saw him dead. I certainly didn't see his dead body."

"But what about you? Do you think he's still out there?" I asked. "Is he sipping piña coladas on some beach in South America?"

Dinic laughed, and then said, "How do we really know?"

Dinic's question was one that I'd been asking all through my search for Arkan. It was the question of certainty. Of truth. What do we believe? Who do we believe? And how can we believe any of it? It made me think of William Faulkner's famous observation that "the past is not dead. In fact, it's not even past."

I'm still not completely sure about everything in Arkan's life. But in the end, that was exactly what had created the legend of Arkan. You could never pin him down, and because of that you never knew what he was capable of doing, even if that meant defying death. Alive or not, he is indeed still making everyone wonder, what next?

NOTES

Prologue

Much of this is a personal account. Background about Arkan and crumbling Yugoslavia is culled from numerous articles in *Vreme,* which the *Los Angles Times* described as "a window on Serbia's puzzling national mind-set and explains the roots and the course of the [Yugoslav] conflict with chilling accuracy and detail." Richard Holbrooke's memoir, *To End a War,* was also useful, and Arkan's interview with Charles Gibson took place on April 15, 1999. My interviews with Ceca took place in November 2004.

PART I: THE EARLY DAYS

1. John Wayne Dreams

I've tried to piece together his early life from interviews with many people familiar with the saga, but I'm most grateful to Milomir Marić, Vladan Dinic, and Marko Lopusina. Accounts of his youth have been reported at one time or another in most of the newspapers and magazines in Serbia. But most definitive for me were: Dada Vujasinovic's "Biographic Data on

Serbian Fighter Arkan," published in *Duga,* February 1, 1993, and Milomir Marić's "Legenda O Arkanu," which appeared in *Profil,* issue 11, 1997. For the stories about how Tito changed Yugoslavia, I relied on Stevan K. Pavlowitch's biography of Tito and Misha Glenny's book *The Balkans,* as well as an extensive biopic that appeared on the Arts and Entertainment Network in 1997.

Jovan Dulovic was a key source for Arkan's early days of crime in Serbia, on how the young criminal got his start and shuttled off to Western Europe. Bozidar Spasic and two other UBDA officers who cannot be named corroborated important details. Unfortunately, I was not able to obtain official prison reports. When I approached the Ministry of Justice, I was told that Arkan's files had been lost "due to a flood." I depended on Dobrivoje Radovanovic for accounts of Arkan's time spent at the prison in Valjevo, from his daily habits to his state of mind.

2.   Taking Europe

Dusko Doder's book, *The Yugoslavs,* draws an intimate portrait of Yugoslavia in the 1970s. Among the most helpful parts of the book was his discussion of how hundreds of thousands of the country's workers decided to pick up and head to Europe in search of wealth and stability. For Arkan's brief foray into England, a key source was an unnamable former Yugoslav state security official. Interviews with Bratislav Grubacic, publisher of *VIP* in Belgrade, were helpful, as were stories in *Vreme, Duga,* and *Profil,* as well as one in *The Washington Post,* "Serbia's Treacherous Gang of Three," which appeared on February 3, 1993.

I had three interviews with Dacovic Milutin, who described his strange criminal career in Italy and was my main source of information about Arkan plunging into Italy's underworld.

Interviews with Milan St. Protic, Budimir Babovic, and Bozidar Spasic were all critical to me in understanding the shadowy UDBA, from how an agent was recruited to the kinds of activities the agent performed for Comrade Tito.

3.   How We Change

Interviews with Dacovic Milutin.

4.   The Case of the Elusive Man

Derived exclusively from my reportage and interviews with dozens of people in Serbia, Croatia, and Bosnia.

5.   The Smiling Bank Robber

Descriptions of Gothenburg are based on personal reporting. Johannes Knutsson, professor at the National Swedish Police Academy, provided me with insight on crime in Sweden through the decades, including the evolution of the country's law enforcement. Hanns von Hofer was also helpful, but I am beholden to Walter Repo for his knowledge about Arkan and how he fits into the country's criminal canon.

In re-creating Arkan's crime spree in Sweden, I relied on Swedish police reports, which provided names and events—early robberies and heists at Gotabanken and Kungalv banks.

6.   We Got You! No You Don't!

This first conversation with Swedish investigators is taken from the official police transcripts, translated from Swedish into English. The interrogation took place in Brussels between April 26, 1977, and April 28, 1977, and involved prosecutor Karl Gustav Pfeiff, Chief of Gothenburg Police Ingemar Stromvall, and a Serb interpreter.

7.   Breakout

For the account of Arkan's return to Gothenburg and Stockholm, I depended largely, if not exclusively, on Swedish police reports. Walter Repo again was key for perspective about how the robberies played out and a part of the country's fixation on the crimes as they unfolded. Most papers in Sweden ran accounts of the courthouse breakout, though the best stories for me were Marina Stagh's piece in *Aftonbladet,* "The Escape Through the Window," which appeared on September 11, 1979, and two stories in *Expressen* on September 12, one by Jerker Soderlind, "The Break Out a Professional Job," and a second by Per Wendel, "*Expressen*'s Man Met the Robbers."

Dutch investigators—S. B. M. Voorhoeve and Y. M. Th.A. Fraser—interrogated Arkan on May 28, 1980, and my re-creation of that conversation was taken directly from transcripts, again translated from Swedish to English.

8. Hit Man

To get a snapshot of the mysterious and somewhat opaque UDBA, I spoke to numerous people inside and on the periphery of the agency. Most important were Budimir Babovic, the former head of Interpol in Belgrade and, of course, Bozidar Spasic. Also helpful in filling out and corroborating several of the assassination stories was Marko Lopusina, as well as several people close to Arkan who asked not to be named.

Vreme published numerous accounts about the UDBA. Among the most helpful to me in describing the agency's iron grip on the Yugoslavian population was Stojan Cerovic's article, "The Long Hand of the Secret Police," June 28, 1993. Again, Dada Vujasinovic's *Duga* article "Biographic Data on Serbian Fighter Arkan" helped flesh out personal details of the young Arkan's involvement, as did Chuck Sudetic's story in *The New York Times,* "A Shady Militia Chief Arouses Serbs," December 20, 1992. Dusko Doder's book also helped sort through the UDBA murk.

Recently released Central Intelligence Agency documents provided a window into Tito's paranoia about domestic terrorism in the 1970s. The September 27, 1972, memorandum, "Yugoslavia—The Ustashi and the Croatian Separatist Problem," warned its operatives "in recent months Tito and other Yugoslav leaders have been giving a great deal of public attention to Croatian émigrés and Croatian separatism. Clearly, the Yugoslav government is treating the issue as if it involved a threat to the regime and to the survival of the federal state."

While local press has extensively documented the Yugoslavian mafia's penetration into Holland, Germany, and Sweden, Michel Van Rijn helped illuminate Arkan's stretch of time in the Netherlands. Van Rijn's ghostwritten memoir, *Hot Art, Cold Cash,* detailed his adventures and run-ins with some of Arkan's men, who at one time wanted him dead. Journalists Harald Doornbos and Jan Portein were also key sources for the Holland adventures.

9. The Man Arkan Didn't Kill

I interviewed Nikola Kavaja over the course of three days in his apartment in downtown Belgrade. Much of the interview appeared later in *The Paris Review,* Summer 2006.

PART II: THE WARLORD

10. My Fixer Milan and Our Search for Truth Among Serbia's Crime Lords

Milan is a pseudonym. To protect Milan's identity, I have changed numerous personal details, including where he lives, what he does professionally, and what he looks like. All of my experiences with Milan are fact.

11. Cruising in the Pink Cadillac

Over the course of three interviews, Marko Nicovic described in colorful and authoritative detail his police years on the hunt for Arkan. I heard numerous versions of Arkan's 1983 encounter with the police, but the most detailed came from Bozidar Spasic. Also important to me in writing about Arkan's life in the 1980s, including his run-in with police in 1986, were Vladan Dinic, Jovan Dulovic, Budimir Babovic, and Vojislav Tufegdzic.

I am grateful to Slavoljub Ninkovic, whom I interviewed two times. Once at his bar, and again at Casino Slavija, where he used to play baccarat and roulette with Arkan. Over those conversations, he narrated the sleepless years of gambling in the 1980s and then his time with the Tigers a decade later.

12. Lord of the Soccer Warriors

Susan L. Woodward's book, *Balkan Tragedy,* provided one of the most extensive discussions of Yugoslavia's economic and constitutional collapse. Also useful to me in describing the country's disintegration were Misha Glenny's two books, *The Balkans* and *The Fall of Yugoslavia.* Deputy Secretary of State Strobe Talbott remarked on the postcommunist chaos at the National Press Club on November 9, 1995.

Louis Sell deftly captured the rise of the former Serbian president in his book *Slobodan Milosevic and the Destruction of Yugoslavia*. Peter Maass' book, *Love Thy Neighbor*, was also helpful, as was Stephen Engelberg's *New York Times Magazine* profile, "Carving Out a Greater Serbia," September 1, 1999.

I spoke to more than a dozen Red Star fans about Arkan's leadership of Delije, but Sloba Markovic was most important. *The Village Voice* and the Sunday *Times* ran stories about the Red Star fan club, but most valuable was Ben Anderson's story in British *GQ*, "A Matter of Life and Death," which provided some practical insight on Red Star history and the club's continued violence even today. Franklin Foer's book, *How Soccer Explains the World*, was most vital to fleshing out the brutal trajectory of the Red Star fan club, including their epic battle with Zagreb fans and the club's involvement in Arkan's Tigers.

13. The Tigers

The story of the Tigers, how Arkan recruited his militia and took them to war, is mythical. Most of the stories here came from my own reporting and interviews with former Tigers. Conversations with Sloba Markovic, Mr. X, Trax, and a man who called himself "The Giant" were especially edifying. In addition, almost every Serbian newspaper and magazine recorded the group's rise, as did CNN and BBC and *The New York Times*.

For the retelling of Arkan's capture by Croatian police in Dvor na Uni, I leaned heavily on news stories in *NIN, Vreme,* and *Vjesnik*. Among the most important was Salih Zvizdic's *Vjesnik* story "Arkan's Life, Crimes, Prison Release Viewed," April 12, 1992.

Many interviews were done regarding Arkan's time spent in Zagreb prison on weapons charges. Most important were Spasic, several Red Star fans, and Daca, who recounted the day Arkan was released.

14. What I Learned at Red Star Stadium

This account was one of three visits I made to the Red Star fan club.

Many books were helpful in getting a grip on why some Serbs described themselves as a "heavenly people" and how the idea encapsulated in the moniker was used as justification for ethnic revenge. Most instructive was Tim Judah's book *The Serbs*.

15. War!

Many of the paramilitary details here come from the UN Commission of Experts, which was established in 1992 on the basis of UN Security Council Resolution 780 and headed by M. Cherif Bassiouni. I interviewed Bassiouni at length on two occasions. Specific battles, like Tenja, come from conversations with former Tigers. Also critical to understanding the authority of Arkan's militia, what they did, and how they did it were Sonja Biserko, director of the Helsinki Committee for Human Rights in Serbia, and Natasa Kandic, executive director of Belgrade's Humanitarian Law Center.

Testimony at the International Criminal Tribunal for the Former Yugoslavia (ICTY) was integral to mapping out the fall of Yugoslavia in human terms. Among the most instructive as to Arkan's role were statements from his secretary, known as ICTY witness B129, as well as the 1998 ICTY trial of Slavko Dokmanovic, a former president of the Vukovar municipality. At that trial, prosecutors exhibited footage of a 1992 interview with General Andrija Biorcevic, the man in charge of JNA's 1991 storming of Vukovar, who spoke about Arkan's militia as an awesome force of destruction.

16. The Dangers Out There

My encounter with the Tigers occurred in September 2005. Names were changed.

17. Camp Erdut

Filip Svarm's Serbia documentary, *The Unit,* was an invaluable source here, as were Bassiouni's UN reports, and interviews with Ruzica Mandic, Bratislav Grubacic, Sonja Biserko, Ron Haviv, and former Tigers. Anna Husarska's report for *The New Republic* in 1995, "Rocky-Road Warrior," was useful for color, as was Arkan's propaganda/recruiting documentary, *Arkanovi Tigrovi.*

18. Vukovar: I Killed Twenty-four Ustache!

Tomislav Simovic's description of how Arkan got trapped behind Croatian lines appeared in ICTY testimony on Tuesday, February 12, 2002. Almost two years later Dobrila Gajic-Glisic, a former Serbian Defense Ministry employee, clarified the story at ICTY. She told the court that she was in fact with Simovic the moment Arkan returned from the enemy lines. When he mentioned killing twenty-four Ustache, she recalled how she expressed horror, which angered Arkan. "Madam," he said, "leave the room if you can't bear to listen to this."

Janko Baljak's documentary, *Vukovar: The Final Cut,* is the most extensive examination of Vukovar's carnage. Both *The Washington Post* and *The New York Times* also published numerous stories about the fall of Vukovar, including solid coverage of the Ovcara farm massacre. Among the best was Chuck Sudetic's *New York Times* story, "U.N. Investigating Croat's Grave Site," November 29, 1992. At ICTY, Bogdan Vujic vividly described atrocities at Vukovar's hospital and the Velepromet storehouse.

19.   Because War Pays

Numerous media and human rights sources detailed the war looting. Stories in *The New York Times* and *Los Angeles Times* and on CNN, the BBC, and ABC helped here, but Arkan's secretary's 2003 ICTY testimony was most vital in grasping the warlord's smuggling operations. In *The New York Times,* Marlise Simons wrote a deft summation of the secretary's testimony on April 23, 2003, "Mystery Witness Faces Milosevic," and on April 13, 1995, Roger Cohen reported connections between Arkan's illicit activities and Milosevic: "Serb Says Files Link Milosevic to War Crimes."

For accounts of the Tigers' death rites and Arkan's dissolving marriage to Natalia, I depended largely on my own reporting.

Laura Silber's book *Yugoslavia, Death of a Nation* was a key source for the end of the first year's fighting in Croatia, as was Misha Glenny's book, *The Fall of Yugoslavia.*

20.   Meeting the Tigers

While all the facts are intact, names were changed.

21.   My Name Is Trax; Arkan Made Me Do It

I am indebted to Trax, whose name was changed—he worried about former

Tigers, as well as The Hague. Trax narrated specific stories about the Tigers in Bosnia, especially the first battle in Bijeljina. Also important to Bijeljina were my own interviews with locals and former Serb and Bosnian Muslim fighters. Christiane Amanpour's CNN documentary was a classic investigatory takedown.

News coverage of the Bosnian conflict was widespread, but reports in *The New York Times, Christian Science Monitor, Los Angeles Times,* and *The Dallas Morning News* were paramount, as was Mark Danner's series about the Yugoslav wars in *The New York Review of Books.* I'm also indebted to Peter Maass's *Love Thy Neighbor* and Chuck Sudetic's *Blood and Vengeance.*

I interviewed Arkan's son Michael in Belgrade, and conversations with former Tigers provided backup.

22.   I Don't Give a Damn

Samantha Power's deeply reported book about genocide, *A Problem from Hell,* is the main source for Jon Western's story and documentation of the international community's resistance to intervening in Bosnia. Warren Zimmerman's book, *Origins of a Catastrophe,* was additionally vital.

I interviewed over a dozen people about Arkan's sanction-busting operations, but most essential were Cherif Bassiouni, Marko Nicovic, and Budimir Babovic. Specific smuggling routes were detailed in the Center for the Study of Democracy's report "Smuggling in Southeast Europe" and the Institute for War and Peace Reporting's Balkan Crisis report, "Speedboats, Cigarettes, Mafia, and Montenegrin Democracy."

The chief source for "naming names" was Elaine Sciolino's *New York Times* story, "U.S. Names Figures It Wants Charged with War Crimes," December 17, 1992.

Stories in the *Christian Science Monitor* ("Young Gangs Rule Belgrade Streets"), the *Los Angeles Times* ("A People Poisoned by Chaos"), and *Maclean's* ("Wild in the Streets") were crucial sources for writing about Belgrade's crime wave. But *Vreme* published some of the best stories about the city of darkness, specifically dispatches from Milos Vasic and Uros Komlenovic. The Serbian documentary, *See You in the Obituaries,* is a classic, as is Tim Judah's book, *The Serbs.*

23. Man of the People

Reports about Arkan's election run appeared in many international newspapers and magazines, though the chief sources for my account were the following: Chuck Sudetic, "Rival Serbs Are Admitting Bosnia-Croatia Atrocities," *The New York Times,* November 13, 1993; John Kifer, "An Outlaw in the Balkans Is Basking in the Spotlight," *The New York Times,* November 23, 1993; "Nationalist Leads Serb Campaign," *Chicago Tribune,* December 19, 1993; Jonathan S. Landay, "New Star of the Serbian Right," *Christian Science Monitor,* December 3, 1993.

Articles in the Serbian *Vreme* were also edifying, including: Stojan Cerovic's, "Arkan, A Man for All Seasons," August 2, 1993; Uros Komlenovic, "On the Spot: Kosovo and the Elections," November 8, 1993; Milos Vasic, "The December Vote: Slobodan and Arkan's Flying Circus"; "War Report," December 1993; and Filip Svarm, "Interview with Arkan: I Don't Like Intellectuals," October, 18, 1993.

I spoke to dozens of people about Arkan's stint in Parliament, but am especially grateful to Bratislav Grubacic, Nesa Pavolovic, and Ceca Raznatovic.

24. Pop Star

Eric Gordy was my personal Google for help on many subjects, but especially on pop culture, the rise of Ceca, and what her rise meant to the region. His book *The Culture of Power in Serbia* was decisive, as was Adam Higginbotham's story for *The Observer,* "Beauty and the Beast," January 4, 2004.

For an account of the marriage, there were dozens of interviews, but Giovanni di Stefano and Ceca Raznatovic were my principal sources. Also significant was the two-hour video of the wedding and Dejan Anastasijevic's *Vreme* story, "Machine Gun Wedding (With Singing)," February 27, 1995.

25. War's Over

Many books contributed to my retelling of the last days of the Yugoslav war, but chief were Misha Glenny's *The Fall of Yugoslavia* and Laura Sibler's book and documentary, *Yugoslavia: Death of a Nation.* Samantha Power's book *A Problem from Hell* was also a key source. The Srebrenica massacre was detailed in a report to the UN secretary general on November 15, 1999, and later at the World Court.

Apart from interviews with the Serbian Tigers, I met Hamdu Abdic in Bihac and spoke to him over coffee one afternoon. Anthony Lloyd's stories in *The Times* corroborated much of what Abdic said, specifically his dispatches "Battles Rage Along Bosnia Front Lines Despite Ceasefire," October 13, 1995, and "Truce at Stake in Embattled Town," October 14, 1995.

Descriptions of the Sanski Most atrocities appeared in Arkan's ICTY indictment, as well as in Bill Schiller's story in *The Toronto Star,* "New Serb Slaughters Uncovered Survivors," February 11, 1996, and Chris Hedges piece in *The New York Times,* "For Some, Hope of Peace Offers Little," October 12, 1995. Witness B-1047's testimony at The Hague on Monday, June 16, 2003, was most damning.

Examinations of the Dayton Peace Accords appeared in most major news media, but I relied on Richard Holbrooke's book, *To End a War.*

Interviews with former Tigers, including Trax and Mr. X, narrated many postwar sagas. Natasa Kandic was also helpful.

PART III: THE ASSASSINATION

26. This Is Serbia, You Wouldn't Understand

I spent about a week with Ceca in November 2004, and her story was published in *GQ* magazine in June 2005.

27. Going Legit

I interviewed Dada's parents one evening and spoke with Milomir Marić over coffee one afternoon at a Belgrade café.

For Arkan's foray into soccer, I depended principally on interviews with former Tigers and an Obilic supporter who referred to himself as the Giant. Foer's book was seminal, as were news stories in *The London Telegraph* ("Warlord's Team Takes on Europe Protest," May 24, 1998), *The Village Voice* ("Among the Thugs," April 7–13, 1999), *The London Independent* ("Spin-Doctor to the King of Ethnic Cleansing," April 26, 1998), and *The Financial Times* ("Not Such a Beautiful Game," October 27, 2006).

For accounts of the KLA and Milosevic's intervention in Kosovo, I leaned on Stacy Sullivan's moving book, *Be Not Afraid, For You Have Sons in America,* as well as Tim Judah's *Kosovo.*

28.   The End

There was widespread coverage of the NATO bombing, but *The New York Times* dispatches were superlative, including Carlotta Gall's "Crisis in the Balkans: Belgrade: Chinese Evacuate a Bombed Embassy in Serbia," May 9, 1999.

Charles Trueheart's April 2000 story for *The Atlantic,* "A New Kind of Justice," was an excellent source of information for the background, function, and reach of ICTY.

For accounts of Arkan's indictment, CNN and the BBC were thorough, but most important were, again, *New York Times* pieces, specifically, Roger Cohen's "Crisis in the Balkans: The Overview," May 28, 1999, and Marlise Simons's piece "Serb on 'Wanted' Lists Suggests Asylum in Belgium but Is Rebuffed," July 14, 1999.

Dinic was my chief source for the last days of Arkan, as was Ceca and Giovanni di Stefano.

29.   If I Had a Magic Wand

From my interview with Ceca.

30.   The Kill

Sources here included interviews with emergency room doctors and assistants, waiters at the Intercontinental Hotel, Ceca, and former Tigers. CNN and the BBC provided extensive coverage of Arkan's funeral. All Serbian newspapers reported on the event, as did *The New York Times,* where Steven Erlanger's piece, "In a Land of Glitz and Crimes," January 23, 2000, was a standout.

Epilogue

Belgrade's independent radio and television station, B92, had the best continuous coverage in English about the capture of Arkan's killers and the trials. For the saga of Serbia post-Arkan and post-Milosevic, I interviewed numerous Belgraders. Among the most significant were Ivana Kronja, Natasa Kandic, Sonja Biskero, and Bratislav Grubacic, as well as several Serbian government officials whom I cannot name.

BIBLIOGRAPHY

BOOKS

Andric, Ivo. *The Bridge on the Drina*. Chicago: University of Chicago Press, 1977.

Arendt, Hannah. *Eichmann in Jerusalem: A Report on the Banality of Evil*. New York: Viking, 1963.

———. *The Origins of Totalitarianism*. New York: Harcourt Brace Jovanovich, 1951.

Avisar, Ilan. *Screening the Holocaust: Cinema's Images of the Unimaginable*. Bloomington and Indianapolis: Indiana University Press, 1988.

Bassiouni, M. Cherif. *Crimes Against Humanity in International Criminal Law*. Cambridge: M. Nijhoff Publishers and Kluwer Academic Publishers, 1992.

Brogan, Patrick. *The Captive Nations: Eastern Europe: 1945–1990*. New York: Avon Books, 1990.

Clark, Wesley K. *Waging War: Bosnia, Kosovo, and the Future of Combat*. New York: Public Affairs, 2001.

Cohen, Roger. *Hearts Grown Brutal: Sagas of Sarajevo*. New York: Random House, 1998.

Doder, Dusko. *The Yugoslavs*. New York: Vintage Books, 1979.

Foer, Franklin. *How Soccer Explains the World: An Unlikely Theory of Globalization*. New York: HarperCollins, 2004.

Gjelten, Tom. *Sarajevo Daily: A City and Its Newspaper Under Siege*. New York: HarperCollins, 1995.

Glenny, Misha. *The Fall of Yugoslavia: The Third Balkan War*. New York: Penguin Books, 1993.

———. *The Rebirth of History*. New York: Penguin Books, 1990.

Glutman, Roy. *A Witness to Genocide: The 1993 Pulitzer Prize–Winning Dispatches on the "Ethnic Cleansing" of Bosnia*. New York: Macmillan, 1993.

Haviv, Ron. *Blood and Honey: A Balkan War Journal*. New York: TV Books/ Umbrage, 2001.

Holbrooke, Richard. *To End a War*. New York: Random House, 1998.

Hukanovic, Rezak. *The Tenth Circle of Hell: A Memoir of Life in the Death Camps of Bosnia*. New York: Basic Books, 1996.

Ignatieff, Michael. *Blood and Belonging: Journeys into the New Nationalism*. New York: Farrar, Straus and Giroux, 1994.

———. *Virtual War: Kosovo and Beyond*. Toronto: Viking Books, 2000.

Judah, Tim. *Kosovo: War and Revenge*. New Haven and London: Yale University Press, 2000.

———. *The Serbs: History, Myth, and the Destruction of Yugoslavia*. New Haven and London: Yale University Press, 1997.

Kaplan, Robert D. *Balkan Ghosts: A Journey Through History*. New York: St. Martin's Press, 1993.

Lopusina, Marko. *Komandant Arkan*. Cacak: Legenda, 2001.

Maass, Peter. *Love Thy Neighbor: A Story of War*. New York: Alfred A. Knopf, 1996.

Malcolm, Noel. *Bosnia: A Short History*. New York: New York University Press, 1994.

———. *Kosovo: A Short History*. New York: New York University Press, 1998.

Mazower, Mark. *The Balkans: A Short History*. New York: Modern Library, 2000.

Mihailovic, Dragoslav. *When Pumpkins Blossomed*. New York: Harcourt, Brace, Jovanovich, 1971.

Neuffer, Elizabeth. *The Key to My Neighbor's House: Seeking Justice in Bosnia and Rwanda*. New York: Picador, 2001.

Power, Samantha. *A Problem from Hell: America and the Age of Genocide*. New York: Basic Books, 2002.

Ridgeway, James. *Burn This House: The Making and Unmaking of Yugoslavia*. Durham and London: Duke University Press, 1997.

Ridley, Jasper. *Tito: A Biography*. London: Constable, 1994.

Rieff, David. *Slaughterhouse: Bosnia and the Failure of the West*. New York: Simon and Schuster, 1995.

Rohde, David. *Endgame: The Betrayal and Fall of Srebrenica, Europe's Worst Massacre Since World War II*. New York: Farrar, Straus and Giroux, 1997.

Sell, Louis. *Slobodan Milosevic and the Destruction of Yugoslavia*. Durham and London: Duke University Press, 2003.

Silber, Laura, and Allan Little. *The Death of Yugoslavia*. New York: Penguin, 1997.

Singleton, Fred. *A Short History of the Yugoslav Peoples*. Cambridge: Cambridge University Press, 1985.

Sudetic, Chuck. *Blood and Vengeance: One Family's Story of the War in Bosnia*. New York: Penguin, 1999.

Sullivan, Stacy. *Be Not Afraid, For You Have Sons in America: How a Brooklyn Roofer Helped Lure the U.S. into the Kosovo War*. New York: St. Martin's Press, 2004.

Thomas, Robert. *The Politics of Serbia in the 1990s*. New York: Columbia University Press, 1999.

Vulliamy, Ed. *Seasons in Hell: Understanding Bosnia's War*. London: Simon and Schuster, 1994.

West, Rebecca. *Black Lamb and Grey Falcon: A Journey Through Yugoslavia*. New York: Penguin, 1995.

Woodward, Susan L. *Balkan Tragedy: Chaos and Dissolution After the Cold War*. Washington, D.C.: Brookings Institution Press, 1995.

Zimmerman, Warren. *Origins of a Catastrophe: Yugoslavia and Its Destroyers—America's Last Ambassador Tells What Happened and Why*. New York: Time Books, 1996.

VIDEO AND TELEVISION

Arkan: Alleged Serbian War Lord, with Christiane Amanpour. Aired June 1, 1997 on CNN. Produced by John Fielding and edited by Cliff Hackel.

Ekonomija destrukcije (The Economics of Destruction). Directed by Mladjan Dinkic. Belgrade, Serbia: VIN, Video Nedeljnik, 1995. Videocassette.

Pretty Village, Pretty Flame. Directed by Srdjan Dragojevic. Brussels, Belgium: Cobra Films, 1996. DVD.

The Cook Report—Arkan. Aired October 27, 1992 on ITV. Produced by Mike Townson and reported by Roger Cook.

OTHER MATERIAL

The Wounds. Directed by Srdjan Dragojevic. Brussels, Belgium: Cobra Films, 1998. DVD.

Vidimo se u citulji (*See You in the Obituary*). Directed by Aleksandar Knezevic and Vojslav Tufegdzic. Belgrade, Serbia: B-92 Radio, 1995. DVD.

Vukovar (Final Cut). Directed by Janko Baljak. Belgrade, Serbia: B92 Radio, 2006. DVD.

Final report annexes, which detail war in Croatia and Bosnia, particularly paramilitary activity, from the UN Commission of Experts, headed by Cherif Bassiouni and established in 1992 "pursuant to Security Council Resolution 780."

INDEX

Page numbers for illustrations are in *italics*